KIT CARSON
A Portrait in Courage

★

KIT CARSON
A Portrait in Courage

by M. Morgan Estergreen

UNIVERSITY OF OKLAHOMA PRESS
NORMAN AND LONDON

To Ila and Elmer
two artists in Taos

LC: 62–1127–4

ISBN: 0–8061–1601–3

6 7 8 9 10 11 12 13 14 15

Foreword

KIT CARSON'S LIFE STORY IS, in essence, the story of the West as that region developed over the first three quarters of the nineteenth century. As such, then, Kit's life symbolizes the story of the American fur trade; of buffalo hunting and beaver trapping; of Indian tribes and Indian wars; of the annual rendezvous in mountain meadows; of the immigrant, the pathfinder, the soldier, and the seeker after gold—all following the Santa Fe, Spanish, Oregon, and California trails; of cantonment, Indian trading posts, and an adobe castle on the Arkansas River; of the caravan, the pack train, the oxcart, the overland stage, and the express by pony; of the conquests of Oregon, New Mexico, Texas, and California; of a wild and unknown West finally explored and conquered; of the march ever westward until the land from the Atlantic to the Pacific was under one flag.

This biography of Kit Carson necessarily includes accounts of some of his contemporaries: Robert, George, William, and Charles Bent; Céran St. Vrain; Old Bill Williams; Thomas Boggs; Tom Fitzpatrick; Ewing Young; Joseph Walker; Milton Sublette; William Wolfskill; Jim Beckwourth; Sir William Drummond Stewart, the noble Scotsman; Lucien Maxwell; John Charles Frémont, the Pathfinder; Josiah Gregg, who "traveled the Santa Fé Trail for his health and made the West live from his pen as the more vigorous Carson made it live with his deeds"; Alfred Jacob Miller, who with his talented brush gave us a lasting record of the culture of the Indian tribes, the exciting life of the mountain men, the beauty and freedom of the wild horses "tameless and swift and proud," and the life in and around the trading posts which dotted the land. There are others, too many to name here. These men, like Kit, were the pioneers of the West: they were roaming the length and breadth of that vast, undisturbed region many years before the hostile Indian was conquered and the settlers moved in to take over the rich valleys and upland meadows.

Where possible, I have allowed Kit to tell his own story, supplementing it with the accounts and impressions of the many narrators of that day. Much of my primary source material was obtained from Blanche Chloe Grant's notes on the life of Carson. These valuable but unclassified notes were given to me by Miss Grant the year before she died, and I have relied heavily upon them in preparing this book. In them are direct quotations from Kit Carson's son Charles, who died in Colorado in 1935; from Teresina Bent Scheurich, who was reared by Kit and his second wife, Josefa; and from Rumalda Luna Boggs, Governor Bent's stepdaughter. Teresina died in Taos in 1920 and Rumalda in Clayton, New Mexico, in 1906. Also included is the story of Governor Bent's murder, and there are copies of letters from Oliver Wiggins, Teresina, Aloys and Charles Scheurich, Charles Carson, and Carson relatives in Kentucky, the Carolinas, Pennsylvania, New Mexico, and Colorado. Miss Grant had examined material in the Huntington, Bancroft, and Museum of New Mexico libraries, as well as army records in Washington and Carson material in the Library of Congress. She had listed old books, journals, and documents containing Carson material owned by various individuals throughout the United States and Europe. From all of these sources she drew a wealth of information and in addition used much of the varied dialogue and unique descriptions of the period.

Copies of documents, letters, and many obscure books had to be obtained before I could certainly separate truth from error in the oft-recorded life of Carson. Fictional material had to be discarded, and this led to many interesting discoveries heretofore overlooked by historians and biographers of Carson. I found some problems, too, such as that of the Broadus operation. Did Kit actually amputate Broadus' arm? Miss Grant said that he did, citing Peters' *Life and Adventures of Kit Carson* as the source of her information, when she edited and published, in 1926, *Kit Carson's Own Story of His Life,* the autobiography of Carson "dictated to Col. and Mrs. D. C. Peters about 1856–57" (I might add here that there was no Mrs. Peters at that time) and sent to her by Charles Camp. In 1943, however, she changed her mind: "I know now that Peters was incorrect [Was he ever correct? He seems to have gone far out of his way to imply that Kit performed the surgery.] about the Broadus operation, for I gained from Kit's family the information that he did not actually wield the saw and razor in the surgery, but he only assisted—it is highly improbable that an inexperienced boy of sixteen would be able to perform such a feat." Kit himself honestly and definitely states (*Kit Carson's Own Story of His Life*): "One of the party stated that he could do it." It is a case, and the first one, when writers have gone astray to create their own Carson, always putting him at the apex.

In addition to the valuable *Kit Carson's Own Story of His Life,* I have used as source material five biographies: *Kit Carson Days,* by Edwin Legrand Sabin, of which there are two versions, the 1914 edition in one volume and the 1935 two-volume revised edition; *Pioneer Life and Frontier Adventures,* by DeWitt Clinton Peters; *The Life of Kit Carson, The Great Western Hunter and Guide,* by Charles Burdett; *Kit Carson the Pioneer of the West,* by John S. Cabot Abbott; and *The Life of Kit Carson,* by Edward S. Ellis. Books about and by John and Jessie Frémont gave a delightful insight into some aspects of Kit's character. These include *Life, Explorations and Public Service of John Charles Frémont,* by Charles W. Upham; *Recollections,* by Elizabeth Benton Frémont; *The Exploring Expedition to the Rocky Mountains,* by Colonel John Charles Frémont; *Jessie Benton Frémont, A Woman Who Made History,* by Catherine Coffin Phillips; and *Exploring with Frémont,* by Charles Preuss, the diaries of the man who was Frémont's cartographer on the first, second, and fourth expeditions to the West.

George Douglas Brewerton furnished first-hand information about Kit in his *Overland with Kit Carson, A Narrative of the Old Spanish*

Trail in '48. And both Ruxton and Garrard gave accounts of meeting Carson on the trail.

My own search for Carson material extended over the states of California, Colorado, New Mexico, Missouri, Pennsylvania, Kentucky, and North and South Carolina, as well as to three European countries: England, Scotland, and Ireland. Many items were obtained from historical-museum libraries, newspaper files, court records, and family Bibles and from the Rare Book Division of the Library of Congress.

There are several versions of where Kit Carson was born and the exact date; the statements used here have been documented from family records and reliable old journals of that day and time.

Edgar Lee Hewett gave my father some of the pictures used to illustrate this volume, while others came from Blanche Grant and the Carson family. It is indeed regrettable that a photograph of Mrs. Carson has not been found. I was able to obtain a photograph of her sister, Mrs. Bent, but the only clue which might lead to the discovery of an unmarked picture of Mrs. Carson is a photograph of her son William, who is reputed to have resembled his lovely Spanish mother. Kit, Jr., was said to have favored his father.

I am indebted to many people who generously supplied material used in this book: Edgar Lee Hewett, Bert Greer Phillips, Charles Carson, John Young-Hunter, Tessie Berry, Francis Marion Morgan, Teresina Bent Scheurich, Rumalda Luna Boggs, and Blanche C. Grant, all of whom are now dead.

Thanks and appreciation are extended to Ruth Rambo, Edith McManmon, and Kitty (Mrs. J. K.) Shishkin of the Museum of New Mexico Library, Gertrude Hill of the New Mexico State Library, and George Fitzpatrick, editor of the *New Mexico Magazine*; Victor White, Dr. V. Mitchell Smith, Lee Roy Johnson, Miss Julia Keleher, Fritz Peters, Sue Engstrom, W. A. Keleher, Charlotte A. Haegler-Stewart, Dr. Irving Lowe, Elmer and Ila (McAfee) Turner, Hazel Spraker, the Reverend John A. Marse, Chris Emmett, Marjorie Pickett Riedl, Mae Reed (Mrs. Clyde) Porter, Edwin L. Sabin, J. Cecil Alter, John Randall, Nedra Brannen, Marshall Dwight Moody, Toni (Mrs. Thomas) Tarleton, and Mrs.

Richard Dicus; and Mrs. Jean (Hal M.) Stevenson of the Harwood Library at Taos, Mrs. Marjorie Reigstad, Mrs. Seed, Dorothy Wonsmos at the University of New Mexico Library, Dr. Charles A. Anderson, Frederick R. Goff of the Rare Book Division in the Library of Congress, and Major Jack K. Boyer, director of the Kit Carson Museum at Taos, who drew the map of Kit's 1829 trip to California with Ewing Young; Colonel and Mrs. John A. Lowe, Joseph and Isabelle Quinn, Burton Harris, Lelle Swann, Constantine Aiello, Lucille (Mrs. Ashley) Pond, Vernon Hendry, and Mrs. C. D. Weimar, and the staffs of the Wisconsin Historical Society, the Huntington and Bancroft libraries in California, and the Helene Wurlitzer Foundation of New Mexico, which granted me financial assistance during the research period.

When Miss Grant began to gather material for the life story of Kit Carson, she asked Edgar Lee Hewett to write an introduction to the biography when it was ready for publication. He readily consented, telling her that he was preparing a paper on Carson for the School of American Research, Archaeological Institute of America, and suggesting that she use all or part of it as her introduction. Professor Hewett completed his paper and it was published in 1946 shortly before his death. Miss Grant received a copy, and in her notes is the request that it be used with her material in a Carson biography. With the permission of the Museum of New Mexico and the School of American Research, Professor Hewett's paper appears as the introduction to this book.

M. Morgan Estergreen

Taos, New Mexico

Contents

Illustrations

Maps

Introduction
by Edgar L. Hewett

MY ADMIRATION for the Great Scout was aroused when I was a small boy. An uncle, James C. Stice, had been a member of General John C. Frémont's command in California. In his later years, his coming to our home was looked for with war whoops. He knew just what small boys liked—tales of adventure, first hand stories of great men and their deeds. Kit Carson was Frémont's chief scout and guide through the years just preceding and during the Mexican War. Uncle Jim liked to live that time over again with the eager youngsters. He fixed in my mind a pattern for heroes—not Napoleonic nor military in the usual sense; not reckless nor spectacular, but of quiet, steel-nerved courage, as far removed as could be from the braggart or gunman of the frontier. Incidentally, it gave me an ideal of what a real man should be.

In later years in the Kit Carson country, I found myself continually on the trails of the frontier men of the generation just before me. Fifty years ago I spent some vacations gathering Kit Carson material, and I found the best of sources. Old associates and the sons and daughters of Kit were still living. In this paper I am not going to publish a new biography of him, but bring out first hand impressions from those who knew what they were talking about. I had read everything I could get about Kit, and have continued to do so. It amounts to a good many volumes, most of them worthless or worse. I have yet to read a good life of Kit Carson. His own story, brought out from a document found in Paris, and published by Miss Blanche Grant, is extremely valuable. But you can depend upon it that modest Kit Carson never gave us an intimate picture of himself or critical evaluation of his own deeds. Much of the stuff written about him is purely legendary, and mighty bad legendary, at that. I am apprehensive that a wholesome, truthful biography of him will never be written. The sources are gone. What I am aiming at now is to give the impressions of Kit conveyed to me by those who knew him in life, checked from one to another and found consistent throughout. First will be my picture of the man physically. Then I want to set this in the outline of his life that has been worked out by the historians, which I found to be approved family history.

He was a little below average height—five and a half feet—and never weighed over a hundred and forty pounds.

He did not impress one as being a small man, being well set up and well proportioned. He walked with easy, natural step, without swagger, all his movements being rather deliberate. He was slow of speech, his voice low and well modulated. He spoke the everyday language that most westerners use today—nothing of the "them thar" vernacular generally ascribed to frontiersmen by writers who never saw one. He occasionally said "done" for "did," as many westerners do, even now. He did not drink, swear nor use coarse language.

You may wonder how such a description of Kit can be written now. Let me tell you. Fifty years ago, when I was gathering information from his old associates and relatives, I made the acquaintance of Jesse Nelson and his wife, a niece of Kit's, at their home in Nine Mile Canyon, some twenty miles south of La Junta, Colorado. They and Kit had lived together at the ranch on the Rayado in New Mexico. They gave me much information about Uncle Kit and the life on the Rayado. With them I met Charley Carson, Kit's second son.[1] When I asked them to describe Kit for me, they said, "Just describe Charley. He is Kit over again—same size, build, complexion, walk, voice, manners. In Charley you have the perfect image of Kit." So, the description of the Great Scout that I have

[1] The Carsons had a son, Charles, born about 1849 or 1850, who died in infancy; two more sons and a daughter followed. Their fourth son was also named Charles (for Charles Bent), and it is he to whom Professor Hewett here refers.

put down here is authentic. It was confirmed by others who knew him intimately.

Charley talked modestly about his father; still more so about himself; wanted to be worthy of the Carson name. He was then a fairly well-to-do ranchman. He had 150 head of cattle and did some farming. He was unmarried, a Mason and wore his father's Masonic ring. He was 33 years old when I interviewed him.

When I was collecting the Kit Carson history, I made the acquaintance of Mrs. William Carson, widow of Kit's oldest son. William had been sheriff of Conejos County, Colorado. On mounting his horse he was killed by the discharge of his revolver. He was well spoken of by everyone who knew him. Mrs. Carson was living in a little adobe house in Antonito. She was a daughter of the famous trail-finder, Tom Tobin. Her son, Billy, was a fine little chap about six years old. He grew up in the San Luis valley, became deputy sheriff of Conejos County. He died a few years ago. Mrs. Carson had in a frame on her wall Kit Carson's commission as a brevet brigadier general. That would be a priceless document now. I do not know where it is.[2] I wish the Boy Scouts of America might have it to hang in their Rayado house.

One of my best sources of information was Tom Tobin, the famous trail-finder and guide of Lieutenant Beall of the United States Army. You may find an account of him in my *Campfire and Trail*. When I knew him, he was living on his ranch on the Trinchera, south of Fort Garland. I wrote of him at that time:

Among men of the western frontier, there was one who ranked with Kit Carson, but who remained comparatively unknown, who his cronies use to say, could track a grasshopper through the sagebrush. Tom Tobin, trail-finder for Lieutenant Beall,[3] was born early in 1823. He was hard and gruff and taciturn and fearless. Unlike the universally

[2] A copy of the document hangs on a wall of the old Carson home, now a museum, in Taos, New Mexico.

[3] Lieutenant Benjamin S. Beall, commander of the New Mexico Military District in 1848 (he was Major Beall then), for whom Carson twice acted as guide in chasing Apaches in New Mexico, should not be confused with Lieutenant Edward Fitzgerald Beale, the naval officer who was with Kit on the famous "crawl" to San Diego in 1846.

loved Carson, he was never too well thought of by his neighbors. They never *knew* him. Underneath that tough shell was the golden hearted *man*. Tobin, too, was a man of few words. Asked if he knew Kit Carson: "I et many a beaver tail with him." Was he as fearless as reputed to have been? "Wasn't afraid of hell or high water." How was he in private life? "Clean as a hound's tooth." Was his word as good as said to have been? "Kit Carson's word was sure as the sun's comin' up." Did he use much profanity? "Kit never cussed more'n was necessary."

Among trail men of the Southwest, I place Tom Tobin head and shoulders above all—not as a scout, the laurel wreath there belongs to modest, soft-spoken, wiry, steel-nerved Kit Carson. Would that someone who knew him had written the biography of that noble son of the Southwestern frontier! Carson was the prince of scouts, the long distance guide without equal.

Kit himself never claimed that he was fearless, as many said he was. In fact, he admitted that he was scared stiff more than once, but he never lost his pluck in a crisis.

Kit Carson was born in Kentucky in the year 1809. Four little boys born that year, the world could not well have done without: William E. Gladstone, the great prime minister of England, to whom Great Britain owes its preeminence as a Christian empire; Charles Darwin, who gave to the world a new and greater conception of the science of life; Abraham Lincoln, the Great Emancipator, who spoke to the world the immortal words, "that government of the people, by the people, for the people, shall not perish from the earth"; and Christopher Carson, plainsman, mountaineer, trapper, scout, soldier, who led the way in the opening up of our great west.

Kit was born in Kentucky, but his boyhood was passed in Missouri. He was apprenticed to a saddle maker, but did not like this job, so slipped away at the age of fifteen.[4] His employer evidently did not mind, for he offered only one cent reward for his return. Kit got his chance to go west with a wagon train, and so commenced his education. It was natural for the Indians to resist the penetration by an alien race of the region in which they had lived and been un-

[4] Kit was sixteen at the time, not fifteen.

molested through many centuries. It was equally natural for the white race to want to carry its civilization into the unoccupied regions. A certain amount of conflict was unavoidable. Kit took his part in battle with the Indians, but was never an aggressor as an Indian fighter. In a few years he came to know the Great Plains, the Rockies, and the far west of California as no other man ever did. He soon found that trapping, especially for beaver and otter, offered great opportunities for exploration and profit. He engaged in this for several years, both as an independent trapper and attached to various expeditions. This led to an acquaintance with the wild western country which was to make him in the future the most capable scout that could be found. That life of camp and trail inured him to all the hardships of the frontier.

Taos was the center for the trapping industry. Striking into the northern and western wilderness with little in the way of food except as much flour as could be carried, the trappers lived a frugal life. Beaver tails furnished the principal meat supply. Trapping the streams for several hundred miles, caching the pelts for the return trip, carrying them on their backs and on mules into Taos, and finally transporting them to the St. Louis market was the usual program. Often the take of a year or two netted a substantial sum of money. Most trappers blew it in before starting on another expedition. Kit is reported to have saved a considerable part of his.

As the trapping business grew, larger expeditions went out, and Kit's knowledge of the western country was extended. He came to know minutely the west to the Pacific and down into Mexico. Even the best equipped expedition often suffered intense hardships. A diet of mule meat was luxury. Mules that died of exhaustion on the trail helped out the commissary. Some had to be sacrificed for food when desperately needed. Those were years of incessant adventure, during which he saw almost nothing of civilization, with practically no food except what he gained with his rifle. He said of that time if he had one meal a year of bread, meat, sugar, and coffee, it was luxury.

Eventually Kit's knowledge of western trails found its place in the opening of the frontier. He met the Great Pathfinder, John C.

Frémont, and that astute leader saw in him the indispensable scout, and promptly drafted him. The trapping business was on the wane anyway, and Kit realized that he was ready for the occupation for which years of exploration had fitted him, and in which he was destined to achieve fame. He became the right hand of General Frémont in the California campaigns and the Mexican War. If official reports were to be carried, he was the trusted courier. The name, Kit Carson, was coming to be known throughout the nation. Considered indispensable by his commanding officers, looked upon by his associates as the keenest and bravest of scouts, beloved by his own people, Kit went his modest way, unconscious of his increasing greatness.

It was inevitable that the scouting phase of his life should come to an end. He wanted to get back to the region that he most loved—northern New Mexico. He settled down at Taos, built his home on the Rayado, and hoped to live out his life in peace. From his ranch various business enterprises were carried on in stock, trading and so forth, with fair success. But his great knowledge of the west, of army life and the Indian tribes, could not be dispensed with. He led a telling campaign against the Navaho. He was in some of the smaller but critical engagements of the Civil War, and later became Indian agent, in which capacity he served for a number of years. His service as a soldier was rewarded by his appointment as brevet brigadier general; but who ever speaks of *General* Carson? No title could add to the simple name, Kit Carson. Wherever that name is spoken, people listen.

In his plains days Kit married an Indian girl. She lived only a short time, leaving him a daughter, Quilina, of whom I could get no trace excepting that she went to California to live. It has been claimed that he then married an Apache woman of not very amiable disposition. I could find no confirmation of this from those who knew him so long and well. He subsequently married Josefita Jaramillo of Taos. She bore him seven children: William, Teresina, Rebecca, Charley, Stefanie, Kit, Jr., and Josefita. Kit and his wife, Josefita, lived out their lives together, and their graves are side by side in the Taos cemetery. When I first saw it, the place was overgrown with weeds, but I thought then, and put down in my notebook:

> Well, here is the end of a long trail. Back to this little old mud village Kit Carson always came from his vast wanderings. Here was his home with the gentle Josefita to welcome him, now to lie beside him under the little wooden cross. I am proud of this homely burial place. I hope no more pretentious monument will ever be erected here. This is where Kit Carson wished to rest, and he never wanted any grandiose inscription on his tombstone. On the modest red sandstone obelisk in front of the federal building in Santa Fe, you read his authentic biography in four words: "He led the way." I never stand at Kit Carson's tomb but there flashes over my mind the picture of a vast granite sarcophagus under the dome of the Hôtel des Invalides in Paris with the hypocritical self-dictated inscription: "I desire that my ashes shall rest on the banks of the Seine, in the midst of the French people whom I have so much loved," all embellished with laudation of his monstrous crimes. Far, far more glorious to be a Kit Carson, beloved, steel-nerved pathfinder, and sleep beneath the weeds under the vast blue dome of the great Southwest, than a Napoleon Bonaparte, under a gilded dome in Paris, with testimonials of his murderings on every hand. As a man I rank Napoleon, the scrubby Corsican corporal, with the loathsome little coward, Billy the Kid, of odious memory in New Mexico.

Kit Carson was more than a rough and ready frontiersman; more than an intrepid scout. I put down the following as told me by those who knew and loved him:

> His loyalty to his country was unshakable. Ingratitude did not disturb him. He was a man of fine sentiment, of boundless love for the region that gave him his opportunities. Sitting on his veranda in Taos and looking across the great valley to the gray hills of the west, he loved to talk of the old trails, of the friendly Indians, the old trapper and soldier associates, and of his beloved commander, General Frémont. As he sat on the porch of the Rayado ranch, he looked with loving eyes to the blue of the Great Plains, talked with deep feeling of the buffalo hunts, the caravans, the courageous traders, the hardships that were only incidents in a busy life. He seemed unconscious of his greatness. He simply "Led the Way."

KIT CARSON
A Portrait in Courage

I ★ Family Background

CHRISTOPHER CARSON always thought he had been born in Kentucky, but both North Carolina and Kentucky claim him as a native son. Perhaps the uncertainty is symbolic, for Kit Carson belongs, not to a particular state, but to the Southwest.

Kit was born on Christmas Eve, 1809. In this year, too, was born Abraham Lincoln, whose shadow would in later years stretch across the slave states, the premonitory sign of a new, yet old, Union. During the Civil War, Kit would fight for its preservation. In the West, the shadow of John Charles Frémont, the Pathfinder, would soon fall upon the vast, unconquered territory to which would come an indefeasible line of pioneers, some of whom would go all the way to the western coast of the continent to establish new homes. The population of young America had doubled in the twenty-five-year period ending in 1809, and before another half-century had elapsed, the United States would extend from the Atlantic to the Pacific. Both Carson and Frémont would play major roles in advancing America's western frontier.

The history of the West is a story of pioneering, of the restless movement of individuals and groups and even communities, diverse, yet common of purpose. People wanted more freedom or more money or better land or a better climate or "another chance" or "a fresh start" or innumerable other things. They gathered, moved, then dispersed. They rejoined, only to break off again. Always, some of them moved on. Pittsburgh, St. Louis, and the small Spanish village of Santa Fe became growing towns instead of wilderness outposts as nineteenth-century America expanded westward. By the end of the century, the land beyond Santa Fe would be settled, and deep ruts in the Spanish, Santa Fe, and Oregon trails would guide the building of a railroad which would bind settlement to settlement in the growing hegemony of people *versus* wilderness. Growing, expanding, moving: these, then, are the words to describe America at the time of Kit's birth.

In one sense, the westward movement can be said to have begun in Europe. Political unrest there, plus a strong desire for free land, free enterprise, and freedom of speech and worship, caused hundreds, then thousands, of dissatisfied Europeans to sail west to the New World. They settled along America's eastern seaboard, and when that area became crowded, many of them pushed toward the setting sun once more, thereby extending and prolonging the westward migration they had begun when they left their homelands. The movement was sustained as new arrivals poured into well-established coastal towns and cities, remained there briefly, and traveled on toward unclaimed lands farther west.

Freedom and opportunity, opportunity and freedom—these were the drawing cards of the New World. A desire for freedom of worship undoubtedly played some part in bringing Alexander Harvey Carson, Kit's great-grandfather, to America, and it might very well have accounted for his preliminary emigration from the west coast of Scotland to that part of Ireland now known as Ulster. Whatever his reasons, he eventually packed a few belongings, gathered his family together, and set sail for the new land across the ocean.

These Carsons were an adventuresome lot. There was always a branch of the family who never stayed long in one place; they heard of distant land, something beckoned, and they pulled up stakes and traveled. For centuries they had been fighters, preachers, and adventurers in Scotland. The less adventurous ones stayed on there, but Alexander and his family fled to freer lands—first Ireland, possibly England, then to America.

Alexander, a Presbyterian minister, presumably fled Scotland after one of the temporary defeats suffered by the Presbyterian Churchmen. The Reverend Carson was one of the "old recalcitrant pastors who fought without compromise for the ascendancy of their kirk" and for their religious beliefs. Such men were persecuted, exiled, and executed throughout the seventeenth century, which was marked by the long and bitter struggle for supremacy between church and state.

There is a tradition among the Young-Hunters of Scotland that Alexander Carson left Ireland after a brief stay and moved to Bradninch, England, near Daniel Boone's grandfather, a humble weaver of Cullompton. By this time the Carsons had four sons. John, Samuel, William, and James were born in Ireland during the approximate years 1710, 1712, 1715, and 1717. A fifth son, possibly named Alexander, Jr., was born in America.

About 1713, George Boone's two sons, Squire and George, went to America. They were not long in writing home, and every letter was filled with stories of rich land, rolling acres of it, to be had for the taking. Pennsylvania, they told their father, was the place to live. Old George noted the enthusiasm of his sons and thought things over. Finally, after four years of what must have been very careful deliberation (or was it indecision?), he made the move across the ocean. Whether or not Alexander Carson sailed with him on August 17, 1717, and landed at the thriving port of Philadelphia on October 10 has been a matter of speculation among the descendants of both families, but sometime before 1735, the name of Kit's grandfather, William Carson, was recorded in Cumberland County, Pennsylvania, at that time a part of Lancaster County.

To people like the Boones and the Carsons, the New World offered religious freedom, and they were quick to take advantage of the opportunity to establish their respective churches. A number of religious denominations sprang into existence in the American colonies during the seventeenth and eighteenth centuries, among them the first Baptist church, organized in Boston in 1682, and the Presbyterian church, which held its first synod meeting in Philadelphia on September 17, 1717. There was a Presbyterian church in Philadelphia as early as 1701, and the earliest Presbyterian colony had been established in Salem, Massachusetts, in 1652. The United Presbyterian Church in America resulted from the union of "Associate" and "Associate Reformed" churches, two offshoot bodies of the Presbyterians of Scotland and Ireland composed of people who were dissatisfied with the earlier church. Theirs was the same restless claim made by Alexander Carson: the state had too much power over the church.

In America, the Carsons settled in a forested area. Only a small part of the land had been cleared for farming, and even then stumps had been left, which necessitated cultivating between them. The Carsons customarily plowed with oxen. Their livestock ran wild, for few farmers could afford fences and barns.

Kit's grandfather spent part of his boyhood in Pennsylvania, and there is specific evidence that life on the Carson farm was the kind a boy would enjoy. Game was plentiful; deer came to the cabin door, and there were bears aplenty. Near-by trees afforded shelter and protection for wild turkeys, and the flutter of their wings could be heard at nearly all hours. Even the buffalo came to water near farms in remote, outlying areas. And, much to the delight and excitement of a boy of that day and age, there were Indians living in the Tylpehocken and Octelaunee valleys, which lay beyond the mountains north of the Carson and Boone farms.

These Indians were friendly most of the time, for the Quaker policy of fair dealings had kept them on good terms. There were occasions, however, when the red man became hostile, as in 1728, when George Boone wrote the governor that the settlers had fled and "there remains about twenty men with me to guard my mill ... and we are resolved to defend ourselves to ye last Extremity." Later, in 1745, John Carson, who founded Carsonville in Dauphin County, was one of the signers of a petition to Governor Hamilton asking for ammunition and arms to enable them to protect themselves against the Indians. In time, peaceful relationships were restored, and the Carsons have recollections of friendly Delawares visiting their grandfather's farm.

The urge to move on to new country was undoubtedly discussed in the Carson cabin, for during the 1750's a steady stream of people flowed out of Pennsylvania through the Shenandoah Valley and southward into North Carolina. When Daniel was about sixteen years old, Squire and Sarah Boone sold their farm and traveled west to the Cumberland Valley, then went down the Shenandoah. Squire moved his family from place to place for nearly two years before he finally settled in Yadkin Valley on the western frontier of North Carolina.

Stories of land grants in the wild area to the south drifted back to the Carsons and other Pennsylvania farmers. Some of them were satisfied with what they had, but others, among them William Carson, seeking to improve their lot or simply for the want of a change of scenery, joined the southbound throng of travelers following the barrier-chain of the Alleghenies through Maryland and the Virginias into the Carolinas. At that time the barrier-chain formed the western frontier of a rugged, thickly wooded country whose tangled slopes compelled the traveler to follow the curve of the long, trough-like valleys that lay between the ranges. There were no roads through the mountains, except, perhaps, "Warriors' Path," a mere trace of a road used by Indian war parties or Indian hunters. Where the few dim paths or trails to be seen led, no white man ever knew.

All along the edge of the mountains the frontier folks established homes and flourished. Thus the areas along the south-trending emigrant trails were becoming well settled when William Carson passed through the Shenandoah Valley on his way to North Carolina, where he stopped in Rowan County, now a part of Iredell County, near the site of present-day Statesville. Here, on December 1, 1761, he established the Carson land grant of 692 acres in the present Loray district. The grant, made by Lord Granville, lay on both sides of Third Creek, or Wind Creek, as it is now called. William, while not a minister like his father, was a faithful supporter of the Presbyterian church and is reported to have donated the land upon which Concord Presbyterian Church was first built. He had apparently decided to stay for a while.

A brief account of William's marriage to Eleanor McDuff was passed down to his great-grandson Charles. It was like other North Carolina weddings in the years 1750–52. The bride-to-be rode to the church on horseback, sitting on a pillion placed behind her father's saddle; when they dismounted, her father placed the pad

7

behind the bridegroom's saddle. After a brief Presbyterian ceremony in the log church, Eleanor was lifted to her pillion by her
new husband, and they rode off to their honeymoon cabin, followed
by friends and relatives who proceeded to toast the happy couple
and feast and sing far into the night.

Lindsey, Kit's father, was the first child to bless this union, arriving on August 1, 1754; then came Andrew on March 1, 1756, Robert on July 20, 1759, and Sarah about 1762. Eleanor followed a
few years later, possibly around 1764–67, and Alexander, who emi-
grated to Mississippi, was born in 1769. His son, Alexander Jr., was
the first Carson on record to go west of the Mississippi River.

In 1753, the Boones acquired land in North Carolina's Yadkin
Valley from the Earl of Granville. King George II had granted the
Granvilles an enormous tract of land but had retained the right to
half of any gold and silver which might be found thereon. The
Earl himself retained the right to half the remainder, which left
one-fourth for the owners. One of many irksome stipulations concerning the land was that the purchaser had to pay an annual rental,
and he was also obliged to clear three out of every one hundred
acres every three years. To clear even one acre of this densely forested land was backbreaking work.

With such practices being the order of the day, it can safely be
assumed that the Carsons and the Boones had a hand in the dis-
sensions which arose over land-grant stipulations. At this time in
North Carolina, the people, through their representatives in the
legislature, began their strenuous opposition to royal authority. They
took more violent action at home when they seized one of the Granville agents, a Mr. Corbin, and, according to historian John H.
Wheeler, "compelled him to give bond and security, to produce
his books, and disgorge his illegal fees." North Carolina's rebellion
against this system of oppression kept her in the lead of the Colonies
in the Revolutionary struggle.

The series of Indian wars from 1758 to 1760, it should be
noted, had been fought mostly on the North Carolina frontier. By
1760, the white man had laid waste the whole Cherokee country,
burning villages and destroying crops, and had driven five thousand

Indians into the hills. It is not surprising, therefore, that these hardy pioneers should take on the British, too, when the need arose.

Lindsey's father had chosen his land by a creek, presumably so that he would have water for his crops and livestock during dry spells, as well as for family use in cooking and bathing. The North Carolina country was wilder than the Pennsylvania William Carson left, and it was more sparsely populated. Trees and undergrowth were thick and tangled, so much so that Lindsey and his brothers had to cut their way along the river to hunt and fish. They soon discovered that the easiest way to travel in this wilderness was to follow the buffalo paths, which they adopted for bridle paths. Later these were widened into roads for carts and other vehicles, for Salisbury was near enough to supply a few commodities for the frontier farmer and to provide the hunter and trapper a good market for his skins and furs.

Game was everywhere; a hunter could kill thirty deer a day, claimed Daniel Boone, without leaving Yadkin Valley. Shaggy buffalo made deep ruts to the river, where multitudes of geese, swans, and ducks swam lazily. Wild turkeys nested in the tall pines, and fur-bearing animals, such as the raccoon, abounded in the woods. Colonel William Fleming wrote in his journal that great flocks of parakeets appeared in these parts in winter. He also tells about the large ivory-billed woodpecker in Kentucky and North Carolina— "birds which have long since drawn back into the remote swamps of the hot gulf coast, fleeing before man as the buffalo and elk have fled."

Shortly before the American Revolution (about 1773), William Carson died suddenly. According to available records, he died from "imprudently drinking cold water from a well in the church yard on a hot day." He was buried in Morrison's Cemetery, a half-mile from Concord Church. After his death, Eleanor married a widower, John Scroggs, whose son John, Jr., married Eleanor's daughter Sarah.

When Lindsey was twenty or twenty-one, he, Robert, and Andrew served in the American Revolution under General Wade Hampton. At the close of 1779, the British transferred the seat

of the war to the southern colonies, where Sir Henry Clinton enlisted some two hundred Loyalists in his army. The fighting in the
Carolinas took on the aspects of a civil war, and the British were
continually harassed by guerrilla bands of patriots under the leadership of such brave men as Sumter, Pickens, and Marion, the Swamp
Fox. Andrew and Lindsey, both captains under Marion, were engaged in the hazardous mission of carrying dispatches between Generals Greene and Marion while Cornwallis waged fierce war on
South Carolina.

Captain Lindsey Carson's war record was not as outstanding as
that of his brother, Andrew. On one occasion a band of Tories made
camp in Iredell County on Hunting Creek (at Cook's Spring) to
await Cornwallis' army, which they would join as it marched up
the west bank of the Yadkin River in pursuit of General Greene.
While passing through the vicinity the Tories took the inhabitants'
best horses, among them a prize horse belonging to Michael Elsbury, a soldier home on furlough. A four-man party was organized
to recover the horse; in it were Elsbury, Andrew Carson, Daniel
Wright, and William Young. The men located the camp where the
stolen horse was tied, slipped past the sentries, recovered the horse,
and cut loose the halters of the rest of the horses. Selecting the best
to ride, they shot into the band and stampeded the herd. Andrew
and his men escaped, leaving the Tories afoot.

Later, Captain Andrew Carson and Captain Caldwell were instru-
mental in bringing to justice a notorious Tory murderer and sabo-
teur named Aldrich. The man had ambushed and killed seven or
eight of his neighbors and had tried to kill Andrew's future father-
in-law, Thomas Young.

Early in the fall of 1780, Andrew again honored the Carson name
at the Battle of Camden in South Carolina by carrying the fatally
wounded Baron de Kalb from the creek in the thick of battle. The
Baron, who, with Lafayette, had joined Washington's army during
the memorable campaign of 1776, was one of many distinguished
Europeans who gave his services—and life—for the American cause.

The war continued to be a bitter struggle, involving not only the
British and the Colonists, but also the Indians. Great Britain had

actively sought an alliance with the Indians soon after the conflict began, for circumstances made them natural allies: the Colonists were advancing deeper into their territory, settling in their sacred hunting grounds.

The Indians were receiving many coveted gifts from the British command. Already approached were the Cherokees, Choctaws, and Creeks, and many of them had joined the fight. Consequent ravages of Indian warfare became so atrocious that the frontier folks grew to hate the British king with a deadly and lasting passion. They saw their children borne away into captivity, their homes burned, their wives outraged, and their friends tortured by Indians armed with British guns, bribed with British gold, obeying British commanders.

When the Creeks, who had held back, saw fifty cartloads of ammunition sent by the British, they joined the Cherokees in a mighty attack which might very well have meant the destruction of the settlers had it not been for a mistake made by the British at the onset of war. The British had prematurely aroused the Indians and had sent ammunition before troops arrived to organize the campaign. The settlers, who were better organized, even though they had less ammunition, fought the Indians and won the war.

As soon as the Carson boys were old enough, something beyond the mountains aroused their wanderlust and they scattered to different parts of the country. Robert Carson went to Kentucky; Alexander, Lindsey's nephew, traveled up the Missouri River and was hunting and trapping there as early as 1809; Lindsey and Andrew moved to the Hunting Creek settlement of Iredell County, North Carolina.

Shortly after the war Andrew Carson married Thomas Young's daughter, Temperance, a relative of the famous Houstons of Iredell County, and they settled in North Carolina to rear their family. At about the same time, Robert and Lindsey Carson moved to South Carolina, and in 1784, Lindsey married Lucy Bradley.

At this time Kentucky was struggling with birth pains. While some of the Revolutionary battles were being fought, Daniel Boone and his companion, Richard Henderson, were busy laying the foundation for the future state. In 1773, Boone attempted to lead a group of settlers into its wilderness. Some of his party were killed by Indians, and the rest lost courage and returned to their homes. In 1774, Harrodsburg was founded. It was soon abandoned but was successfully resettled in 1775 a fortnight before Boone and Henderson began to erect their fort at Boonesborough.

"Neither the Royal nor the provincial government were factors in the various settlements which simultaneously sprang up on Kentucky soil," Theodore Roosevelt pointed out. "Each group of pioneers had its own leader, its own settlement, its own motives. These individual settlements could not have become permanent had it not been for the comparatively well-organized settlement of Boonesborough" and the temporary safety from Indian raids afforded by Henderson's Treaty of Sycamore Shoals.

When the treaty was finally signed on March 17, 1775, with some twelve hundred Indians present, including Chiefs Dragging Canoe, the Raven, Attakullaculla, and Oconostota, who was head chief of the Cherokees, it merely transferred an imperfect title, which the Indians held by squatters' rights, to an indefinite boundary. Both Dragging Canoe and Oconostota told the white treaty-makers that the land which they had bought for £10,000 was a "dark and bloody ground." They warned that beyond the mountains dwelt the northwestern Indians, who were at war with the Cherokees and who would show the white settlers as little mercy as they showed the Cherokees, their enemies.

The treaty title included all of the land lying along and between the Kentucky and Cumberland rivers. Henderson named the new domain Transylvania, and it was, as the chiefs had said, a dark and bloody ground. The people who went there were constantly attacked by the Indians, and on many occasions entire settlements were wiped out. Part of the difficulty lay in the fact that Kentucky, or Transylvania, was virtually an island in a wilderness, separated from the extreme outposts of the seacoast by two hundred miles of virtually impenetrable forests. Elsewhere, most new settlements were formed when people moved a short distance from their neighbors and thus had at least some protection, but this was not the case with the isolated settlements in the wilderness of Kentucky. Here there were no settlements back to back.

In April, Henderson's settlers arrived at the fort which Boone and his men were building. Dogwood whitened the forests, and the banks of the streams were crimson with redbud blossoms. No doubt the beauty of such a background and the promises of hundreds of acres of rich soil gave the settlers new hope, for they soon finished the fort and constructed log homes around it.

Boone's fort was rectangular, about 250 feet long and half as wide. At each corner were loopholed two-story blockhouses which served as bastions. The sturdy log cabins of the settlers were placed so that their outer walls formed part of the fort's walls. Between the cabins, high stockade fences, also loopholed, were built. A double wooden gate, closed with stout bars, was flanked without by the blockhouses and within by the cabins. In case of Indian attacks, each cabin was separately defensible. The inner courtyard was used for a corral.

While Kentucky was being settled, Lindsey Carson and his wife, Lucy, were rearing a family in South Carolina. Their five children were William, born in 1786; Sarah, born in 1788; Andrew, named for his distinguished uncle, born in 1790; Moses Bradley, born in 1792; and Sophie, born in 1793.

Just before Sophie's birth the Lindsey Carsons moved to Boone's Kentucky, settling near the present-day site of Richmond. That part of Kentucky had undergone rapid changes since the founding of Boonesborough some nineteen years before. Four years after Kentucky was settled, the population was reported to be about three thousand. Now there were more people than that in one settlement.

On April 5, 1793, shortly after Sophie was born, Lucy Carson died. For about three years Lindsey managed alone, relatives helping with his five children. Then on February 11, 1796, he married Rebecca Robinson of Greenbrier County, Virginia.

Christopher (Kit) Carson was the sixth of ten children, six boys and four girls, to bless this second marriage. First to arrive, on November 29, 1797, was Elizabeth; she married Robert Cooper of the Kentucky and Missouri Coopers. Nancy, who married a Mr.

Briggs of Fort Briggs in Missouri, was born on August 28, 1801. Robert, born November 10, 1803, married a Calloway, and Matilda (or Mathilda) M., born on November 4, 1805, married an Adams. Hamilton, who was born January 18, 1808, was married three times; to a Smith, to a Campbell, and to a Cook. Christopher (Kit) was married twice, and his date of birth was December 24, 1809, and not the twenty-fifth, as some historians have stated. Hampton, probably named for General Wade Hampton, was born on May 23, 1812, and married Annita Crews; Mary Ann, Kit's favorite sister, was born May 25, 1814, and married a Rubey; Sarshall C., born June 16, 1816, married an Arnich; and Lindsey, Jr., was born on September 11, 1818, a week after his father's death.

After Nancy was born in 1801, Lindsey purchased from John Berry 115 acres of land for £250. The acreage, purchased on November 25, was located at the corner of Tate Creek and Groggin's Lane in Madison County. It was here that Kit spent the first year or so of his life. According to Mary Ann, his cradle was of peeled hickory bark and was the same hand-hewn cradle used by the five Carson children who preceded him.

The Carson cabin was reported to have been the usual two-story log cabin of that day, with a huge stone fireplace at one end of its large living room. In addition to the living room, which was also used as a dining room, there were a small bedroom and a storeroom. A ladder led from the living room to a loft above, where the children slept. The floor was probably made of puncheons, great slabs of wood carefully shaped, and the roof was probably of clapboards. Antlers driven into the joists supported ever-ready rifles, and long pegs of wood in selected corners held jackets and family clothing. The long dining table was made of one or more huge clapboards set on wooden pegs. Benches and three-legged stools were used for chairs, and the Carson cabin was reported to have had the luxury of a hand-made rocking chair. This, plus the upstairs loft, placed the Carson dwelling in the nicer class of frontier homes.

2 ★ Kit's Early Life

CAPTAIN ANDREW CARSON, Kit's uncle, related that Kit was born in Iredell County, North Carolina, while Lindsey and Rebecca were visiting in the home of Christopher Houston on Hunting Creek and that Kit was named for their host. The same tradition has been handed down in the Young family, with the added information that Kit was born two months before he was due, suggesting that this fact might account for his small stature. In height he was only five and a half feet, six inches shorter than any of his brothers.

Whether he was born in Kentucky or North Carolina seemed to have been immaterial to Kit. When Colonel Peters took notes at Fort Massachusetts, New Mexico, Kit began the story of his life with the statement that "I was born in Madison County, Kentucky, December 24, 1809." When people asked Kit where he was born, he at once said Kentucky.

In 1809, there were many places in Kentucky so thick with trees and undergrowth that it was impossible to cut a path through the hills or by the streams, which were bordered with luxuriant grass and wild flowers. At times, wild turkeys, pigeons, and quail swept through the air in cloudlike flocks; wild geese, ducks, and other water fowl swam rivers and lakes which no paddle wheel—or even a keel—had yet disturbed. And there were buffalo.

The buffalo meant many things to the frontier family. They used his flesh as food and his skin as robes and covers. They made moccasins of his hide, fiddle strings of his sinews, and combs of his horns. They spun his coat into yarn, and out of it they wove a coarse cloth which looked like rough linen and was almost as warm as wool. Every home had a loom, and every woman was a weaver.

The towns springing up in Kentucky did not differ much from those in remote parts of Pennsylvania. The settlers' harvests were abundant, and they were anxious to export the surplus. They had already cut roads and trails from one settlement to another. Once in a while an adventurous hunter would stop at the Carson cabin to give accounts of the new land where Daniel Boone was living. There was no other way for the Carsons to know about "Upper Louisiana," as Missouri was then called, for there were no newspapers in Kentucky then and Zebulon Pike's book, published in 1810, had not yet reached Kentucky. Nicholas Biddle's book on the Lewis and Clark explorations was not published until 1814.

Indians were still a scourge to Lindsey and his family. Although they rarely attacked a town or settlement of any size—life was reasonably safe in the thickly populated areas—the remote river routes and isolated farms were beset by them. The wooded riversides, where the hunter had to go for game, were ideal hiding places for marauding Indians.

The vanishing frontier and the scarcity of game undoubtedly played some part in the next move of the pioneering Carsons, for the record of a deed in Madison County Court House lists the sale, on October 6, 1811, of Lindsey Carson's cabin and land in Kentucky to John and Rebecca Grugett, or Gingett, for the sum of one thousand dollars. Years later George Carson, son of William, wrote to Edwin L. Sabin that he remembered his father's telling of the sale of the cabin and the trip to Missouri, which was made in the summer of 1812. Both Teresina Bent Scheurich and Charles Carson claim that the trip was made in the spring of 1811, which seems more likely because of the war.

The Boones and the Coopers, already settled in this wildly beautiful country, might have influenced Lindsey's decision to move to Upper Louisiana. The Carsons and Boones were closely associated and intermarried when Kit's older half-brother, William, married Millie Boone, Daniel's grandniece, in 1810. Millie passed away when their first and only child, Adaline, was born in 1810. When the Carsons prepared to follow the Boones to Missouri, William left his daughter with his sister-in-law, Cassandra Boone, and joined the family group on the long journey to claim some of the new land.

The trip was certainly arduous, but not dangerous, since the Indians rarely attacked large groups of travelers. The trail had been steadily traveled since the turn of the century. Most of the family walked, for there were not enough horses or oxen to accommodate all of them. Little blue-eyed Kit rode on the saddle in front of his mother while the older Carson children walked or rode in the baggage carts. They lived off the land as they traveled, and Lindsey was thus always in the lead, with the men, scouting for game.

It took most of the summer and fall to make the trip, and only once did they experience an Indian scare. It was dusk and the families had stopped at the edge of a stream to camp for the night when some Indians were seen across the creek. Everyone was apprehensive, even though the men stayed on guard all night, but the Indians passed by without molesting them.

Daniel Boone was given a large tract of land for his settlers by the Spanish officials, who proposed it as a townsite. Daniel named the new town "Daniel Boone's Palatinate." For a while it prospered; then the Missouri River shifted and much of the land was washed away.

As magistrate under the Spanish crown, Daniel held court under the "Justice Tree," near his cabin. Whipping posts were common, but the lash was Boone's principal penalty and he saw that it was well laid on. The culprit was "whipped and cleared," Missouri tradition states, and thus restored to a reputable standing in the community.

On March 9, 1804, Spain formally transferred sovereignty of Upper Louisiana to France. The next day, France turned it over to the United States. When Lindsey arrived, it had not yet been christened Missouri, and the Americans were a long time in settling it.

There was plenty of land, so Lindsey claimed a large tract in the central part of what is now Howard County. While the land was being cleared and their cabin built, the Carsons lived at Fort Hempstead, Fort Kincaid, and Fort Cooper. There was still Indian danger in this wild new country, so the cabins were barricaded, loopholed, and bulletproofed. Each planting season the men made a careful search for lurking Indians. Half the men stood guard while the others plowed, sowed, and, later, harvested. For many years ripe fields were burned or otherwise destroyed by marauding Indians who were reluctant to give up their homeland to the white settlers.

Kit lived the ordinary life of the frontier child: little formal schooling, much chasing of buffalo and fighting Indians. The excitement of hunting, the peculiar habits of the deer and buffalo, the ways of the Indians—these elements symbolized Kit Carson's subsequent life. Legend has it that Kit's first toy was a wooden gun whittled by his brother soon after they arrived in Upper Louisiana. It wasn't too many years until the toy gun was exchanged for a real one, which Kit's father taught him how to use. Daniel Boone, now an old man who spent his time hunting and fishing, taught young Kit much about the skills of shooting and the ways of the Indian.

Not all the Indians in the vicinity were hostile. At the age of six, Kit was beginning to learn the habits and character of the friendly Indians. He was learning to think as they thought, mastering their particular psychology, which in later life enabled him to know exactly how to trail them and what to expect.

An incident remembered in Carson family circles and passed down from Kit's niece shows his complete lack of fear of Indians. One June day when he was playing by the river, he suddenly realized that he was not alone. At first he saw no one; then, through the bushes, he saw bright black eyes, set in little brown faces, peering at him. He motioned his watchers to come closer. Very cautiously, at first, they came to stand at a safe distance from him, then, little by little, they came closer. None of the little Indians was over seven years old, and one was so small that he could barely toddle. Their only piece of clothing was a deerskin tied around their middles.

Nothing was said at first because Kit knew no Indian words, nor did he know their sign language. Finally he devised a way to make himself understood. He pointed to his chest and repeated his name. Nothing happened. Not a child changed expression. Again, he repeated his name, then he pointed to the little Indian nearest him.

It worked. The Indian child murmured something, and as he pointed to another of his fellows, the latter spoke his name. This continued until all the children had told Kit their names. They taught Kit a game played with sticks, and he showed them how to play games he and his brothers played. Kit spoke in his language and the Indian children in theirs, but they seemed to understand one another.

According to another story in the Carson family, Kit gave the alarm for an Indian raid and helped his father and older brothers fire from the cabin's loopholes until the Indians fled. And the following story of young Kit's Indian experiences comes from his favorite sister, Mary Ann. She told her granddaughter, Mrs. Hawley, how Kit saved her from the Indians:

> Indians were a constant peril in those days, and we always were afraid of them. When we would go to school or any distance away from our house, we would carry bits of red cloth with us to drop if we were captured by the Indians, so our people could trace us.
>
> When we were asleep at night and there was the slightest noise outside the house, Kit's little brown head would be the first to bob up. I always felt completely safe when Kit was on guard duty, even when he was a boy, or when he slept near me.
>
> I will never forget the first time that I thought he saved my life. We were on horseback and came to a stream that had flooded into a raging torrent. It was dangerous, and I screamed to Kit that I never would be able to get across. "Get on my horse behind me," he said. "Then close your eyes and hold on for dear life." I did as he said, and he took me safely across the raging stream.

Kit's mother, it can be assumed, did not dream that such acts of courage by her son would win him fame. True, Kit was shorter than his brothers, but he possessed the best disposition in the Carson family. He was the silent, reliable member of the family, even as a child. He also possessed the fine features of his ancestors; wavy blond hair, a high forehead, twinkling blue eyes, and strong, well-shaped hands. And he had a magnetic personality.

Lindsey and Rebecca Carson wanted and planned for Kit to study law. As Kit grew older and as his remarkably retentive memory developed, his father's desire that he should have such an education increased. All of the Carson girls were sent to school, but Kit was the only Carson boy who attended school regularly through the third grade. This was intended to prepare Kit for a legal career, a dream his parents never realized because he chose his own career.

It was natural for Kit to become a trapper, Indian scout, and soldier. Most of the Carsons went west to trap beaver and hunt buffalo, and Kit's childhood was crowded with Indian stories his older brothers brought from the western frontier. This was reason enough for Kit to want to go west; the problem was, how could he get there? Well, he would find a way.

The first Carson to receive literary mention in connection with trapping was Alexander Carson, whose name, along with some of his deeds, appears in Washington Irving's *Astoria*. According to Irving, Alexander and a fellow trapper named Benjamin Jones joined the Wilson Hunt Price expedition in May, 1811. The two men had been trapping together for at least two years before that, but they seem to have split up sometime after meeting Price's group. Elliott Coues gives a brief account of them in his *New Light on the Early History of the Greater Northwest*.

Still another Carson who went west to make his fortune was Charley, Kit's nephew. Ben Arnold said that "he was a market hunter and served fresh meat to bull trains." Arnold's account of Charley's death at the hands of "a war party of fifteen or twenty Blood Indians" near Fort Benton is included in L. F. Crawford's *Rekindling Camp Fires*. And Kate L. Gregg, in *The Road to Santa Fe*, lists Andrew and Robert Carson as members of the 1825 expedition surveying for the proposed road to Santa Fe. She also says that Andrew Broadus was with the party.

On the Missouri frontier, Kit's father continued his accustomed life of farming, hunting, and fighting Indians. He and his older sons, Moses and Andrew, served in the militia from Fort Kincaid during the War of 1812. At this time, Lindsey owned a large-bore rifle. Most of its stock had been shot away, along with two of Lindsey's fingers on his left hand, in a skirmish with Indians. Lindsey killed two, one with his rifle and the other with the Indian's own knife in hand-to-hand combat. Despite the increased hostility of the Indians, young Kit, who was as fearless as his father, took his turn at guard duty with the men.

William Carson returned to Kentucky for his daughter, Adaline, in 1816 and brought his sister-in-law back with them. The Howard County tax records list both William and Lindsey, and the marriage bureau dates William's marriage to Cassandra in 1818, when he established a farm near his father's at Cooper's Bottom. There Adaline became Kit's favorite playmate for the next few years.

When Kit was eight, a tragedy befell the Carson family. It was early September, 1818. Lindsey and a Negro boy were clearing a field for cultivation near Fort Cooper when the woods caught fire. In the attempt to extinguish the blaze, a burning limb fell on Lindsey, killing him instantly.

After the death of his father, Kit joined the older boys in plowing the fields and taking care of the large Carson family. Seed had to be planted, crops harvested, and the animals fed and watered. As a result of his share in such responsibilities, Kit was unable to attend the one-room frontier school steadily. But by going when he could and with Mary Ann's assistance, he was able to gain approximately two more grades in grammar school.

F. Tom Carson related that although Kit was said to have had a fairly good common-school education for his time, and to have written a good hand, and spelled acceptably, it was a known fact that he did not care for the classroom and its confinements. He once described the end of his schooling to his friends in the following manner: "I was a young boy in the school house when the cry came, 'Indians'! I jumped to my rifle and threw down my spelling book, and there it lies." Mary Ann came to his defense with the declaration that "Kit was always a smart little fellow at his books, and father meant to make a lawyer out of him, but soon after we moved out of the fort and were getting along pretty well, father was accidentally killed."

The Carson girls continued to go to school when there was a teacher. Mary Ann said she was a good reader and often read to Kit after supper by candlelight. The subject was always the great

West: the buffalo hunters, the Indian fighters, the trappers, missions, and forts in faraway territory under the flag of Spain. It was recorded, whether correctly or not, in Carson family tradition that the Pike and Biddle books, or parts of them, had been read to Kit by his sister. However, neither Pike nor Biddle gave the romantic impressions recorded by Kit's sister. Pike described the West as a desert everywhere, and Biddle used the word "treeless" often.

Kit's older brothers were all actively engaged in the fur trade. During the War of 1812 and shortly after, the fur trade along the Missouri River was nearly devoid of profits and interest, but Manuel Lisa, Moses Carson's early employer, was actively trading there just after the war. In 1819, Moses became an officer in the Missouri Fur Company when it was reorganized.

Moses established quite a reputation in the trading journals of his day. He would return home with tales of Indian fights (Joshua Pilcher made him a temporary officer in the Arikara campaign) and stories of the high prices received for beaver plews. These stories undoubtedly added fuel to the fire of Kit's ambition to go west and become a trapper and Indian scout, but his dream would not be realized for some years.

At the death of Kit's father, Mrs. Carson became the seventh widow at Fort Hempstead. She remained a widow for four years, then married Joseph Martin. Soon there were more children—Kit's half-brothers and a half-sister. And it seemed as if Kit were doomed to spend his life in Missouri, for in 1824, when Kit was fifteen, his mother and stepfather apprenticed him to two saddlers. "He didn't like it," Mary Ann said. "About the only use he had for a saddle was on a horse's back."

3 ★ Caravan at Independence

By 1826, Kit had already served one "distasteful" year as a saddle-maker's apprentice to William and David Workman in Old Franklin, directly across the river from Boonesville. Kit's older brothers, who had been trading between St. Louis and Santa Fe, were making preparations for a trip to Independence, or perhaps farther west, with a caravan of trade. Kit begged to go with them, but his mother refused to give him permission, promising that if he would wait another year, he could then go west.

Kit later told his niece that he felt at that time that he had already waited too long. He said that while he worked in the saddle shop he had listened to trappers, hunters, and mountain men tell tales of the new West, of hunting paradises, undreamed-of freedom, and thrilling Indian encounters. He told her how he had longed, during his year of apprenticeship, to travel to the great wilderness, to join the buffalo chases, and to live the life of a trapper, floating down some distant stream in a long canoe filled with valuable furs. It was while he was learning to use the awl that he overheard traders talking about a caravan going to far-away Santa Fe. The men had said, according to Mary Ann, that they were going to the Spanish province to trade because there goods sold at profit of 200 per cent and beaver pelts were better exchanges than gold.

When Kit's brothers, with their pack animals, left Franklin to accompany the caravan as far as Independence, they refused to let him accompany them. Kit rebelled. He borrowed a neighbor's mule and started for Independence, about one hundred miles away. He caught up with the caravanners early one morning when they were camped just outside Independence. He was told that he would have to return home. Obediently, he rode out of camp toward the east, turned the mule loose, trusting that it might eventually find its way back to Franklin, and trudged back to camp on foot. Such determination must have softened the hearts of his brothers, as well as that of Charles Bent, for they agreed to let him go with them to Santa Fe.

Years later, Kit told his niece that it was Charles Bent whom he sought out to ask for a job and Charles who gave him the opportunity to go west. Stephen Turley, he said, was wagon master, and William Bent, who was seven months younger than Kit, also made the trip. However, he told Teresina that Charles Bent did not go all the way to New Mexico, but left the caravan soon after it crossed the Cimarron.

Kit had often heard his older brothers speak, with great respect, of Captain Charles Bent. The Bent brothers had not grown up in a "semi-literate cabin-in-the-clearing" atmosphere, as had most of the traders and trappers, but had been reared in St. Louis. The Bents lived in a large house set amid deep lawns and fragrant fruit trees, and their meals were served, by slaves, on open verandas overlooking the wide Missouri. In the Bent stables were blooded horses, and near by were kennels for the hounds, while the vast farmlands included dovecots, beehives, and orchards of wild plums and crab apples. Judge Silas Bent had managed to keep seven of his eleven children in this atmosphere. Charles, William, George, and Robert followed the Santa Fe Trail.

A few weeks after Kit made his unannounced departure from the saddle shop to join the caravan, the following insertion appeared in the *Missouri Intelligencer*:

NOTICE TO WHOME IT MAY CONCERN: That Christopher Carson, a boy about sixteen years old, small for his age, but thickset, light hair, ran away from the subscriber, living in Franklin, Howard Co., Mo., to whome he had been bound to learn the saddler's trade on or about the first day of September last. He is supposed to have made his way toward the upper part of the state. All persons are notified not to harbor, support, or subsist said boy under penalty of the law. One cent reward will be given to any person who will bring back said boy.

(signed) David Workman
Franklin, October 6, 1826

By the time the notice appeared, Kit was well on his way west.

When Kit arrived at Independence, the caravan was ready to begin the long trip across the prairies. Rifles had been checked, powder horns filled, and water containers loaded on the wagons. The supply wagon had been packed the night before. According to Josiah Gregg, each man's allotment of food for an overland trip to Santa Fe usually consisted of about fifty pounds of flour, as many more of bacon, twenty of sugar, ten of coffee, and some salt. Beans, crackers, and a few trifles were sometimes added to the larder, but they were looked upon as dispensable luxuries. Buffalo and other game killed along the way furnished fresh meat.

As the first streaks of dawn lengthened across the Missouri sky, the caravan started on the long, dangerous journey over the plains and into the mountainous country of the Santa Fe Trail. It was the custom to strike the trail away from the muddy Missouri River, traveling through the country of the then friendly Osage Indians, where not even a house dotted the bleak landscape, and head for the Arkansas River, there to cross into the vast prairie beyond. This part of the journey was not too dangerous because a treaty with the Osages had been signed in 1825. It allowed the United States government and the Mexican Republic to build a road through the Osage country and granted the "unmolested use thereof" to travelers. Be that as it may, the wise traveler was always prepared for Indian trouble, regardless of any treaties which might have been made.

Every night during the trip to Santa Fe, the wagons were parked in a hollow circle, the front wheels of one wagon overlapping the rear of another. An opening was left in the circle through which the animals could be driven in case of Indian attack. With as few as seven wagons forming a circle, a hundred animals could be held in the makeshift corral at one time. Campfires were usually built outside the wagon enclosure, and the men slept on blankets in the open. Tents were rarely used on these trips; in case of rain, the men retired to the wagons for shelter.

In addition to marauding Indians, there were many perils that could befall travelers on overland journeys. Animals might stampede, and rain, hailstones as big as hen eggs, or snowstorms could strike with such violence that the trail would be lost for days. Rattlesnakes, always numerous on the prairies, sometimes struck at horses and caused confusion among men and beasts. Miscalculation of water and supplies resulted in great hardship at times. Confusing the lead-wagon driver of the caravan were deep paths made by buffalo, imprints of numberless generations of the animals who had followed their leaders from place to place across the plains.

Just before the Bent caravan reached the Arkansas River, as the men were preparing to camp one evening, a teamster named Andrew Broadus jerked his rifle out of the wagon, muzzle first, to shoot a wolf. The gun discharged, and the ball lodged in his right arm. There was no doctor on this trip, so the arm was neglected until gangrenous infection set in. If Broadus were to live, his arm would have to be amputated.

Kit and two others assisted the men who offered to perform the operation. Whiskey was used as an anesthetic; the surgical instruments consisted of a butcher knife and a handsaw. The knife was honed to razor sharpness, and the coarse teeth of the saw were filed down to a fine proportion. The "surgeons" opened the arm around the bone, which was then sawed off. After they had cauterized the wound with a red-hot iron bolt, they applied tar, taken from a wagon wheel and heated to the proper consistency, to the stump to serve as a seal against dirt and infection. The stump was then bandaged, and the caravan proceeded as if nothing unusual had happened. Despite the crude surgery, the arm healed rapidly and Broadus was well in a few weeks.

A day's journey after the accident, the caravan arrived at Pawnee Rock, the "blackboard of the plains," where travelers inscribed their names and the date of arrival on its lower edge. For many years the red, jutting cliff, which was capped by a mound of stones, had been used by Indians and white men alike to indicate they had passed by, *paso por aqui.*

Pawnee Rock was in the heart of the buffalo country. Indian hunting parties—Comanches, Sioux, Arapahoes, and even the northern Blackfeet and Crows—were to be seen following the drifting herds of bison. Now the cavvy, or animal herd, of any wagon train was a tempting prize for Indian raiders, and Kit's position as herder, or wrangler, following the cavvy was therefore one of the most dangerous jobs in the caravan.

Authors of old western romances tell of the 1826 Bent caravan's having an Indian scare at Pawnee Rock, wherein young Kit shot his mule instead of a Pawnee. This incident was also proclaimed by Jim Bridger, Buffalo Bill, Daniel Boone, and others. It was a perennial joke for the rough traders to tell of the green cavvy boy's first trip—their way of initiating the newcomer. Completely ignorant in the ways of warfare on the plains and in the open, Kit apparently learned a great deal on the way to Santa Fe. According to available records, he proved himself an excellent marksman, dependable, honest, and courageous in every way. His year of saddle-making served him well, not only on this trip, but also in later years when he had to make his own clothing and moccasins of skins and hides.

Kit told Teresina how proud he was to have been herder, saddlemender, and cavvy boy with Charles Bent, who was destined to become New Mexico's first civil governor under American rule. Kit was to be Charles Bent's lifelong friend, as well as his brother-in-law, for Kit and Charles were to marry the Jaramillo sisters in Taos many years later.

Many miles beyond Pawnee Rock, the Bent party forded the Arkansas. Ahead lay the arid wastelands of southwestern Kansas, the most trying stretch of the overland trail to Santa Fe. The area was drier in the fall of the year, for the water holes nearly always dried up under the blistering summer sun, and forage for the horses and mules was scarce. The traders called it the "water scrape." Moreover, it was a favorite haunt of the fast-riding Comanches. From here on, the caravan would be in Mexican territory.

After three days of hot, dusty travel, the Cimarron River was

27

reached. Here there was a spring, the first water the group had encountered since leaving the Arkansas, and it was hereabouts that they would most likely meet the first *cibolero*, or Mexican buffalo hunter. The hunters and trappers always said that meeting a *cibolero* was a good-luck omen. From him they heard news of Santa Fe markets and how many Indian war parties were in the immediate vicinity. The captain customarily went to the Mexican's camp, where the latter's companions and their families were busy drying buffalo meat. From them he would purchase meat for his caravan, as well as some bags of coarse, overcooked bread.

Charles Bent, his brother William, and some of the other men left the caravan at the Cimarron, and Kit did not see Charles Bent again for three or four years.

Where Oklahoma now joins New Mexico, mountains were visible in a hazy outline to the northwest. Although the party skirted the main ranges, many a pine-covered slope had to be negotiated before Santa Fe was sighted. According to custom, the captain sent runners ahead when the caravan was two days out of Santa Fe. These men, who left at night to avoid Indians lurking in the vicinity, were generally agents whose mission was to obtain an agreeable understanding with the customs officers and arrange for storehouses, as well as to send back provisions, if such were needed.

Within sight of Santa Fe, the caravan halted. Kit probably helped clean the dust from the wagons and carriages while each teamster replaced the old whip cracker with a new one. All the men changed to clean clothing before entering the village: the mountain man to his fringed buckskin suit, the city-bred merchant to his fashionable fustian frock, the farmer to his jean coat, and the teamster to his flannel-sleeve vest. Store hats and round beaver hats were taken from buckskin bags to put on freshly combed hair. As perhaps at no other time, water was used lavishly on both hair and faces.

It was late November, 1826, when the Bent caravan reached its destination. To the rear of the long line of wagons and carriages, herding the animals, rode young Kit Carson.

The entire populace gathered on the outskirts of the capital to view the arrival of the caravan. Bright-eyed children ran in and out of the crowd. Their mothers and aunts wore black *rebozos* draped over the faces stained crimson with the juice of the alegria plant. Fathers, uncles, and brothers, customarily leaning against adobe walls, drew serapes closely around their shoulders, smiling as the Americans passed, then scowling at them behind their backs.

The resentment of Americans by the Spanish and Mexican male populace had some justification. The brusque, uncouth mountain men ridiculed the courtesy of the Spaniards. *Los Americanos,* most of them taller than the Spaniards and Mexicans, were admired by the women—sufficient reason for them to be hated by the men. As hostilities between the United States and Mexico increased, the feeling of animosity toward the gringo flared into open resentment.

The arrival of Kit's party was an important event in the history of Santa Fe; it changed the aspect of the place at once. This was one of the largest caravans to arrive in the capital up to that time. Captain William Becknell brought the first wagons over the Santa Fe Trail in 1822; whether he arrived with the three original wagons or only one of them has been disputed in various journals of the day. In 1823, only pack animals were used, but the following year, 26 wagons made the trip; the year after that, there were 37. Henceforth, only wagons were used. In 1826, some $90,000 worth of merchandise was brought to Santa Fe in 60 wagons accompanied by 100 men. By then, caravans and expeditions were traversing the Santa Fe Trail as often as three times a year.

The village of Santa Fe was clustered around a central plaza where everyone met for *fiestas,* fairs, and trading. At the east end of the plaza stood the small adobe church, while on the north side, one could pass through a low doorway into the Palace of the Governors, which was rumored to contain festoons of Indians' ears. Square, flat-roofed adobe houses encircled the plaza, each of them built around a patio, or inner court. Around this was a gallery upon which the rooms of the house opened. Because of the thickness of their walls (three to six feet), these simple houses were cool in the summer and warm in winter.

Kit did not remain long in Santa Fe. Soon after his arrival, he joined a group of traders going to Taos. Sometime during the first

29

week in December, the party arrived in the small village of Don Fernandez de Taos, or San Fernando, as it was sometimes called, some eighty miles north of Santa Fe in the Sangre de Cristo Mountains. Here Kit spent the winter of 1826–27 with one of his father's friends, an explorer and trapper named Kincaid, the same man who had established Fort Kincaid in Missouri. Kincaid had already experienced a great deal of Indian fighting while trapping in the Far West, and his name was well known in trapping circles from St. Louis to Santa Fe.

Kit and Kincaid had a mutual liking for each other from their first meeting. The winter was an interesting and beneficial one for Kit, for during the long evenings, Kincaid taught him the Spanish language, as well as various Indian tongues. Kit also learned sign language, which was understood by nearly all Indians, regardless of tongue or dialect. In later years he would find it a valuable tool.

Kit was an apt student and soon learned the ways of the Southwest Indians. He became familiar with the places in the sandy hills where they were likely to attack; he learned how to detect an ambush. It became easy for him to tell, by the degree of flatness of trodden grass, how recently horses or men had passed that way. He devoted much attention to geography; true, he and Kincaid had no maps or books, but Kincaid was a renowned explorer. With a stick he would "draw on the ground all that was needful of a chart."

The two men trapped the streams near their cabin and chased buffalo on the plains. Kit made his own clothing of skins and furs, trimming his jackets, leggings, and moccasins with long fringes of buckskin. These were not solely for ornamentation, but served the purpose of furnishing strips of leather to mend moccasins and harness in an emergency. Sometimes he adorned his leggings with porcupine quills of bright colors. His caps were made of warm beaver pelts, and his moccasins were lined with fur, for the snows piled high in this mountainous part of New Mexico and temperatures dropped far below zero.

Kit and his host made couches of corn husks and covered them with buffalo robes—luxurious beds for healthy, weary men! Pitch pine and piñon illuminated the cabin at night and gave it a pungent aroma. A day's hunting with Kit's skillful aim provided a week's supply of meat for them. Kit learned to cook their meals, as well as to cure, dry, and freeze meat for future use. The process of curing, or "jerking," was a very simple one at the high dry altitude in which they lived. It consisted of slicing the meat and hanging it in the sun for a few days. If the weather was wet, the sliced meat was dried indoors by placing it on a pan before the open fire. Although Kit must have seen jerked meat and pemmican, a finely ground dried buffalo meat, when he was a boy in Missouri, he also had an opportunity to see plenty of the long strings hanging on each side of the covered wagons during his trip to New Mexico.

One day as Kit and Kincaid were hunting some distance from Taos, they discovered a large herd of buffalo feeding in the tall grass. The prairie was black with *cibola,* as the Spanish called them. It was with difficulty that the two men approached the herd, for it took a bit of maneuvering to keep downwind from the animals. To avoid being seen, they leaned forward in their saddles.

When they had worked their way fairly close to a group of young bulls, Kincaid decided to fire. Almost before the shot hit its mark the herd stampeded, the frightened buffalo running in every direction. Kit snapped a quick shot at a fleeing cow as the sea of black rushed past and saw the cow fall in the midst of a cloud of dust and flying hoofs. In seconds the herd had gone, and Kit was off his horse with his knife unsheathed, ready to skin his prize. As he looked up to see if Kincaid had made a kill, he heard the latter's cry of alarm. Kincaid had hit his bull, had seen it fall, but when he drew his knife to skin it, the animal had raised itself with its forelegs doubled beneath it. Kincaid, within a foot of the wounded, gore-covered buffalo, dropped his knife and jumped back with a yell of surprise, for he had thought the animal dead. Kit grabbed his rifle and put an end to the angry bull.

They ate the liver and marrow, Indian fashion, made a fire of buffalo chips to cook some choice parts for their noon meal, and quartered the remainder to take back to the cabin.

Years later, Kit told Teresina that it was after this buffalo hunt that he met Father Antonio José Martinez, whose life spanned three periods of New Mexico history—Spanish, Mexican, and American—and was interwoven with every important event of nearly fifty fateful years of transition. Although he was officially the priest of Taos parish, he also said Mass at the large San Geronimo mission church at Taos Pueblo, three miles north of Taos village.

Kit visited the pueblo with Kincaid and saw the tall, Arab-like Indians standing on the rooftops of their five-story adobe fortress. San Geronimo de Taos, the northernmost Tigua pueblo, nestled at the foot of the Indians' sacred peak. It had no doors or windows; ladders, made of strips of buffalo hides and small poles, were used to scale the high walls and were then pulled up to the roof. One entered a room by descending a ladder through the roof. These ancient apartment houses (for this is what they were and are) were built around a plaza through which flowed a clear mountain stream that bisected the two main buildings. Tall willows, which turned fiery red in the fall, lined the stream, and from these, the Indians selected a name for themselves: People of the Red Willows.

The village of Taos, surrounded by majestic mountains, was small. Its adobe houses looked much like the houses of Santa Fe. They had earthen floors, and their ceilings were made of peeled logs, called *vigas*, with herringbone *latillas* or split cedar, between. The roofs, also made of earth, were flat and usually leaked when it rained, which wasn't often. Some of the ceilings (in rooms where the roof was inclined to leak) were covered with coarse muslin pasted on with a mixture of flour and water. A cord or wire fastened to the muslin terminated in a bucket on the floor. Water from leaks flowed down the cord (or wire) and into the bucket. Glass windows were an unheard-of luxury; the few openings were high in the walls, to be used as loopholes in case of Indian attack. In the yard or enclosed patios of each home stood cone-shaped adobe ovens in which the women or their Indian slaves baked bread and cakes.

Kit learned to love Taos and the handsome Indian people. After each expedition he returned there, and for forty-two years Taos was his home.

4 ★ Trip to California

EARLY IN THE SPRING OF 1827, Kit bade his friend Kincaid farewell in Taos and joined a party going to the States. When they reached the Arkansas River, Kit was persuaded by a group of trappers to return with them to Santa Fe; when they arrived there, he learned of Kincaid's death.

In early summer Kit joined a group of traders going to El Paso del Norte, hiring out as a team driver at wages of a dollar a day. After the long, hot trip, Kit collected his pay and walked through the dusty streets of the village. In physical appearance he found it to be little different from Taos or Santa Fe: the houses were constructed of adobe, their earthen floors hardened with ox blood, and the people were mixed, part Spanish and part Indian. In other ways, however, El Paso was much different. For one thing, it was the chief center of trade between the States, the territories, and Mexico. For another, it lay in the rich Río Grande Valley, and the vineyards near by had become famous for fine brandy and *Vino del Paso*. Thus it was a much busier place, most of the time at least, than Taos or Santa Fe.

There was no work for Kit in El Paso, so he returned to Taos in the fall of 1827. He spent his second winter in Taos as a cook in the quarters of a well-known trapper, Ewing Young. Young's store was a gathering place for men to buy tobacco, gunpowder, lead, and other supplies. Here the returning hunter, trapper, and trader congregated to tell of success or failure and to discuss the common, always serious problem of Indian war parties on the prowl.

No doubt Kit and the mountain men heard, by moccasin grape-

33

vine, rumors that the Bent brothers and Céran St. Vrain had begun to build an adobe fort on the north bank of the Arkansas River. Already the large mud bricks, in which wool, instead of straw, was used as a binder, were drying in the sun. Much of the material for the large, rectangular fort would be hauled from Santa Fe, and hundreds of workmen would be transported from near and far to work on the project. Work began, but a smallpox epidemic, along with much difficulty in hauling materials, delayed completion of the fort until 1832.

In the spring of 1828, Kit hired out as interpreter on a trading caravan with Colonel Tramell. Their destination was Chihuahua, by way of El Paso. Chihuahua, founded between 1703 and 1705 as a mining town with the title *San Felipe el Real de Chihuahua,* was made a *villa* in 1715. It was the capital of the Mexican province bearing the same name and was situated on a tributary of the Río Conchos. The streets were broad, some paved with a crude type of brick. In the center of the town plaza stood a great stone cathedral surmounted with a dome and two towers. Its beautiful façade was decorated with statues of the Apostles. Near the town were ore smelters for the silver mines, which were the basis of an extensive silver trade between Chihuahua and the United States.

In Chihuahua, Kit met one of his brother's friends, Robert McKnight, who had returned to Missouri in 1822 after nine years' imprisonment in the Mexican state. McKnight, James Baird, Samuel Chambers, Benjamin Shrive, Alfred Allen, Michael McDonough, William Mines, Peter Baum, Thomas Cook, and Carlos Miera, an interpreter, had each received a prison sentence for taking goods across the border. Spain had slammed the door on foreign trade; she wanted economic monopoly, not realizing that her shortsighted policy was destroying her empire. In 1821, however, Mexico gained independence from Spain. The new government released McKnight and his party and invited Americans to its territory.

When he met Kit, Robert was in Chihuahua trying to recoup his losses by trading and by mining in the Santa Rita de Cobre, in southwestern New Mexico near the Río Gila. Robert had declared, as had Baird, "I will go back to Mexico . . . and become a citizen. I have resided the prescribed term of years (in jail!) and there is a better chance for obtaining justice from the Mexicans, scoundrels though they are, than from my own government." He achieved his objective and lived to make a fortune in the copper mines.

Kit accompanied McKnight back to the mines in order to work that winter as a teamster. Wagons and pack trains were continually hauling between Chihuahua and McKnight's outpost at Santa Rita. Now Santa Rita was in Apache country, and the Indians were about as tame as the rattlesnakes which infested the area. Guards were much in evidence around the mine, which was worked by pick and shovel. The gold in the ore paid the expenses of digging, hauling, and refining; the copper, present in abundance, was clear profit for McKnight.

Christmas Eve, 1828, found Kit and the McKnight group in Chihuahua. Perhaps they watched the church procession by torch-light and the strange native miracle play on Christmas Day. There was no trading over the holiday, so it was undoubtedly an enjoyable occasion for young Kit. On the twenty-ninth, the wagons started on the trip back to the mines. There Kit stayed, in the village of low adobe huts at Santa Rita, until the spring of 1829. He then made his way back to Fernandez de Taos, probably returning that spring with the Wolfskill group, who had made a trip to El Paso for wine and brandy the previous fall.

While Kit was working for Robert McKnight, Ewing Young, who was later associated with David E. Jackson and Dr. David Waldo in the firm of Jackson, Waldo and Company, had sent a party of trappers to the Río Gila area in Arizona to trap beaver. The Apaches had beaten the trappers off their hunting grounds, chasing them out of the country. When Kit arrived in Taos, he joined the forty-man trapping party Young was recruiting to take back to the Río Gila. Young planned to chastise the Indians and resume the trapping venture.

Kit had at last gained the opportunity for which he had come west. Already he had established a reputation among the mountain men in Santa Fe and Taos. Young, knowing Kit's skill with a rifle, made him an offer to trap in Arizona and then go to California. Kit eagerly accepted.

Young did not take out a trapping license before leaving Taos. He believed that if he didn't have a license, the Mexicans wouldn't know he was trapping unless they caught him in the act, and he planned to take every precaution to prevent that. He told his men that in the previous year when he and Milton Sublette were trapping with a license issued by Governor Narbona, they had both been arrested and their furs confiscated by order of the Mexican government. In the course of the seizure, a Mexican, one Luis Cabeza de Vaca, had been shot. When Sublette saw the twenty-nine packs of furs (which were worth about $20,000) being spread out to dry on the Santa Fe plaza, he noticed that several of them were his personal property. He seized them and escaped, undetected, in order to take them to St. Louis.

To conceal their intentions and to throw the Mexicans off their trail, the Young party left Taos without traps and took a devious route through the wild, high country of northern New Mexico. In his autobiography, Carson states: "We traveled in a northern direction for fifty miles, and then changed our course to southwest, travelled [*sic*] through the country occupied by the Navajo Indians, passed the village of Zuni, and on to the head of the Salt River, one of the tributaries of the Rio Gila." They were in Apache country.

The trappers were alert for Apaches, but they saw none until they made camp, according to Kit, "on the head waters of the Salt River." When the Indians were discovered, Ewing Young laid an ambush for them: he ordered most of his men to hide in advantageous positions and await his order to fire. "The hills were covered with Indians," says Kit in his autobiography, "and, seeing so few [of us], they came to the conclusion to make an attack." It would be a great coup for the Apaches—or so they thought. The trappers, however, had other ideas.

Young watched them swoop down the slopes toward him, heard their bloodcurdling war cries, and waited. When they were within a few yards of the camp, he sprang his trap. The Indians were caught

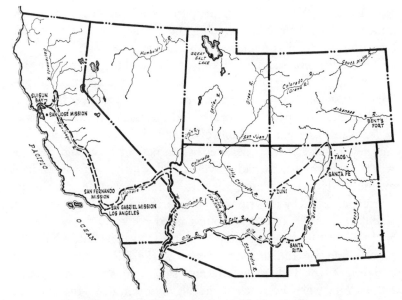

TRAPPING WITH EWING YOUNG, 1829

in a deadly crossfire, and before they could extricate themselves, fifteen of their number, including their chief, lay dead and perhaps as many more were wounded or unhorsed. And all the while the trappers were pouring a steady stream of rifle fire into their ranks.

It was too much for the Apaches. They fled in wild confusion, those without horses zigzagging from rock to rock until they were well out of range. It was the only open attack made on the trappers, although the Indians exacted some measure of revenge in the days that followed by crawling into Young's camp at night to steal traps, kill or steal horses and mules, and otherwise perform malicious acts of vandalism.

This was Kit's first Indian battle, but he fought like a veteran, and his bravery won warm praise from his companions. As a mere stripling, Kit had been known as one of the most skillful shots in Missouri, which produced some of the finest marksmen in the world. Now he had been put to the test.

At the head of the San Francisco River (the Verde River of cen-

37

tral Arizona), Young divided the party, sending part of the group back to Taos for traps and holding the other section, of which Kit was a member, for the journey to California.

The California party, which consisted of eighteen men under the leadership of Young and Kit, remained in camp a few days to prepare for the journey. Game was scarce, and the three deer they managed to kill were packed carefully and their skins made into water bags.[1] With this small amount of food and water, they began the journey across a barren, deserted wilderness of rocks and canyons where few white men had traveled and which even the Indians avoided. Many years later, Kit told Teresina that he felt the adventure afforded by the trip was well worth the suffering it entailed.

Before they broke camp, Young asked Kit to find out what he could about the desert country from the Navahos. Kit, who knew how to find the Indian camp, rode into the hills alone. What he had learned of Indian dialects and sign language from Kincaid helped him when he reached the Navaho camp. To the chief he conveyed that he had come in friendship. The chief answered that it was good and that Kit would not be harmed.

When they were seated in the chief's hogan, the pipe of peace was brought out. While it was being passed around, Kit asked about the land through which Young's group was to travel. The chief answered Kit's question by telling him that he would not find many deer, would find less water. He advised Kit to stay away from the trails to the east.

Kit stayed the night at the Navaho village to learn the locations of water holes and where the beaver could be found. Next morning, he thanked the chief and the men of the tribe, mounted his horse, and returned to camp to make his report.

The first four days, they traveled over sandy, barren country with no game or water. The water they carried in the deerskin bags was now rationed: one sip per man. Guards were placed over the scant supply to make sure no man driven by thirst would help himself, for with the loss of this water, the destruction of the whole party

[1] In his autobiography, Kit says they killed three bears. Sabin and Peters list three deer, and Stanley Vestal says they killed deer, with no mention of bears.

would be a probable consequence. About the fourth day, the thirsty mules suddenly rushed forward with all the force their exhausted strength could muster. Ahead of them, almost a mile away, was a water hole fringed with grass.[2]

For two days Young's party camped by the water, and when they were rested and refreshed, they started out again across much the same type of barren desert through which they had just traveled. Although the deerskin bags had been filled at the stream, it was not long until the group was without water again. Both animals and men suffered. The animals became thinner and thinner and the men's skin, dried out by now, tautened over their cheekbones; their mouths were dry and their tongues swollen. Kit, who was in the lead, maintained a punishing pace, for he realized that they had to find water that day or perish. He saw cool lakes on the afternoon of the fourth day, but he closed his mind to the mirages and led the men and their half-dead mules and horses on.

Some time later, Kit came to the rim of a canyon. His heart must have leaped at what he saw below him, for at the bottom of the canyon flowed the mighty Colorado River of the West. He signaled his companions, and soon the desert echoed with their shouts as both men and animals rushed headlong toward the canyon.

As soon as camp was made, Kit and three others went hunting. They had not been out long when they came upon a party of friendly Mohave Indians. In sign language, Kit told the Mohaves that he was hungry, and after much bargaining he purchased a mare, heavy with foal. This made a wonderful feast for the men, who had meanwhile found wild oats for their mules.

Early the next morning, Kit and the others prepared their traps, for they had seen gnawed branches of trees strewn along the banks of the river and knew that beaver swam therein. Selecting a likely spot, Kit waded to it (entering the stream some distance away) with a trap, set it, then anchored it. At just the right distance from its jaws, he drove an upright stick lightly into the bottom and baited it with some of the essence which would attract beaver. (When he had no essence, or "castoreum," he used the fresh roots of sassafras or spice

[2] This may have been Peach Springs.

bush, both of which beaver like.) He had learned from Kincaid how to run a horsehair from the stick to the trap so that the beaver would pull the decoy into the water when the trap was sprung, thus preventing other beaver from being decoyed to a dead trap, and this he now did. The trap was ready.

A band of Mohaves had been watching Kit intently. As they made signs to let him know that they were friendly, he noticed among them the two Indians who had sold him the mare. No doubt Kit was glad the Mohaves had sought him out: he wanted information about the trail ahead. In sign language the leader told Kit that it was bad country and that a hard march lay before them, but if they followed the river and then turned west, they would find the Spanish trails to the valleys of California.

After three days of trapping and preparing for the next part of the journey, Young gave the word to break camp. They took the route the Mohave chief had outlined and in three days struck the bed of the Mohave River. Following this dry basin for six days, they finally found water; then they turned west and four days later arrived at San Gabriel Arcángel Mission.

The Spanish mission, with its cultivated fields and large herds of fat cattle and sheep, must have seemed like Paradise to Kit and his group after such barren country. At the mission at that time were 70,000 head of cattle, 200 horses, 3,000 mares, and hundreds of oxen, mules, and sheep. The priest in charge told Kit and Young that sales of wine made from the mission's grapes netted about $12,-000 each year, the vineyards producing some 600 barrels annually.

The trappers remained at San Gabriel for a day to purchase beef and other commodities. From there, a day's travel over the mountains brought them to the mission of San Fernando, where they found more luxuriance. Here ran streams of crystal water, teeming with fish and bordered by grass and wild oats. They found antelope, elk, deer, and other game in abundance.

When they arrived at the San Joaquin River, they began trapping for beaver. Near the place where the San Joaquin empties into the Sacramento, Young halted his party to make camp for a few days. Here they met another trapping party of sixty-one members commanded by Peter Skene Ogden of the Hudson's Bay Company. The two groups, although rivals in business, showed good sportsmanship and met on friendly terms, trapping near each other until they came to the Sacramento. By then they had become good friends and were exchanging knowledge of the country and the ways of the beaver. As John S. C. Abbott points out in his *Kit Carson, the Pioneer of the West,* this exchange of information proved valuable to Kit:

Here again the peculiarity of Kit Carson's character was developed. Instead of assuming that he knew about the wilderness and the business in which he was engaged, he lost no opportunity in acquiring all the information he could from the strangers. He questioned them carefully and his experience was such as to enable him to ask just such questions as were most important.

There is scarcely a man in America who has not heard the name Kit Carson.[3] His wide-spread fame was not the result of accident. His achievements were not merely impulsive movements. He was a man of pure mind, of high morality, and intensely devoted to the life-work which he had chosen. . . . He had also gathered and stored away in his retentive memory all that the veteran ranger Kincaid of the woods could communicate respecting the geography of the Far West, and the difficulties to be encountered, and the mode of surmounting them. And now he was learning everything that could be learned from the Canadian boatmen and rangers.

Already young Carson had attained eminence. It was often said, "No matter what happens, Kit Carson always knows at the moment exactly what is best to be done."

Both as a hunter and trapper, though he had not yet attained the age of manhood, he was admitted to be the ablest man in the party. And his native dignity of person and sobriety of manners commanded universal respect. In this lively valley both parties lived, as trappers, luxuriously. They were successful with their traps, and the deer, elk and antelope were roving about in such thousands that any number could be easily taken. These were indeed the sunny festive days of our adventurers.

[3] Kit was not nationally known at the time of the California trip. He achieved such recognition in 1846 when John Charles Frémont sang his praises of Kit to the nation.

Peter Ogden and his group departed, going up the Sacramento to the Columbia River, while Young and his trappers camped all that summer in northern California near Suisun Bay. It was while they were thus camped and enjoying hunting and fishing that forty Indians ran away from San Rafael Mission (a few contemporaries name San José) and hid out in an Indian village whose inhabitants were hostile to the mission. The mission priest had sent fifteen loyal Indians to bring back the runaways, but they were unsuccessful. Kit and Young were asked to assist. Young explained that it was important that these Indians be returned to the mission, for if they were not made to return, such a victory would "puff up all the Indians" in the area, render them insolent, and encourage them to make war on white settlers.

Kit selected eleven men to help him bring back the renegades. He decided to make a surprise attack on the village; the battle raged all day. Many of the warriors were slain before they had time to get their weapons, and the rest finally fled to the hills. The next day, Kit demanded the return of the runaway Indians. His request was complied with, and the prisoners were brought to Kit, who returned them to the mission.

At the mission Young and Kit had the good luck to meet the captain of a trading vessel who purchased, for cash, all their furs. Young must have been very happy about this transaction because the Mexicans' policy, based on the "favorable trade balance," drained money from the provinces, with the result that no one had any cash. Thus business was generally conducted on a barter basis.

Young bought much-needed horses and mules, but that night a party of Indians stole sixty of the horses. Kit took eleven men and followed the trail a hundred miles into the Sierra Nevadas, surprising the Indians as they were eating some of the animals. The trappers recovered all of the horses except six eaten by the Indians.

On the first day of September they broke camp, retracing the route by which they had come. They visited the mission of San Fernando briefly, then traveled on to Los Angeles. Here "the Mexican authorities demanded . . . passports," according to Kit's autobiography, but since there is a record of Young's 1829 passport signed by Secretary of State Henry Clay, it is more likely that the officials demanded a trapping license, which, of course, Ewing Young could not possibly produce.

The Mexicans threatened Young's party with arrest; however, they seemed to be afraid to take that action. Pretending friendliness, the Mexicans brought whiskey to the trappers' camp while Kit and Young were absent. Presumably, the purpose of the liquor was to get the men so drunk that arrest would be easy.

Early the next morning, Young found it necessary to get his men away from Los Angeles as quickly as possible. They had engaged in a drunken brawl with the Mexicans, knives had been drawn, and blood had been shed. Kit was sent ahead with three of the more sober men, all the pack mules, horses, and the trapping equipment, furs, and food. Young told Kit that he would catch up as soon as he could. If he failed to show up after a reasonable length of time, Kit was to proceed to New Mexico and report that the rest of the party had been killed. Young knew that this incident was what the Mexicans had been waiting for in order to make their arrests. He would not, however, leave his drunken trappers to the mercy of the Mexicans.

Finally, Young got his men together and the alcohol-dazed group started out. The Mexicans followed on horseback with more liquor, but a subsequent event frightened them away. James Higgins, who was very drunk, aimed his rifle at Jim Lawrence and pulled the trigger before Young could stop him. The display of gunfire frightened the Mexicans, all of whom fled. Jonathan T. Warner describes the incident in his *Reminiscences of Early California*:

> Big Jim was left in the road where he fell upon receiving the fatal shot. These men were both Irishmen, and when under the influence of liquor Jim was intolerable, and Higgins in like condition was uncontrollable. The men were all suffering from the effects of days of debauchery and the major portion of them were intoxicated at the time and could not be controlled by Young who, fearing that still more blood might be shed, as well as apprehensive of trouble with the authorities and people of the country, did not stop to bury the dead, but continued his march.

It is to be presumed from this and other records that Young and Kit did not join in the "debauchery."

Sergeant Pico of California reported the killing on October 7, 1830, and explained in his report that the group of Mexicans which he commanded was too small to detain the American trappers.

Young's group finally joined Kit's forces after dark and they pursued nearly the same route by which they had come. Safely away from the Los Angeles authorities on October 10, Young wrote to Captain Cooper:

> Dear Sir: I received yours of the 8th and am verry sorry that I did not see you[.] I had like to have Lost all the french that I have with me when . . . an Irish Man and an English man in the rear had a falling out about some frivolous thing and one shot the other dead of [off] his horse and I could not stop to do anything with him [but] Left him Lying in the rode where he was kild. . . .
>
> Nothing more at present But Remain
yours Respectfully
E. Young

Nine days later the Carson-Young group arrived at the Colorado, where they camped for a few days to trap and hunt. On the second day there, Kit and six other men were left in camp to guard the horses and equipment while the others trapped the river. The men worked in camp with a heartiness and cheerfulness which probably resulted from their regret over their debauch in Los Angeles. They undoubtedly realized that but for the discretion of Young and Carson, they might well have lost their lives.

Suddenly a group of about five hundred Chemehuevi Indians appeared, crowding around the men in camp and pretending friendship. Kit mistrusted them, for he saw that each warrior had a weapon hidden under his clothing, hoping that it would not be noticed by the trappers. For a while Kit did not make his suspicions known; however, when it became apparent that the Indians intended to murder the whole group, then steal the horses and supplies, Kit unflinchingly ordered the Indians from his camp. He told them that if at the end of ten minutes an Indian remained, he would be shot.

Kit called his men to one corner of the camp and ordered each man to aim at a chief; he himself took aim at their head chief. Although the Indians knew that they could overpower the little group of white men, they also knew that before they could made a move they would lose many of their most honored chiefs. So they turned and left the camp. Only when they were beyond range did Kit and his men relax.

The trappers who had gone with Young returned that evening with many furs, and Kit told Young about the unfriendly Indians. It was immediately decided to push on down the west side of the Colorado, trapping as they traveled. As they came up the Gila near the mouth of the San Pedro, they saw a large herd of horses and mules, so they presumed they had overtaken the same Indians who had tried to murder them. Kit, rememberinng how near a massacre they had been, decided to deprive the Indians of their stolen stock. A short search revealed the Indians' camp, and with galloping horses and blazing guns, the trappers charged it. The attack was such a suprise that the Indians fled in every direction, the trappers taking possession of their animals.

That same evening, while the other trappers were asleep, Kit heard a strange noise. Uncertain of its cause, he pressed his ear to the ground and clearly heard the thunder of many hoofs. He awakened the men, who sprang up, rifles in hand, to discover a band of Indians driving some two hundred horses past the camp. Young knew that the Indians had stolen the horses from the Mexicans in Sonora, and the opportunity to give the horse thieves a lesson was too good to pass up. The trappers took aim and greeted the astonished Indians with a volley of shots. They fled, leaving the horses to find their own way. Kit and the group rounded up the horses, and Young, remembering their recent treatment at the hands of the Mexicans, decided to keep them. They picked out the best ones for personal use, killed ten more for meat, and released the rest. Young figured the thieving Indians would capture them.

Trapping these many months had been profitable; the mules and pack horses were laden with furs and pelts which Young had secured in Mexican territory without a license. He decided to head for the copper mines in what is now Grant County, New Mexico, and leave the furs with Robert McKnight until he could get a license in Santa Fe and return for them. Young knew that McKnight hated the unfair trade laws and that the furs would be safe with him.

Young and Kit remained at the copper mines for a few days after the others had gone to Taos. Then the two men went to Santa Fe, where Young obtained a license to trade with the Indians near the mines. He returned to Santa Rita, got the furs, and sold them in Santa Fe for twelve dollars a pound. His profit was a good one, for the furs were reported to have weighed a ton.

Back to the full life of Taos in the late fall of 1830, Kit and his friends probably stood around the wagons just arrived from the States, watching the men buy hardware, the women silk material or perhaps a pair of silk slippers from distant Paris. Taos was, at that time, the commercial center of the trappers' and traders' world in the West. It was Kit's kind of world. He saw men outfitting for trips into the mountains, swapping horses or mules, replacing saddles and girth belts, buying new traps, packing dried meat, sharpening their hunting knives, and cleaning their weapons. That was what he did, too.

Of interest also was the Indian pueblo located some three miles to the north of the Taos village. Kit had previously witnessed some of the Taos Indian dances. Half-pagan, half-Christian, the spring dances were prayers for rain and fertile crops—prayers for the germination of the seed—dances staged to "maintain cosmic harmony." The Taos Indians recognized the Sun Father, a personification of the sun, as the greatest creative force in the universe. The Sun Father rose in the east, so that was the sacred direction. White, a composition of all colors, was the Sun Father's radiant life-color.

Kit gathered a smattering of the Indians' beliefs and way of life on these short visits to the pueblo. Although they were usually peaceful, the Taos Indians were given to periodic uprisings, so that even the priest who said Mass at the huge San Geronimo mission church was in danger of losing his life. Since 1631, priests assigned to the church had been murdered. In that year Pedro de Miranda was killed, along with Luis Pacheco and Juan de Estrada, two soldiers acting as his guards.

On May 3, 1830, Kit had been honored with an invitation to visit the pueblo and witness the spring races, in which, early in the morning, the Indians raced from east to west—as the sun travels. Although he was an anglo, most of whom the Indians disliked, the Taos Indians felt Kit's sympathy and understanding of their problems. (Later in his life, Kit would become their agent.) The story of Kit's courage, his unerring honesty, and his indomitable spirit had already been told in Taos and the West, and the Indians had undoubtedly heard it. He was liked and respected by all who knew him, for his was a loyal friendship. He once said: "I never turn my back on friend or foe."

Charles Bent was in Taos when Kit arrived. He was delighted to see Kit and hear of the trip to California. The two must have talked of Bent's desire to return to St. Louis and bring back goods in ox-drawn wagons, since the "oxen wouldn't stampede like horses and mules." Therefore the Indians couldn't steal them, and the oxen would provide food in case of need. And Kit and Charles probably discussed the huge adobe trading post under construction on the Arkansas, which, when finished, would be the largest in the country. All of this must have furnished interesting conversation for the young trapper and his friend.

Charles went to St. Louis, and in August of the following year, 1831, he is credited with bringing the first ox-drawn caravan from St. Louis to Santa Fe. With him on this historic trip was the poet and writer Albert Pike. The nation would hear much about the West from him in the coming years.

The year 1831 also marked the arrival in Taos of another Carson— Big Moses, Kit's older half-brother.[4] According to family tradition,

---

[4] Dates here are somewhat confusing. In *Kit Carson's Own Story*, the date of Kit's return to Taos is given as April, 1830, and his joining Fitzpatrick as the fall of that year. If Sergeant Pico's report, dated October 7, 1830, and Young's letter to Cooper, dated October 8, 1830, are correctly dated (and there is no reason to doubt these two documents), then Kit must have returned to Taos in 1831 and joined Fitzpatrick that fall. According to Blanche Grant, the 1831 dates check with Carson family records.

he spent the summer there, and both he and Kit made frequent trips to Bent's Fort on the Arkansas, where Kit worked on the large adobe trading post soon to be completed. On one occasion in Taos, they visited Ewing Young, who had recently married a Mexican woman named Josefa Tafoya. Young and Moses tried to persuade Kit to accompany them to California and Oregon, but for some unrecorded reason Kit declined the proposition. In October, with a party of thirty, they left Taos to trap through to the coast by the Gila route, arriving at Los Angeles in April, 1832. Moses settled in California, and Young went on to Oregon, where he established the "Wallamet Cattle Company."

5 ★ The Carson Luck

YOUNG KIT CARSON had been in the West for nearly five years when, in September, 1831, he joined a Rocky Mountain Fur Company expedition as a free trapper. That he was now a free trapper is testimony to the skills and knowledge he had acquired during those years, for the free trappers were experts in mountain craft. They had to be: they worked for themselves (though they might sometimes contract to sell their plews to a particular fur company), and since they were thus on their own, the amount of their annual earnings depended, for the most part, upon their individual abilities. They assumed great risks, for a single Indian raid could wipe out the year's profits—or perhaps their lives. And there was always the possibility of poor trapping seasons, when they would find few beaver in the streams they chose to trap. Or they might find fur-company brigades trapping ahead of them in nearly any given area. Only the most courageous and skilled mountain men, therefore, could afford to gamble on free trapping and expect to win.

Heading the party Kit joined was Tom Fitzpatrick (called Bad Hand or Broken Hand by the Indians), who, with four others—Jim Bridger, Jean Baptiste Gervais, Milton Sublette, and Henry Fraeb—had earlier bought out the fur interests of the Jedediah Smith–David Jackson–William Sublette partnership. Casting about for new business prospects, Smith and his partners decided to concentrate on trading and set out for Santa Fe in the spring of 1831 with a freight caravan. Fitzpatrick joined them at Lexington. On May 27, Smith was killed at the Cimarron River by a band of Comanches (his body

49

was never found), and Bill Sublette sold out to Dave Jackson soon after their arrival at Santa Fe, but not before he had outfitted Fitzpatrick. Bad Hand picked up a few trappers in Santa Fe, then went on to Taos.

The group was not long in setting out from Taos, for the fall trapping season was upon them. They rode north, crossed the South Platte, and trapped across to the North Platte to the site of the future Fort Laramie, where they met Henry Fraeb with a pack train of supplies. Fitzpatrick traded places with Fraeb, who had been searching for him (Fitzpatrick was on his way to St. Louis for supplies when he joined the Santa Fe–bound Smith-Jackson-Sublette caravan at Lexington, and Fraeb knew nothing of this change in Fitzpatrick's plans), and left for St. Louis to get next season's supplies, leaving Fraeb in charge of the trappers.

After a day or two of rest at the fort, Fraeb led the trappers and his belated pack train up the Platte to the Sweetwater, one of its tributaries. They traveled up the Sweetwater a short distance, then crossed the Continental Divide at South Pass. From here they pressed on across the headwaters of the Green, touched Jackson's Hole, crossed Teton Pass and the Snake River, and skirted the southern and western flanks of the Divide (the boundary of present-day Montana). On November 3, they reached the Salmon, where the main body of Rocky Mountain Fur Company trappers, under the able leadership of Jim Bridger, had gone into winter quarters. According to Kit, the Bridger party was camping with a band of Nez Percés.

The trappers, warmly clad, pursued their hunting and trapping when the weather permitted. They trapped the streams into Oregon before these froze, and when the winter blasts swept down from the north and snow piled up around their winter quarters on the Salmon, they stayed indoors and made moccasins, cleaned equipment, and cooked buffalo steaks.

Sometime during the winter, four of the trappers went hunting and were surrounded and killed by a large party of Blackfoot warriors. No effort was made to avenge their deaths, for Bridger and

Fitzpatrick knew better than to go out looking for trouble, especially in Blackfoot country and at this time of year.

As soon as the streams thawed sufficiently in 1832, Kit and the others began the spring trap. This time their destination was the upper Snake River and its tributaries, a journey which took them through rough and jagged country. The wildly rushing Snake wound through stretches of lava, and in some places its bed lay in deep, inaccessible canyons, a thousand feet below the rim. Three massive waterfalls, all of them rivaling Niagara, made travel difficult, but they were "a sight to see," and Kit often said that they were the "grandest of any, he had ever seen."

From the upper Snake country the party crossed over to the Bear and trapped eastward to the Green, where they met fifteen trappers under the command of William Sinclair and his brother, Alexander. They had left Taos shortly after Fitzpatrick's group and had, according to Kit, winter-camped on the Little Bear River, though he might have meant the Bear. Kit wanted to join John Gantt, and when he learned from the Sinclairs that Gantt was in the vicinity of New Park, he took three men and set out to find him.

Gantt and some fifty men, including Kit, trapped the upper Arkansas and some of the tributaries of the Green with fair success and without being bothered by the Indians. In the fall they set up their winter camp on the Arkansas. Gantt and a few men took all the plews and started for Taos, while Kit and the others remained behind to trap. Gantt was back in less than two months with a load of supplies, and the group continued the fall trap until the streams began to freeze.

There was a lot of snow along the upper Arkansas during the winter of 1832–33, but buffalo were plentiful. Thus the only problem facing Gantt's party was that of finding food for their animals. Deep snow covered the available grass, and the men had to cut sweet cottonwood bark for their horses. Otherwise, they seem to have fared quite well.

One day in January, 1832, they turned the horses out to graze, and some Crow Indians, ranging south from the Big Horn River, succeeded in driving off nine of the animals. Kit, as usual, was elected leader of a group of eleven men, two of them Cheyennes, chosen to recover the animals. For forty miles the pursuit was continued with as much speed as possible in an effort to catch up with the Indians. The trail was almost completely lost at one place: the snow was deep and a large herd of buffalo had crossed, obliterating all signs of a path. At length they picked it up again, but it was dusk and the horses were very tired—and so were the men. Kit pointed to a grove of trees about a mile ahead and suggested that they camp there until morning. Just as he spoke Kit saw some dim fires about a half-mile away. They had found the horse thieves.

The Indians had fled from the north, and they would expect their pursuers to come from the north, or so Kit thought. The southern part of their camp, he reasoned, would be less guarded. Kit and his men decided to make a wide circuit in the snow in order to approach it from its south side. This took some time, but it was time well spent for the snow aided them by muffling the sound of their approach. Very cautiously the trappers worked their way to a spot within a hundred yards of the half-faced log forts where the Indians were camped. Silently they crouched in the snow behind some bushes and watched the Crow warriors—painted and plumed with colorful feathers—dancing, singing, and celebrating their victory over the white man. It was evident from their actions that the Indians had no idea of the trappers' being anywhere in the vicinity.

The stolen horses were tethered a short distance from the camp. The very sight of them was anything but soothing to the indignant trappers. The war whoops and wild dancing continued until long after midnight; then, one by one, the warriors threw themselves down by their fires to sleep. As the trappers watched, it grew colder, but they dared not move until the Indians were all asleep.

At last all was quiet in the Crow camp. Kit and five men crawled to the place in the trees where the horses were tied, leaving the other trappers in the rear to cover them should the Indians awaken. They silently cut the ropes and, by throwing snowballs at them, drove the horses to the edge of the timber, where they were taken over by waiting men.

It was a skillful maneuver, accomplished without even a neigh or the stamp of a hoof. When the horses were safely out of sight, Kit and his men shivered in the snow, not fifty yards from the sleeping Indians, wondering what action to take. Some of the men were in favor of leaving without a fight, while Kit and two others wanted "satisfaction for the trouble and hardships" they had endured in pursuit of the horse thieves. Seeing that Kit and the other two men were determined to fight, the rest of the trappers agreed to join them. As Kit explained, "there is . . . a brotherly affection . . . among the trappers and the side of danger [is] always . . . their choice."

Sending one of their number to help guard the horses and to inform the others of the plan to attack, they turned their attention to the Indian fort. All was quiet. When they were within a short distance of the sleeping Indians, a dog barked. The warriors scrambled to their feet, only to face a volley of shots from Kit and his men. One of the warriors was killed before he could return the fire, and the others fled to the north fort. Kit and his men took up positions behind the trees and waited. When the warriors rushed them, they drove the Crows back with another volley of gunfire and rejoined the guards and horses at the edge of the timber to wait for another attack. It came, and again the trappers drove the Indians back to the fort, where they remained. Kit and his men returned to camp.

There is a story among the Cheyenne Indians, supposedly passed down from the Cheyennes involved, that only two Crows were killed in the fight. Although, it was said, the Cheyennes chided Kit on his failure to kill more warriors in the battle, they bestowed upon him the name of *Vih-hiu-nis,* which means "Little Chief."[1]

Before starting on their spring trapping, Kit's party cached their beaver furs, the catch amounting to about four hundred pounds.

[1] Much has been written about the Crow fight. In his autobiography, Kit says: "We killed nearly every Indian in the fort." If we believe George Bird Grinnell's report from the two Cheyennes who accompanied Kit and the testimony of those who knew Kit best—that he was never known to brag or lie—then we can only conclude that Colonel Peters elaborated on the information Kit gave him for the autobiography and that the trappers did not kill "nearly every Indian in the fort."

Kit directed the digging of a funnel-like hole in the earth, narrow at the top and large at the bottom. Into this the men put branches and leaves as a lining. The tightly rolled furs were carefully packed into the hole, and it was then covered with poles, straw, and finally earth. The horses were tethered above the spot for many hours of tramping. The men built a fire, leaving the ashes over the cache so that no one could see that the earth had been disturbed. The dirt dug out of the hole was placed on a buffalo robe, carried to the river, and thrown into the water.

Satisfied that no one could possibly find the cache, Kit and his men rode off to trap the south fork of the Platte. Shortly after they arrived there, two of the trappers deserted. Kit, suspecting their reason, took two men and the fastest horse and went in pursuit. The deserters had a day's start, so Kit and his companions were not able to catch up with them. When they got back to the old camp, the furs were gone, and so was a canoe they had made during the winter. The deserters and the furs were never heard of again; Kit concluded that the Indians killed the men and stole the furs. He did discover the two horses the men had used, however, and took them back with him.

The two thieves probably belonged to that reckless breed of hunters and trappers called *coureurs de bois*. Washington Irving describes their restless habits in his *Astoria*:

> A new and anomalous class of men gradually grew out of this trade. These were called *coureurs des bois*, rangers of the wood; originally men who had accompanied the Indians in their hunting expeditions and made themselves acquainted with remote tracts and tribes; and who now became, as it were, pedlars of the wilderness. These men would set out from Montreal with canoes well stocked with goods, with arms and ammunition, and would make their way up the many and wandering rivers that interlace the vast forests of the Canadas, coasting the most remote lakes, and creating new wants and habitudes among the natives. Sometimes they sojourned for months among them, assimilating to their tastes and habits with the happy facility of Frenchmen; adopting in some degree the Indian dress, and not unfrequently taking to themselves Indian wives.

Twelve, fifteen, eighteen months would often elapse without any tidings of them, when they would come sweeping their way down the Ottawa in full glee, their canoes laden down with packs of beaver skins. Now came their turn for revelry and extravagance. You would be amazed, if you saw how lewd these pedlars are when they return; how they feast and game, and how prodigal they are, not only in their clothes, but upon their sweethearts. Such of them as are married have the wisdom to retire to their own homes; but the bachelors do just as an East Indiaman and pirates are wont to do; for they lavish, eat, drink, and play all away as long as the goods hold out; and when these are gone, they even sell their embroidery, their lace, and their clothes. This done, they are forced upon a new voyage for subsistence.

The *coureurs de bois,* or *voyageur* type of trappers, flourished in the early 1800's when John Jacob Astor was rising to power. In 1831, many of them were working for American fur companies, having drifted down from Canada to partake of the profits from over-stocked Rocky Mountain streams. With the advent of the Missouri trapper and the Kentucky hunter, such men as Carson, St. Vrain, the Bent brothers, and others of their kind became models of proper conduct in the trapping and trading professions.

In *The Personal Narrative of James Ohio Pattie of Kentucky,* Timothy Flint wrote of the American trapper and hunter:

There was a kind of moral sublimity in the contemplation of the adventures and daring of such men. . . . They tend to re-inspire something of that simplicity of manner, manly hardihood, and Spartan energy and force of character which formed so conspicuous a part of the nature of the settlers of the western wilderness.

Even the most crude of the American trappers were fundamentally honest; they dealt fairly with each other and certainly would never steal another trapper's cache. There was among the mountain men a code of honor which did not include the Indian; long before Kit Carson came west, the *coureur de bois* had done his part in debasing the latter.

At the winter camp on the Arkansas, Kit and a companion "took possession of the buildings" to await the arrival of John Gantt's partner, Mr. Blackwell, and his trappers, who came in about a month later. The two men fortified the camp, and, according to Kit's report, "being by ourselves we never ventured very far from our fort, unless for the purpose of procuring meat. We kept our horses picketed near and, at night, slept in the house, always keeping a good lookout so that we might not be surprised when unprepared."

Gantt evidently did not know of Kit's plan to stay at the camp, for soon after Blackwell arrived, there appeared four trappers from the Gantt camp who thought Kit and his partner had gone under. They had been sent out to locate Kit and his companion.

From the Arkansas the combined groups set out for Gantt's camp at the Bayou Salade, Colorado's South Park, in the high mountains. On the fourth morning of their trip, while they were having breakfast at dawn, raiding Indians attempted to steal the hobbled horses by stampeding them. Kit and his men were instantly on their feet, their rifles blazing. One Indian was killed and the rest turned and rode wildly away. With the yelling Indians went one of the trapper's horses, which had broken its hobble or had been cut loose by an Indian. It was decided not to try to capture the stolen horse, since the Indians had most likely prepared an ambush.

The trappers were in the heart of the Indians' hunting grounds; they expected trouble and were always ready for it. Many powerful tribes were ready to combine forces for their destruction. Thus it was not luck that enabled them to come out of this section of Indian country with their scalps intact. It was wise precaution.

After traveling some fifty miles, Kit thought they were out of danger but took the same careful precaution to picket all the animals before retiring. All during the night their little dog barked, which warned them that Indians were close. The next morning, Kit and three of the men, having heard much about "a large number" of beaver in a certain rather inaccessible section, determined to explore and trap that area. To reach it, they had either to traverse a lofty mountain or take many hours to ride around it. They decided to take the short cut, leading their horses.

The climb, straight up rocky cliffs most of the way, soon proved exhausting to the trappers as well as to the animals. Finally, after hours of laborious effort, they reached the top of the ridge, beyond which was a broad valley. They made their way to the stream and examined it. There was no sign of beaver. Their hard work had been in vain.

Rather than descend the steep cliff, the trappers decided to take the long way around the mountains. They let their horses walk leisurely while "they joked about the beaver they hadn't found." There was no need for haste, for they knew they wouldn't be expected back at camp for many hours.

Suddenly there appeared before the mountain men four mounted warriors. Their hair was ornamented with colored eagle feathers, their faces stained with yellow, black, and crimson paint, and they were fully armed. In short, they were on the warpath. When the warriors saw the trappers, they turned and galloped away. Without a moment's hesitation, Kit and his companions spurred their horses in pursuit. The race continued in open country until the Indians dashed past a hill where more than fifty warriors rode out to intercept the trappers.

Kit was in the lead; on he rode, as if to charge the entire war party. Just before he reached the Indians, Kit swerved his horse sharply and threw himself forward, at the same time leaning to the protected side of his mount and urging him forward with all possible speed. The other trappers followed Kit's example, and, amid a hail of fire from the Indians, they ran the terrible gauntlet. Not a shot was fired by Kit and his men, for if unhorsed, each wanted to have a loaded rifle in his hands with which to make his last defense. Kit's daring act so amazed the Indians that by the time they realized what he was doing, it was too late to surround the trappers, who were already galloping to safety. Some of the Indians had kept up a steady stream of fire and two of the trappers were wounded, but their escape was one of the most extraordinary on record. Kit admitted that he was never more utterly deceived and entrapped by Indians in all his life.

The men in camp had their own story to tell. That morning, soon after Kit and the others had left, a band of hard-riding Indians came thundering toward the trappers' animals, running off all the horses that were loose. Four of the men immediately rode out after the marauders, firing on the run. The Indians fled, leaving the horses behind, whereupon the trappers broke off their chase and rounded up the animals.

When Kit, Blackwell, and the others started for the Gantt camp, only one of the wounded men was able to ride a horse; the other had to be carried on a crude litter. In four days they found Gantt at Bayou Salade and remained with him until the wounded men recovered. Meanwhile, the Blackwell-Gantt partnership was reported insolvent, so Kit and two companions left the failing company and traveled into the timber region to trap on their own.

Both the Utes of the mountains and the Arapahoes of the plains claimed Bayou Salade as their hunting grounds. It was an ideal place: large herds of buffalo, elk, and deer roamed as far as the eye could see. Many battles had been fought for the right to hunt this game; red men fought red men, and when trapping parties were in the area, the mountain men took on all the Indians. Most of the time, however, the place was left to the Indians.

While the Indians were hunting buffalo, they always left their women and children in charge of old men in mountain retreats. Kit knew that as long as the Indians were hunting, he could safely trap in the remote regions of the mountains. Few trappers took advantage of this opportunity, and for a very good reason: the Indians would leave the trapper alone while he trapped the streams, but when he came out of the mountains, heavily laden with pelts, they would band together to steal the valuable furs. Many trappers lost their lives trying to protect their catch. Kit knew this, but he had a plan. On they trapped in the high country, unmolested.

Their path led directly into the heart of the mountains. It was a wild and beautiful country with flower-bordered streams and plenty of tall grass for the horses. The higher they climbed, the more turquoise the sky became. They found game and beaver in abundance and spent many days hunting and trapping. They had made a good catch when Kit announced that it was time to get out of the mountains.

Leading their animals, which they had loaded down with furs, the trappers headed for Taos. Out of the mountains they came and onto the open prairie. These lone men and their wealth were perfect targets for roving Indians, for as they went, they were sharply outlined against the horizon. There wasn't even a boulder or a bush to protect them should the Indians attack, but Kit had timed their descent from the mountains to coincide with the return of the Indians to their mountain retreats. He hoped that he had calculated the time correctly, so that the Indians would be busy storing their buffalo meat and preparing the hides for the women to tan. He guessed right. Not an Indian was seen along the way.

When the trappers reached Taos, furs were in great demand. They sold the beaver skins at top prices ($6.00 a pound), divided the profits and went their separate ways. Kit had been in luck again, for between the fall of 1832 and October, 1833, beaver-skin prices dropped from $6.00 a pound to $3.50 in the states.

John Jacob Astor might have influenced this price drop when he returned from England in 1832. He reported that Englishmen had stopped wearing beaver hats and were now wearing silk ones. This comment was significant in St. Louis and the East. Fashion abandoned the beaver hat, and the change grossly affected the earnings of the mountain men.

The Missouri Fur Company, in which Big Moses, Kit's half-brother, had served, failed in 1830, forced out by the Rocky Mountain Fur Company. Six years later, the Rocky Mountain Fur Company suffered the same fate when it was pushed out of business by the incoming American Fur Company, which, under Astor's control, had Ramsay Crooks directing from New York and Pierre Chouteau, Jr., overseeing details from St. Louis. With the best organizers and traders in the business, not to mention unlimited funds, Astor's fur company absorbed the fur trade in the Southwest.

In the spring of 1832, the Rocky Mountain Fur Company, the American Fur Company, and the Hudson's Bay Company locked in a bitter contest for supremacy, while Captain Benjamin Bonneville, Nathaniel J. Wyeth, and others vainly attempted flank marches. The Rocky Mountain Fur Company subsequently failed, and such men as Sublette, Bridger, Fraeb, Gervais, Jackson, and Fitzpatrick parted company and went their separate ways. This left the American Fur Company dominant on the plains and in the mountains.

In the beginning of the fur-trade era, the Hudson's Bay Company had forbidden its employees to bring alcohol into Indian territory, but as rivalry became keen, the Hudson's Bay Company changed its policy: the fetish of the fur trade became alcohol. Kit once said that the only gifts the white man had given to the Indian were alcohol and smallpox. As a free trapper, he was not involved in the bitter conflict between the various fur companies; he took a firm stand against alcohol for the Indians. He was never known to sell or give an Indian liquor, and his advice to the Indians about alcohol gained for him the respect of both mountain men and Indians alike.

Late in October, 1833, Kit and Captain Stephen Louis Lee accepted a commission to take trading supplies by pack train from the trading firm of Bent and St. Vrain Company. Their destination was the Uintah country of northeastern Utah, and their route was the Old Spanish Trail, which had been retraced two years previously by William Wolfskill.

Part of the trail led over heavily wooded mountains. Where they left Wolfskill's path and followed the course of the original Spanish Trail, the country grew more rugged. Snow was falling in the passes. At the forks of the Uintah River, Kit and Captain Lee came upon Fort Uintah, which was owned and operated by Antoine Robidoux. In the fall of 1833, the fort was headquarters for some twenty trappers, traders, and their wives and families. Since winter was setting in early, Kit and Captain Lee decided to make winter quarters with some of the Robidoux men at the mouth of the river. At this time the fort itself was a crude collection of lodges and huts, so Captain Lee and Kit erected their own lodge of heavy buffalo hides in which to store their supply of fuel and provisions. The lodge also served as sleeping quarters.

Early in February, 1834, Antoine Robidoux enlisted Kit's services in tracing a California Indian employee who had disappeared with six horses valued at six hundred dollars. Robidoux warned Kit that the Indian was agile and crafty, but knowing his reputation for courage, Robidoux also knew Kit would return with the horses.

In an Indian village near their camp, Kit stopped to recruit help in catching his quarry. The Indians knew Carson and respected him as a great white warrior, so he could have secured the services of a score of warriors had he wanted them. He chose only one—a wiry brave he thought he could depend on in any emergency.

The trail led down Green River toward California. The thief had a head start of many hours, and his horses were fleet. It was apparent from the condition of his tracks that he had lost no time on the road and was going at a full gallop. The chase gave all indications of being a long one.

Kit and his Indian companion spurred their horses to a fast gallop. Across a long stretch of prairie they rode, then around a mountain; they urged their horses between the rocks with no slackening of speed. After a hundred miles, Kit felt sure they would overtake the thief the next day. His horse had withstood the fast pace admirably, but the Indian's horse was badly jaded. It slackened pace, staggered, and trembled so violently that the warrior leaped from its back. If it didn't die then and there, it would not recover for days. Under the circumstances, he had no choice but to wish the Indian good luck and continue the pursuit alone.

At the end of twenty miles of hard riding, the flanks of Kit's horse glistened with sweat, but he knew the thief was not far ahead and it would not do to stop to rest now. He urged his mount on for another ten miles before he caught sight of the fugitive.

The powerful California Indian was riding leisurely amid the stolen horses when he saw Kit. He leaped from his horse and ran toward a clump of sage, at the same time raising his rifle to fire. If the Indian could gain the protection of the sage, he would have Kit at his mercy—and there was no mistaking his purpose. Kit was in the open and had not the slightest cover against the Indian's aim. It was Kit's life or the Indian's.

Kit spurred his horse in one last burst of speed to get within rifle range. The Indian, with the fleetness of a deer, had bounded across the open space and now made a leap for the sage as he turned to shoot at Kit. All of this happened in seconds; the Indian's gun went off as he pitched to the ground, dead, for without checking his horse,

Kit had fired a split second before the Indian. Kit's bullet had found its mark, while the bullet meant for him whipped harmlessly above his head.

Kit rounded up the stolen horses and took them back to Robidoux. He and Captain Lee had not yet sold the Bent and St. Vrain goods, so when they learned from some trappers that Bridger and Fitzpatrick were in winter quarters on the Little Snake River, they headed there. There they sold the supplies to Broken Hand, their payment being beaver pelts, which Lee loaded on the pack horses and took to Bent's Fort. Kit stayed with Fitzpatrick.

After a month of trapping with Fitzpatrick, Kit decided to trap on his own; he took three men with him on the venture. One evening he was out hunting game to replenish a dwindling larder when he came upon a herd of elk. He took aim and fired. As the victim of his unerring aim dropped to the ground, Kit heard a loud noise behind him. He turned, and there, on a dead run toward him, were two huge grizzly bears. Realizing that he could not possibly reload in time, he dropped his rifle, made for the nearest tree, and hastily scrambled up it to the topmost branches. At this point, he must have been extremely thankful that grizzlies cannot climb trees (their claws grow out of the top of their paws, and they cannot grasp a tree trunk). The Carson luck again!

Both bears tore up the earth around the tree where he perched. One bear finally lumbered away while the other continued to uproot small aspens growing near the big evergreen. He made several attempts to get into the tree where Kit crouched, but when he found he could do no damage, he finally followed the other bear into the woods.

After waiting a while to make sure the bears were gone, Kit slid down the trunk of the tree to look for his rifle. Reloading it when he found it, he made his way back to camp as fast as possible. It was long after dark when he arrived, and the hungry trappers wanted to know why the great Kit Carson had returned late and empty handed. Kit related the details, concluding with a remark about "never having been so scared in my life." Teresina said that Kit referred to this as his "worst difficult" experience.

Kit and his men trapped the headwaters of the Laramie River and some of its tributaries for another two weeks or so before Jim Bridger came by. He was on his way to rendezvous, which was set for Green River some distance above Henry's Fork, and Kit's party fell in with him. They arrived in due time, sold their plews, and waited for the pack train of supplies to arrive.

In September, the rendezvous broke up, and the trappers, divided into a number of groups, set out for their favorite trapping grounds. Kit joined the Bridger, Sublette, and Fitzpatrick group, which included some fifty men, to trap the headwaters of the Missouri.[2] They found the Blackfeet as numerous and hostile as ever. It was nearly impossible for them to set traps without being ambushed, and even if they succeeded, the Indians would steal the traps as soon as the trappers were out of sight. The Blackfeet were excellent marksmen and had plenty of guns and ammunition, thanks to the *coureurs de bois* and a few white traders who supplied them.

On one occasion Kit and a party of men were setting traps when they were attacked by a band of Blackfeet. They swiftly retreated to a stand of trees, hid in the underbrush, and maintained a steady stream of fire. This kept the Indians in check, but the fight continued throughout the day. In their desperation to get at the trappers, the Indians set fire to the underbrush. The foliage was too green to burn well, however, and the fire soon died out. About that time, Bridger's main party arrived on the scene, and the Indians fled.

On another occasion, the Blackfeet surprised a group of men setting traps and killed five of them before they could get away. "A trapper could hardly go a mile without being fired upon," said Kit. "As we found that we could do but little in their country . . . we started for winter quarters."

[2] According to Sabin, Kit is supposed to have met Joseph Gale on a tributary of the Gallatin in the fall of 1834, but evidence from Osborne Russell indicates that the meeting could not have taken place before January, 1835. In *Kit Carson's Own Story*, the event falls under the spring of 1839, which is obviously wrong.

6 ★ Eventful Years

LATE IN 1834, Kit and the Bridger group went into winter camp with a band of friendly Flatheads on the Snake River. For their winter quarters the Indians had chosen a grove of trees on the southern slope of a chain of hills skirting the river. It was an ideal place to camp, and Old Gabe's trappers lost no time in setting up their lodges. Nor were they tardy about laying in a supply of meat and trapping until the streams froze. Their hunting trips were quite successful, and they managed to add a few more beaver pelts to their bales before severe snowstorms blocked the passes and bitter cold froze all the streams.

In February, 1835, Kit got into a fight with some Blackfeet. It was a bitter struggle, and Kit very nearly lost his life. It happened one night when the Blackfeet sneaked into the trappers' camp and ran off eighteen or twenty head of their best horses, among them Jim Bridger's prize steed, Grohean. So quiet was the theft that the night herder did not discover the loss until morning. Kit took thirty[1] trappers in pursuit of the thieves. It was snowing and the drifts were deep. Kit could tell by the Indians' tracks that there were many warriors leading the horses, but he knew, too, that the Indians had to break a path through the deep snow and that this would slow their progress.

When Kit's party finally caught up with the Indians, the horses were grazing on a hillside where there was little snow. Kit looked the situation over: there were thirty warriors, and they had the ad-

[1] Edward S. Ellis says that Kit took only twelve men; Kit says that "twelve of us followed them." Blanche Grant's notes list thirty-one men, including Kit.

vantage of snowshoes. After an exchange of shots (none of which was advantageous to either side), a parley was arranged. As was the custom, one man from each side proceeded halfway to smoke the pipe of peace—in this case the Blackfoot chief and Kit. The chief told Kit that the Blackfeet had no desire to rob the white man; they supposed that they were robbing their enemies, the Snakes. He added that they certainly wouldn't rob *him*, Vih-hiu-nis, the mighty white warrior.

The Blackfoot chief had him at a disadvantage and Kit was well aware of it. Be that as it may, Kit put on his bravest front and told the chief that he wanted no further talk until the Blackfeet gave him the horses they had stolen. The longer the parley lasted, the more the chief smiled. He was mockingly courteous and affable, but he would not yield on any point. At last, more in a gesture of peace than anything else, he ordered five broken-down crowbaits brought to him. He offered these to Kit, saying that the Blackfeet wanted to be kind to the whites and if they wanted horses, they could have these and no more. Smiling no longer, he added that the white man had no right to be in Blackfeet country. The parley was over.

The chief walked back to the Blackfoot camp and Kit moved toward the trappers, but before he could reach them, a bullet whizzed past. He took cover behind a tree, and the battle was on.

Kit was aiming, in fact was about to fire, when he noticed that Markhead was well covered by one of the Blackfeet. He shifted his aim and dropped the warrior in his tracks. This momentary diversion gave Kit's original target time for a better shot. Kit says he dodged, but he was hit anyway. The ball tore through his shoulder, shattering the bone, and he fell to the ground. For the first time in his life, he was a mere spectator; the fighting continued without him, and he had to be content with watching it.

When it became too dark to see clearly, the Indians withdrew to their camp. The trappers also pulled back, selecting a place about a mile from the Blackfeet. Although it was extremely cold, they dared not light a fire for fear of revealing their position to the Indians. Sometime before dawn, they held council and decided that with Kit out of the fighting, they would be wise to accept their loss and return to camp before the Blackfeet attacked again. They tied the wounded Kit on his horse and rode away before daylight.

Back at camp, Kit's wound was packed with snow and bandaged with soft deerskin. Jim Bridger, still reluctant to give up his favorite mount, took some trappers and started after the Blackfeet to try to recover the stolen horses. In a few days they returned, empty handed. The Blackfeet had made a hasty retreat into their own country, where the trappers dared not follow.

Old Gabe and his men began to trap the thawing streams in early April, for spring and fall were the ideal times to trap. In mid-summer, beaver fur was worthless, and in deep winter, the beaver holed up in a frozen mass of sticks and earth—a fort as impregnable as adobe walls. One evening, near St. Vrain's Creek on the Little Snake River, Kit and five other trappers had a strange experience. This is Kit's description of the events as he told the story to Colonel Meline in 1866:

It was . . . let me see . . . yes, 1835. There were six of us hunters out after buffalo, up in the Snake country. We had made a pretty good hunt, and came into camp at night, intending to start in [to Fort Hall] next morning. . . . Well, we camped. Had a good many dogs with us, some of them good dogs. They barked a good deal, and we heard wolves. As I lay by the fire, I saw one or two big wolves sneaking about camp—one of them quite in it. Gordon wanted to fire, but I would not let him, for fear of hitting some of the dogs. I had just a little suspicion that the wolves might be Indians, but when I saw them turn short about, and heard the snap of their teeth, as the dogs came too close to one of 'em, I felt easy then, and [was] sure it was a wolf. The Indian fooled me that time. Confound the rascals . . . you think he hadn't two old buffalo bones in his hand that he cracked together every time he turned to snap at the dogs? Well, by and by we dozed off asleep, and it wasn't long before I was awoke by a crash and blaze. I jumped straight for the mules, and held 'em. If the Indians had been smart they'd 'a had us all, but they run as soon as they fired. They killed but one of us—poor Davis. He had five bullets in his body, and eight in his buffalo-robe. The Indians were a band of Sioux, on the war path after the Snakes, and came on us by accident. They tried to waylay us next morning, but we killed three of 'em, including their chief.

It was time to start for rendezvous. Kit, Old Gabe, and the other trappers packed their equipment and their furs and headed for the valley of the Green. It is safe to assume that they did not tarry along the way, for the mountain men always looked forward to the summer get-together and made every effort to be there before (or soon after) it started. To them, it was the one big event of every year, and they made the most of it.

This year's debauch (a better, more accurate word to describe the typical rendezvous would be hard to find) would, in general, be little different from those which had preceded it. There would be plenty of whiskey (it was really watered alcohol and was made even more dilute by the fur company's always-sober clerk as his customers became progressively drunker), at five dollars a pint, an item the trappers saw little of except at rendezvous or established trading posts. There would be dancing (any style but mostly Indian), of which the mountain men were very fond, so much so that they would dance with absolutely anyone and often did. There would be games, races, and all manner of sporting events and contests, including wrestling, foot races, and (though they went beyond bounds when human targets were used) shooting matches. There would be gambling, arguments, and fist fights. There would be women, Indians, of course (the first white women, both missionaries' wives, to appear at a rendezvous would come the following year), but women nonetheless, and many a trapper would leave the rendezvous with an Indian wife. And last, but by no means least, there would be trade goods, on which, sooner or later (depending on how long and how well his "money" and/or credit held out), the trapper would have to focus his attention, for he would need to outfit himself for the coming year with traps, capotes, blankets, powder, lead, flints, and other necessaries. In sum, things would be pretty normal— except for Kit and Old Gabe. They would figure in a couple of momentous (at least for that time) events.

In the summer camp of 1835 was an agent of the American Fur

Company, Captain Andrew Drips, and he had with him a huge, swaggering Frenchman (or French-Canadian) named Shunar,[2] who made a practice of beating or otherwise mauling anyone and everyone who crossed his path when he was in what Bernard De Voto calls his "alligator phase." He was both feared and hated by every person who knew him.

One day after Shunar had severely beaten two men, he loudly announced that he could lick any man in camp, be he Mexican or French, white or Indian. As for Americans, he said, he needed only a small switch to whip the lot of them. He was drunk, it seems, not only with alcohol, but also with power. This time, however, he had gone too far.

Kit, probably the smallest American in camp, accepted the challenge. He went to his lodge, snatched up a pistol, got on his horse, and galloped off toward Shunar, who by this time was also mounted. Shunar had apparently realized (or had he simply sobered up in a hurry?) that he had made a very bad mistake by the time Kit rode up because when Kit asked if he was the American who was about to be whipped, Shunar said no. "Our horses were touching," says Kit. "We both fired at the same time; all present saying that but one report could be heard. I shot him through the arm and his ball passed my head, cutting my hair and the powder burning my eye, the muzzle of his gun being near my head when he fired. During our stay in camp we had no more bother with this bully [of a] Frenchman."[3]

Jim Bridger figured in another more or less exciting incident at the rendezvous: Dr. Marcus Whitman removed the three-inch iron head of a Blackfoot arrow from Old Gabe's back. Samuel Parker, who watched the operation, described it as "difficult," adding that

[2] The name has been spelled variously (as, for example, *Shunan* and *Shuman*) in other accounts.

[3] There are many versions of the outcome of this fight. One is that Kit got a second pistol from his lodge and killed Shunar; another holds that Kit spared Shunar's life. Sabin, Vestal, and De Voto (who points out that fur-trade tradition says Kit killed Shunar) accept the first version. Samuel Parker says that "while he [Kit] went for another pistol Shunar begged that his life be spared." Kit makes no mention of a second pistol in his autobiography. The story as presented here is based on *Kit Carson's Own Story* and Blanche Grant's notes.

"the Doctor pursued the operation with great self-possession and perseverance; and Captain Bridger manifested equal firmness." After this successful bit of surgery, Dr. Whitman was sought out by trappers and Indians alike to remove imbedded arrowheads. When he returned the following year with a wife and another missionary couple, he was warmly welcomed by the mountain men, and some years later Old Gabe sent his half-Indian daughter to live with the Whitmans at Waiilatpu, their mission post among the Cayuses.

Camped a short distance from the trappers' lodges was a band of Arapaho Indians who had come to the rendezvous to trade. With them was a beautiful young maiden named Waa-nibe. Kit saw her one day and at once concluded that it was high time he took a wife. He broached this idea to the girl's family, and after the dictates of Arapaho custom had been fulfilled, Kit and Waa-nibe (he called her Alice) were married.[4]

Kit's friend Charles Bent also took a wife in 1835. She was Ignacia Jaramillo, the widow of Rafael Luna, to whom she had borne a daughter named Rumalda. As was the custom for widows at that time, Ignacia had again assumed her maiden name, and during their short courtship, Charles did not have to undergo a *dueña*-supervised waiting period. He bought a home in Taos (it was north of the plaza) for his bride and stepdaughter.

When the rendezvous broke up, Kit, Old Gabe, and their men headed for Jackson's Little Hole, arriving there on August 23. Samuel Parker and his party were with them. From here they went to Pierre's Hole by way of Teton Pass. The two groups separated at Pierre's Hole, Parker and his companions going northwest and the Carson-Bridger party northeast to the Yellowstone. After trapping the Yellowstone and the Big Horn, they crossed Three Forks and went on to the Snake. They seem to have moved their winter camp several times, for when Osborne Russell joined them in February, 1836, they were on Blackfoot Creek (Blackfoot River on present maps), about fifteen miles above Fort Hall.

---

[4] It has been said that there were no Arapahoes at the 1835 rendezvous, but both Sabin and Vestal indicate that Kit's duel with Shunar was fought because of Waanibe. Blanche Grant's information is used here; she got it from Rumalda and Teresina.

Tom McKay, a Hudson's Bay Company man then at Fort Hall, proposed a trapping expedition to the Humboldt River country. Kit, Antoine Godin, and four other trappers went with him. They undoubtedly trapped the Raft River on their way to the Humboldt; it was good beaver country, and plews were getting scarce. Kit says they followed the Humboldt (or Mary's, as it was then called) to "where [it] loses itself in the great basin." They traveled back up it for fifty or sixty miles, then turned north toward the Snake. When they reached it, McKay left them to go to Fort Walla Walla.

After a short rest, Kit and his five trappers started to Fort Hall. A desolate journey lay before them, with little or no prospect of game. Long before reaching the fort they were on the very verge of starvation and were forced to search out edible roots and drink the blood of their emaciated mules to stay alive. Kit dared not kill their animals for food because the men were too weak to walk. Four days from the fort, they chanced upon a rather destitute band of Indians who had a few extra horses. Kit bought the youngest of these with his hunting knife, and the hungry trappers had a feast on it.

At the fort, Kit and his men built temporary lodges outside the walls and settled down to repair saddles (Kit's year of apprenticeship stood him in good stead), clean rifles, and otherwise relax for a few days. They were in high spirits, then, when they set out to hunt. The weather was perfect and luck was with them. On the second day out, they passed through a thick forest. Beyond it stretched a prairie, and scattered over that vast expanse were hundreds of buffalo. Other game—elk, deer, and antelope—was also abundant.

Kit selected a campsite at the edge of the woods and picketed the extra horses. A few days' hunting supplied enough meat to load all of the pack animals; the buffalo alone would supply the fort for a month or more. Their success counted for more than they knew because a calamity befell the occupants of Fort Hall shortly after the hunters returned.

When they got back from the hunt, Kit and his men put all of their animals in the main corral and retired to their lodges. Next morning, not a horse or mule remained. The night herder said he saw two men turn the animals out of the corral late at night, but, thinking they were Kit's men, he did nothing. Instead of stampeding the animals, the Indians had acted like trappers coming to let their mounts out to graze.

If the fort was without transportation, at least there was plenty to eat, thanks to the trappers. The situation was relieved a month later when Tom McKay rode in with horses to spare, although, of course, he had no way of knowing about the fort's loss. According to Kit, McKay's party and the trappers joined forces and headed for the 1836 rendezvous, which was to be on Green River again, this time at the mouth of Horse Creek. They arrived six days later.

This year's rendezvous differed from those which had preceded it in one highly significant way: two white women, Mrs. Henry Spalding and Mrs. Marcus Whitman, were present. They were traveling with their husbands to missionary posts among the northwestern Indians. They were the first white women to cross the Continental Divide (and thereby the first through South Pass), and certainly they were the first white women ever seen by most of the Indians present. From all accounts, their presence caused the usually rampageous trappers to use a measure of restraint in their conduct.

Among others who came to the summer camp were missionary William H. Gray, Tom Fitzpatrick, Nathaniel Wyeth, who was in McKay's party, Sir William Drummond Stewart, the Scotsman, and Lucien Fontenelle. As was to be expected, Joe Meek was there, too, and so were Moses Harris, Joshua Pilcher, Jim Bridger, and Osborne Russell, all of them masters in mountain craft.

Following the rendezvous, which lasted about three weeks, McKay returned to Fort Hall and Kit joined Jim Bridger, Lucien Fontenelle, and a group of some one hundred other trappers heading for the Yellowstone. Indian signs were everywhere, and Joe Meek and Dave Crow were attacked while running traps in the "plum-thicket bottoms." Sixty Blackfeet chased two other trappers (both on horses) into the river. One of them, a man named Howell, was wounded and later died in camp. Twenty trappers and a number of Nez Percés and Delawares chased the Blackfeet to an island in the Yellowstone, where the battle continued all day.

It was a bad season for the trappers. They encountered plenty of Blackfeet but few beaver. After trapping the Yellowstone and its tributaries to the mouth of Clark's Fork, they went into winter camp on the Powder River. For their campsite they chose a thick stand of cottonwoods and were assisted in putting up their buffalo-hide lodges by some Crow Indians whose village was near by. The trappers could count on their help in case of Blackfoot attack, for the Crows and Blackfeet were bitter enemies.

The winter of 1836–37 turned out to be extremely cold, with much snow. The trappers, however, fared better than their mounts. The snow was so deep in the valleys that grazing was impossible, and the men had to strip frozen bark from the cottonwoods and thaw it to feed the near-starving animals. It was hard, cold work, but it kept the horses alive.

Spring came at last, and with it the breaking of winter camp. Kit sent two men to Fort Laramie for supplies. After waiting for some time for the men to return, Kit decided that the Indians had struck again. The men had disappeared and were never heard of again.

The spring campaign began in Wind River Valley. The trappers hunted buffalo on the plains, for buffalo hides were becoming as valuable as beaver pelts. With the advent of silk hats, beaver prices had dropped, and now buffalo robes were in demand. Only cow and bullock hides were taken, the hides of full-grown bulls being too heavy for ordinary use, though they served as excellent material for lodges or tipis. (In 1840, the American Fur Company shipped 76,000 robes down the Missouri River, and in 1844, Josiah Gregg had foresight enough to warn of "the prospect of their total extinction" if the wanton slaughter of the buffalo continued.)

One day Kit and his companions found signs of many Indians who had passed a day before them. Kit took five men to ascertain the strength of the enemy. Cautiously, they followed the trail until they came to the Indians' camp, where they watched the warriors make preparations to move their women and children. There was a great deal of agitation in the Indian camp: the Blackfeet were preparing for war. Hurrying back to their own camp, Kit and the five held council with the others. It was decided to attack at once, for the trappers knew that the Indians were aware of their presence. Kit had a score to settle with the Blackfeet, anyway, for he carried a scar on his shoulder, and now he was sure that these same Indians had killed the men he sent to Fort Laramie for supplies.

Leaving sixty men to guard the furs and camp equipment, Kit, Lucien Fontenelle, Jim Bridger, and about forty trappers set out for the Indian camp. The sixty men at camp had orders to move up slowly in order to act as a reserve force should Kit and the men need them. As the trappers charged the Indians' camp, it was evident that they were expected. The Blackfeet were armed to the teeth and far outnumbered the whites. The battle raged for hours, and then the trappers started to run low on ammunition. Kit's order was to retreat, but to keep firing, making every ball count. The Indians sensed the situation and rushed forward. The trappers held fire until the Indians were within rifle range; then they opened up with a volley of shots. Still the Indians came on, and the trappers retreated. Suddenly a horse fell, spilling Cotton Mansfield and pinning him underneath. Six Indians rushed for Cotton's scalp. Kit dismounted and fired into the group. One Indian fell dead and the rest fled, but Kit's frightened horse had bounded away. As the last of the trappers, a Mr. White, came dashing by on horseback, Kit called to him. He stopped and Kit sprang up behind him as Cotton remounted. All rode swiftly back toward their camp.

The Blackfeet posted themselves behind rocks near camp and continued to do battle, though their shots fell short. Meanwhile, the other trappers had arrived on the scene. With fresh supplies of ammunition and sixty more trappers to help them, Kit and his men led a new assault, Indian style. They dodged from tree to tree and rock to rock. The battle raged on, an Indian on one side of a rock or tree and a trapper on the other, each waiting for the other to make a move. The trappers finally conquered; the Blackfeet were dislodged and scattered in every direction. Kit said later: "It was the prettiest fight I ever saw."

During periods of inactivity, the trappers would try their luck at "creasing" wild horses. The feat consisted of hitting the horse with a well-aimed bullet in the upper edge of the neck in order to paralyze it momentarily. If the bullet struck a fraction of an inch too high or too low and failed to "crease," it killed the animal. There were few trappers who were expert enough to make the crease shot. W. E. Webb, in his *Buffalo Land*, expressed the opinion that "creasing" was only possible with one who was "able to shoot away the breath of a pigeon or hit the eye of a flying hawk."

Kit had once managed to crease a beautiful stallion after laying a trap for him. He tied a mare to a tree which a band of wild horses passed on their way to water. When the stallion stopped near the mare, Kit, who was hidden in the tree, got a perfect "crease" shot. When the stallion regained the use of his feet, they were securely tied and a lariat was drawn tightly around his neck. Kit gently rubbed the horse's forehead and nose, breathing into the animal's nostrils so that the trembling stallion could get the "man smell." When the taming process was finished, the proud stallion proved to be swift and of great endurance. He was Kit's favorite mount for many years.

The 1837 rendezvous was set for the valley of the Green, twelve miles below the mouth of Horse Creek. Kit, Bridger, Fontenelle, and their trappers arrived in due time—after trapping a fork of the Missouri with undreamed-of success. It was the only luck they had run into since the previous rendezvous, for they found beaver mighty scarce around the Wind and Powder rivers. That last trap on the Missouri, plus the buffalo hides they had taken, saved them from a very poor year.

William H. Gray was in summer camp again this year with two other white men, an Iroquois, a Nez Percé, and three Flatheads, "one of whom," says Sabin, "was an educated chief, The Hat." (The Indian had acquired that name when he became the proud possessor of a tall silk hat, which he wore at all times, even when he wore no other clothing except his breechclout.) Against the strongly worded advice of the mountain men, the Gray party set out for the States. Just as the trappers had warned, they ran smack into Indian trouble. A large party of Sioux attacked them, pinned them down, and surrounded them. There are several versions of what happened after that, but the tangible outcome is that the five Indians in Gray's party were killed, whereas the three whites escaped.

A warm friendship had sprung up between Kit and Baronet of Grandtully Sir William Drummond Stewart. This year they renewed their acquaintance. Like Kit, Stewart loved the mountains and held in high esteem the men who had dominated them and their hostile residents so well. He had been in the mountains several years, had attended rendezvous, and would be drawn to this region again from his native Scotland in a later year. The mountain men liked and respected him, for he was a man of their own kind in courage and endurance. Kit wrote of him: "Sir William Stuart [*sic*] . . . will be forever remembered for his liberality and his many good qualities, by the mountaineers who had the honor of his acquaintance."

With Sir William was Alfred Jacob Miller, whom he had met in New Orleans that spring and commissioned to do a series of paintings for Murthly Castle. Here in the West he was to meet, first hand, his most fascinating subject matter: the Plains Indian and his way of life and the mountain man and his crude and interesting fight for survival. Miller painted these things in two hundred exquisite water colors (later copied in oils for Stewart's castle) while the trapper was at the height of his career, the culture of the Plains Indians in its golden age, and the western scenery wild and beautiful. Kit, who had never seen an artist at work, asked to accompany Miller on some of his field trips. He showed the artist wild sheep in the mountains and buffalo on the plains and told him much about the Indians.

In the winter of 1837–38, Fort Davy Crockett, located on the left bank of Green River in Brown's Hole, was a popular gathering place for trappers, traders, and other adventurers. The fort, a one-story adobe building with three wings but no stockade, had been completed that spring by William Craig, Phillip Thompson, and William Sinclair. After the rendezvous, Kit and seven others journeyed to the fort, where Kit took employment (as the fort's official hunter) for the winter.

Kit's job was an easy one as such jobs go, for in a month's time he and his men could supply the fort with a four to six months' supply of meat. Buffalo were plentiful, and there were other kinds of game to relieve what might become a monotonous fare of buffalo meat. Thus he had plenty of free time to relax and catch up on the news from men passing through. One such item was of special interest to him; he learned that William Bent, one of the builders of Bent's Fort, had married a Cheyenne woman of great beauty and intelligence. Her name was Owl Woman, and she proved to be an excellent wife for a man of William's temperament.

Sometime in 1837, either on Horse Creek or at one of the forts, Alice gave birth to a baby girl. Kit's dark, elfish daughter was named Adaline (or Adeline, as Kit spelled her name) for the niece—daughter of his elder half-brother, William Carson—who had been his childhood playmate in Missouri.[5] In 1869, Captain James Hobbs wrote of her: "This girl was ... born at Bent's Fort on the Arkansas River. . . . she married . . . George Stilts of St. Louis, Mo., and went to California in 1849 [1851]. . . . She was a noble looking woman, of mixed complexion, black eyes, and long black hair, and could excel most men in the use of the rifle."

From Fort Davy Crockett, Thompson and Sinclair organized a trading trip into the Navaho country of present-day New Mexico. Kit accompanied them. Navaho rugs and blankets were widely known throughout the Southwest and sold for high prices. Kit, Sinclair, and Thompson bought a number of the colorful blankets, procured thirty mules and some horses, and returned to Fort Davy Crockett.

Kit says he joined Jim Bridger in the spring of 1838. If so, he did not stay with him very long because Old Gabe moved westward from his winter camp on the Powder, and Kit specifically mentions trapping in the Black Hills region—*east* of the Powder—with "Dick Owens and three Canadians." The five of them split into two groups, with Kit and Owens pairing off and the three Canadians forming the other party. They "trapped for three months, made a good hunt and then started to find the main camp." The "main camp" was undoubtedly Bridger's outfit, which had experienced an

[5] In Blanche Grant's notes is a statement from Mrs. J. F. Hawley that the daughter's name was Adelaide.

extremely poor season. According to Kit, the two parties joined forces and in July headed for rendezvous at the mouth of the Popo Agie.

In early fall, Kit, Alice, and Adaline set out for Bent's Fort on the Arkansas. Soon after they arrived, Alice fell ill with a fever and died, leaving Kit with an infant daughter and an empty heart. Kit placed Adaline under the care of an Indian woman and took employment as a hunter for the fort.

A story was circulated in later years that Kit married a Cheyenne woman of bad disposition, but there is no solid evidence that this happened, other than in the mind of some ambitious biographer who wanted to add zest to Kit's already colorful life. From the Carson family comes an emphatic denial of such a marriage. A letter from Teresina Bent Scheurich states:

> Uncle Kit was very angry when the man he had given the interview to said that he was married to a Cheyenne woman named *Making Out Road*. He said there was no truth in that story, and there was no truth in the story about an immoral white woman whom he met in Santa Fe when he was sixteen years old. There are so many tales written about Uncle Kit that it is hard to know what the truth really is. I have [had] to ask him many times, is this true or is that a fact? I wonder if the real truth about my Uncle will ever be written, or will he be blamed for things he did not do? Who can tell?

Twice a year, the hunters at Bent's Fort filled their powder horns, loaded necessary supplies on a few of many pack animals, and rode out to hunt buffalo and other game. They might well be called upon to hunt more often, but the spring and fall hunts comprised their major efforts. To Kit, as to nearly everyone who hunted them, there was a thrill and a challenge in hunting the shaggy buffalo. Although he liked to hunt deer, elk, antelope, and grizzlies and to take geese on the wing, none of this held the excitement of the buffalo chase.

While Kit and his men were hunting on the plains of Kansas in the fall of 1838, they met a large caravan under the command of Captain Blunt. The Captain was delighted to see the hunters because the Kiowas were on the warpath again and the caravan was fast approaching Kiowa country. Many of his men were greenhorns—poorly

77

armed ones at that—and would be no match for the Indians should they attack. He was therefore both thankful and relieved when Kit agreed to accompany him.

Among the greenhorns was a fifteen-year-old cavvy boy named Oliver Wiggins. He had run away from his brother, who operated the Wiggins Ferry in St. Louis, to go west. When he joined the caravan, he would tell no one his name (for fear of being sent back to his brother), so, for want of something to call him and because he was dressed in faded blue denim, the men dubbed him "Blue," a nickname which stuck with him through the years.

Perhaps Kit was thinking of a sixteen-year-old saddler's apprentice who ran away to join a Santa Fe–bound caravan twelve years before. Maybe he remembered that boy's job with the caravan: taking care of the cavvy. Possibly he recalled the boy's feelings when he reached Santa Fe—a measure of homesickness mingled with apprehension about the future. Whatever his thoughts and reasons, Kit took an immediate liking for Blue and the two became fast friends. In fact, Kit virtually adopted Oliver Wiggins; in return, Oliver idolized Kit and looked upon him as a father. For twelve years he was a Carson man, and in 1842, he accompanied Kit on Frémont's first expedition. He also went along on the second expedition but was one of those who turned back at Fort Hall.

Two days' travel brought the wagon train into Kiowa country. Here Kit baffled the caravanners by dismounting his men and placing them by pairs in each of the wagons. Blunt and his men may well have thought the hunters were cowards when this move was made, but they soon learned differently. The Kiowas, sure that they had a small party of teamsters at their mercy, swooped down on the caravan. When they were sufficiently close, Kit gave the order to fire, and the mountain men went to work. A number of warriors fell at the first volley, and the others, taken by complete surprise, soon broke off the charge and fled in wild confusion, whereupon Kit and his men jumped on their horses and chased them far into the hills. The caravanners, not to mention the Kiowas, had learned that Kit Carson was no amateur when it came to fighting Indians.

All the while, Blue had been crouching behind a wagon, firing his pistol without hitting a single Indian. He was extravagant in his praise of the clever way in which Kit and his lieutenant, Ike Chamberlain, had handled the situation. He had heard of Kit long before, had dreamed of meeting him, and now he had seen Kit in action. That evening, when the caravan came to the forks of the Santa Fe and Taos trails, Ike asked Blue if he would like to go with them to Taos instead of traveling on to Santa Fe with the caravan. Would he like it? Blue said he would love it! Thus it was that Oliver Wiggins became a Carson man, a decision he never regretted.

Charles Bent owned or leased a building on the south side of Taos plaza; here he had furnished Kit with two rooms and a corral for his horses and mules. Kit used one of these rooms for living quarters, and the other, which had a door opening onto the plaza, was made into a storage room and office from which he could outfit his men and dispatch them on hunting, trapping, or trading expeditions. Sometimes he went with them, especially when they were hunting for Bent's Fort. During these trips and his short stays in Taos, he left Adaline at the fort, visiting her whenever he could.

Kit was, then, beginning to conduct business for himself by 1839. He had established trade connections with the Bents and the St. Vrains (Charles Bent's home was north of the plaza, and Céran St. Vrain lived on the east side of the plaza across from Kit), and this, together with the experience and knowledge he had acquired since coming west, provided a solid foundation for his venture. It was a wise move on Kit's part, for the fur trade was declining rapidly. This year would see the last regular rendezvous; there would be one more, in 1840, but it would be a token affair—a small, brief, friendly get-together more than anything else—and there would be no active trading. For all intents and purposes, the beaver trade had, as the mountain men put it, "gone under."

Among the first Carson men were Ike Chamberlain and Solomon Silver, who acted as Kit's chief aides. Chamberlain was a huge man, somewhat red of face and strong as an ox. His speech and manner marked him at once as a veteran mountain man. Silver, so called because of the large silver earrings which dangled from his thick lobes, was a swarthy Mexican who had been captured by the Comanches when he was a baby. They had sold him to the Kiowas at an early age, and so it was that he never knew his real name. Escaping from the Kiowas, Sol drifted to Taos and was there employed by the Bent brothers. Quick, alert, and a crack shot, he also possessed a fiery temper. But he was loyal, and because of this and his uncanny knowledge of the Indians, Kit considered him a valuable employee.

Kit accompanied his men on the spring and fall hunts in order to fulfill his contract as official hunter for Bent's Fort. He sometimes went with them to the mountains to trap, although such excursions were becoming less and less profitable. Beaver plews were still bringing a fair enough price at Taos and Santa Fe in 1839, but the following year would dry up even those outlets. Trading and contract hunting seemed to be the only way for Kit to make a go of it, and this meant that he would have to do some shrewd bargaining and calculating—and a lot of riding.

In all of his travels, Kit never failed to help anyone in need, Indian and white man alike. The Comanches, the Arapahoes, the Utes, the Cheyennes, the Kiowas, the Sioux, the Flatheads, the Blackfeet, and the Navahos knew him either personally or by reputation. He had sat by their lodge fires, had talked to their chiefs, had sung to their children. He had fought back viciously and effectively when they attacked him, but in their eyes, his was always a fair fight. In council with their chiefs, he had always spoken with a "single tongue." Sometimes he averted wars by his peace talk, as once when the powerful Sioux rode down from the north to drive the Comanches and Arapahoes from their own hunting grounds. The Comanches sent a messenger to Bent's Fort to bring Kit to the combined Arapaho-Comanche war council. The war chiefs told their story, and Kit promised to go to the Sioux camp to talk peace. Kit bound his horse's feet with buffalo hide, and the Sioux were so overwhelmed with wonder at a white man who could ride into their camp "without sound" that they listened to him far into the night. The next day, they left in peace.

In the summer of 1839, Kit made his way to Fort Nonsense[6] for

---

[6] Fort Bonneville. It was built by Captain B. L. E. Bonneville in 1832 and was located on Horse Creek a little less than five miles above its mouth.

the rendezvous. It was a somber gathering which bore little resemblance to the gay, carefree performances of previous years. Although a sizable number of trappers attended, they were disheartened almost to the limit of their endurance and disappointed beyond their most fearful expectations. Only a handful of them had had a good year—beaver mighty scarce; plenty of Indians, though—and now the bottom fell out: prices were so low that profit was impossible. A man could consider himself lucky to break even, and many a good trapper wound up deep in debt. Kit stayed long enough to greet his friend Fitzpatrick and a few other acquaintances, then headed for Bent's Fort. Kit noted that the slack season had brought a number of visitors to the fort. Most interesting of all was one of the first white women to visit the adobe outpost on the Arkansas: sixteen-year-old Félicité St. Vrain, niece of Céran St. Vrain. Her father, Félix, had been killed by Indians a few years before. Félicité fell madly in love with Kit, and although Céran liked Kit very much, he objected to his niece's marrying a widower with a child—a half-Indian child at that. A St. Vrain, scion of nobility, to marry a *squaw man?* Never! Félicité was hurried back to St. Louis. She later entered a convent.

That same year, Céran built Fort St. Vrain on the South Platte River. Although it was smaller than the Bent post on the Arkansas, the fort (called Fort Lookout and also Fort George, for George Bent, who helped to build it) was constructed along similar lines. Its high adobe walls measured 130 feet on the north and south and 60 feet on the east and west. Within them was a deep well; the corral was at the rear of the fort. Céran and the Bent brothers, his partners, established a monopoly on trade south of the North Platte when they completed arrangements with near-by Fort Lupton.

The Bents and St. Vrain may have had control of trade on the Platte, but they were also having their troubles—in Taos and Santa Fe. Governor Manuel Armijo had levied a duty of five hundred dollars on each wagonload of merchandise the "foreigners" brought in but had exempted the "native citizens" from paying the duty, thus throwing the whole burden of taxation on the Americans and "naturalized" residents. As an American, Kit was interested in these arrangements, for he wanted to see his fellow countrymen treated fairly, "foreigners" though they were.

Charles Bent, Céran St. Vrain, and Carlos Beaubien had established three merchandising stores in Taos, which made their position in Mexican-dominated territory indeed precarious. When Armijo and other Mexican officials bought supplies and ammunition from their stores, the Taos Pueblo Indians accused Bent and Beaubien of plotting against the Indians for their land—which was ever a cause for Indian revolt. It was foolish logic to accuse Charles of unfair dealings, but then many issues were confused at this time. In their turn, the Mexicans charged that Texas-inspired gringos had armed the Indians as a first step toward absorbing New Mexico. After the Santa Fe revolution of 1837–38, feelings had run high on all sides; they would smolder until 1847, when another revolt would erupt, this time in Taos.

Kit may have read the letter, written December 10, 1839, which Charles Bent sent to Senator Daniel Webster of Massachusetts, a friend of his father, complaining that the harassments suffered by Americans were motivated by Armijo's desire to ruin his American competitors. Charles claimed that Armijo had refused to do anything about the murders which had been committed in Taos. Taking up the issue of law and order, Charles sent the following dispatch to Alvarez for Governor Armijo: "It is the request of the foreigners residing heare, that you will present the accompanying petetion to the Governor, and impress upon him the necessity of having William Langford tried for the murder of Simon Marsh immediately." Armijo replied that he was too busy to attend to trifles!

Charles set out for Taos, and Kit and his men remained at Bent's Fort to prepare for the fall hunt. Scarcely had he reached Taos when an express was sent to the fort with a report that he was in jail. Kit and a heavily armed rescue party rode toward Taos at once. In Taos Canyon they were surprised to meet Charles, who had just been released, with no charges against him. The authorities had apologized to him, calling the arrest a "mistake." Charles knew that the Mexicans would strike again and would use the Indians as an excuse next time; he therefore asked William Clark[7] to write to the Commissioner of Indian Affairs to ask for the six medals which Colonel Henry Dodge had promised the Indians in 1835. Dodge had apparently run short of medals while at Taos and had forgotten his promise to send them. Two months later, Charles presented the medals to White Cow, Yellow Wolf, and Whirlwind of the Cheyennes and Left-handed Soldier, Raven, and Buffalo Belly of the Arapahoes. Needless to say, this improved Bent's relations with the Indians considerably and strengthened his position against the Mexicans.

To inaugurate the spring campaign, the Carson men rode into Blackfoot country. Now ordinarily this would be inviting trouble, lots of it, in the form of innumerable skirmishes with and raids from the Blackfeet, but this year was different. The Blackfeet were unusually inactive, were so *friendly*, in fact, that the trappers engaged Blackfoot women to tan buffalo hides and cure beaver pelts. It would seem that the smallpox epidemic which had decimated the tribe in recent years had sobered at least some of those who lived through it. At any rate, they did not harass the trappers. The boys made a fair catch of beaver, took what they wanted and needed for immediate use in the way of buffalo and other game, and ranged back toward Taos and Bent's Fort. Their major effort was expended on the way back, for they were obligated to garner a good supply of meat for the fort. They did so, and Kit earned a reasonable profit on the plews they brought in.

There was peace talk among the various tribes in 1840. Encouraged by Kit and Charles Bent, the Indians began congregating for a big meeting in the summer of 1840. First to arrive were the Cheyennes and Arapahoes. They began setting up tipis about three miles from the fort on the north bank of the Arkansas and were soon joined by Kiowas, Comanches, and a few other tribes from the plains. More arrived. And more. The prairie on either side of the river was thick with Indian villages whose inhabitants raced, played ball and other games, and feasted. There was dancing and the counting

[7] Clark added the following note to the letter: "Mr. Bent is an enterprising, respectable man . . . and if occasion requires would, from his knowledge of the country, and of the Spanish and French languages, combined with his general intelligence, prove useful."

of coups and some drinking, but not much, for Charles and William Bent wanted to keep things peaceful. They traded with the Indians, of course, but alcohol was strictly forbidden as a trade item. Even so, the Indians still managed to procure some.

Kit rode out to the Arapaho village to greet Alice's father, who was getting on in years. He was happy to see his son-in-law, and the two of them smoked, talked, and enjoyed themselves generally. Kit had brought gifts, the usual custom, and these were distributed among his late wife's relatives.

Acting as hosts to the various tribes were William and Charles Bent, assisted by Kit. The various chiefs and some of their warriors were conducted, ten at a time, on a tour of the fort. First they saw the Bent trade brand (Quarter Circle B), then, in the center of the courtyard by the well, the huge press for baling buffalo robes and beaver pelts. The fort's offices and living quarters were open for inspection, as was its large kitchen, where Charlotte, a jolly but quick-tempered Negress who was famed for her bread and her pumpkin pies, presided. Charlotte was the wife of Dick Green, who, with his brother, Andrew, served meals and performed general work at the fort.

The chiefs were taken to the cupola of the headquarters room, where each of them looked through the fort's large telescope. After being shown the cannons commanding every approach to the fort, they were convinced it needed no soldiers to protect it. As the chiefs left the fort, they were shown the sentry box above the gate and the six-pounder brass cannon which could sweep fire either inside or outside the fort, a final reminder that the fort's occupants were well armed and would kill many warriors if they were attacked. The Indians were impressed and the Bents were pleased, as well they should have been, for what better way could you practice diplomacy with the Indians than by showing them your great strength (providing you had it, of course)?

The day set aside for the peace council arrived, and Kit, who knew more Indian tongues than any other white man present, did much of the talking for the whites. One of the old chiefs said that the older people of his tribe wanted peace, but the young braves argued against it. If they could not fight and take scalps, they said, how could they count coups?

A younger chief from another tribe wanted to know what there would be for his young warriors to do if they could not fight. More talk of peace and friendship the next day, and then the Indians disbanded and started home.

Charles and Kit rode to Taos, and William settled down again at the fort, his wife and children with him, to trade and manage that section of the Bent business. George Bent, who had just returned from Old Mexico with a Mexican wife, was a partner in the trading business and stayed with him.

In January, 1841, Charles and Kit were having more trouble with Governor Armijo than with all the Plains Indians combined. The Governor had exempted native residents from taxes on their storehouses and shops and had encouraged informers to report American violators. Mexican officials in Taos regularly conducted raids on the Bent–St. Vrain–Beaubien stores to look for contraband. The sales rooms were turned upside down, and much of the merchandise was rendered unsalable. Protests to the American representative in Santa Fe brought no relief.

On October 15, a daughter, Teresina, was born to Charles and Ignacia Bent in Taos; they had lost two children in infancy. Their son, Alfredo, was now nearly four years old, and Mrs. Bent's daughter, Rumalda Luna, was almost ten years old.

One day during the same month, Charles Bent's youngest brother, Robert, was riding horseback with a wagon train when he sighted some buffalo in the distance. Spurring his horse, he rode out alone to kill one. Out of sight of the wagons, Robert rode smack into a Comanche ambush. The Indians who had talked so glowingly about peace the year before killed him, scalped him, and rode off into the hills. Robert's companions found his body and bore it to the fort. "Peace with the Indians," said William Bent bitterly, "there will never be peace!"

Kit, Charles Bent, Ike Chamberlain, Sol Silver, and Oliver Wiggins rode to Bent's Fort for Robert's funeral. George Bent, two years older than Robert, was also there, as were William and a few acquaintances of the family. The gloom brought on by the occasion was not dispelled for several days.

The year 1841 marked a great advance in weapons and a greater decline in beaver prices. Oliver Wiggins became the first man in Taos to own a percussion-cap rifle. It was a gift from Kit, who had purchased it from Golcher & Butler, a Philadelphia firm, for sixty dollars in gold. Beaver prices dropped so low that a season's catch would not pay for the cost of the traps. It was starvin' times for the mountain man who had no other job.

As a young man among such prominent citizens of Taos as Lucien Maxwell, Charles Bent, Carlos Beaubien, Céran St. Vrain, and Thomas Boggs, Kit was introduced to the social life of the village. In Charles Bent's home, Kit met Mrs. Bent's sister, the strikingly beautiful Josefa Jaramillo, who was then only fourteen years old but already a woman by Spanish standards. Josefa was the daughter of Don Francisco Jaramillo and Maria Apolonia Vigil, two of the most prominent Spanish Catholic families in the Southwest. Kit himself became a Catholic on January 28, 1842, and was baptized by Padre Antonio Martinez, who had come to Taos the same year Kit arrived.

Another interesting young lady in the Bent home was Rumalda Luna, Mrs. Bent's daughter, not quite ten. A bright child with dancing eyes, she later married Thomas Oliver Boggs, oldest son of Panthea (Daniel Boone's granddaughter) and Lilburn W. Boggs, governor of Missouri from 1836 to 1840. In 1870, Thomas Boggs became the first sheriff of Bent County (Colorado), and the following year he was elected to the territorial legislature.

In April, 1842, Kit joined a Bent caravan bound for Missouri. According to family records, he took Adaline, who was by now five or six years old and ready for some kind of schooling, along with him. One of the family stories connected with this event (traditionally related by Mary Ann) has it that when Kit and Adaline arrived in Missouri, Kit had misgivings about how his family would receive his half-Indian daughter. So, when he was a day's journey from his destination, he left Adaline in the care of a family with whom they had spent the night and traveled on alone. He was warmly welcomed, whereupon he returned at once for Adaline, who was described by Rumalda Boggs as being a "dark exotic looking child resembling her mother." Kit was very proud of her. She remained with his family, and they later enrolled her in Howard Female Seminary at Fayette, Missouri, where she received a liberal education.

After visiting relatives and making a trip to St. Louis, Kit decided that he had had enough of civilization. "Being tired of settlements," he says in his autobiography, "I took a steamer for the upper Missouri." Kit knew no one on board and no one knew him, but he struck up a conversation with a distinguished-looking man slightly younger than himself. It marked the beginning of a friendship that was to last a lifetime.

7 ★ Exploring with Frémont

THE STRANGER ON SHIPBOARD introduced himself as Lieutenant John Charles Frémont of the United States Corps of Topographical Engineers and explained that he had been commissioned by his chief, Colonel J. J. Abert, "to explore the country between the frontiers of Missouri and the South Pass in the Rocky Mountains and on the line of the Kansas and Great Platte Rivers." In St. Louis he had made arrangements for a party of twenty-one men,[1] among them Kit's friend, Lucien Maxwell, who had been engaged as hunter. Charles Preuss, a native of Germany, was to be Frémont's cartographer. Also going along were Henry Brant, nineteen-year-old son of Colonel J. B. Brant of St. Louis, and twelve-year-old Randolph Benton, son of Missouri's Senator Thomas H. Benton and young brother of Frémont's wife.

There must have been some aspect of Kit Carson's bearing which inspired Frémont's confidence, for he asked Kit if he knew where he could find a guide, explaining that Captain Andrew Drips, who had promised to guide the party, had failed to make an appearance. In answer, Kit told him that he thought he could take him wherever he wanted to go. After making a few inquiries, Frémont engaged

[1] The twenty-one men engaged in St. Louis are listed in Frémont's *Report* as follows: Clément Lambert, J. B. L'Esperance, J. B. Lefêvre, Benjamin Potra, Louis Gouin, J. B. Dumés, Basil Lajeunesse, François Tessier, Benjamin Cadotte, Joseph Clément, Daniel Simonds, Leonard Benoit, Michel Morly, Baptiste Bernier, Honoré Ayot, François Latulippe, François Badeau, Louis Ménard, Joseph Ruelle, Moise Chardonnais, Auguste Janisse, and Raphael Proue. The reader will note that there are actually twenty-two men in the list; the extra man is François Latulippe, who joined the expedition on June 28.

Kit as guide for the expedition at wages of a hundred dollars a month.

The expedition arrived at Chouteau's Landing on June 4, 1842, and remained there until June 6, when it moved to Cyprian Chouteau's trading post, some twelve miles from the mouth of the Kansas River. Here the party was delayed by unfavorable weather. The wait was annoying to everyone but young Randolph Benton, whose high spirits and sunny disposition added a note of gaiety to even the darkest situations. Randolph became an immediate favorite with Kit, Lucien Maxwell, and Basil Lajeunesse. The other men, most of them French Creoles or French Canadians, soon followed suit in taking a liking for the fun-loving boy.

Kit sent an express to Taos asking certain of his men to meet him at Fort Laramie and to bring equipment with them. Oliver Wiggins says that he, Sol Silver and twelve other Carson men set out at once for the fort. They were, he says, quite eager to go along with the expedition, even though they would do so in an unofficial capacity.

By Friday, June 10, the weather had cleared enough for the group to move on. An Indian guide conducted them forty miles along the Kansas River, a route with which Kit was not familiar. Frémont studied the character of the river, and Charles Preuss made topographical maps of the river and the country surrounding it.

On the afternoon of the fourteenth, they prepared to ford the river, an operation rendered hazardous because heavy rains had swollen the stream. Frémont had brought along "an India-rubber boat . . . twenty feet long and five broad, and on it were placed the body and wheels of a cart, with the load belonging to it, and three men with paddles." Basil Lajeunesse swam the river with a line attached to the boat and from the opposite bank helped to pull it across. Six of the expedition's eight carts were safely ferried across in this way. Since it was beginning to get dark, Frémont ordered the two remaining carts and their contents to be placed on the boat for a last trip. The boat tilted, and its cargo was dumped into the water. The men on shore leaped into the river post haste, and nearly everything of importance was saved. Some sugar and a bag of coffee were lost, and Frémont recorded that later on they "remembered and mourned over our loss [of the coffee] in the Kansas." It was a tribute to his men that anything at all was saved from the swift-running current.

The following morning, Lucien Maxwell and Kit, both of whom had been in the water as much as their fellows or more, were ill, so the company remained in camp that day and part of the next. They were visited by a number of Kaw Indians, who brought vegetables and butter. Frémont traded a pair of oxen for a cow and calf and was able to buy about thirty pounds of coffee from a halfblood "near the river."

On the evening of the seventeenth, a hunter from an Oregon-bound party of emigrants under Dr. Elijah White rode into camp. He was on his way back to St. Louis and offered to take letters and messages back with him. Kit wrote a few lines to his daughter; Frémont wrote a letter to his bride of six months and sent a report of his progress to his father-in-law, Senator Benton. Charles Preuss wrote to his wife; and Randolph and Joseph penned short notes to their families.

The next day, the expedition arrived at Vermillion Creek. From this point Frémont and his party turned northwest and traveled into Pawnee country, whose inhabitants were noted horse thieves. They were fairly well into Pawnee lands when Frémont set up the expedition's first night guard. Kit was in charge of the ten-to-midnight shift, and two of his guards were Henry Brant and Randolph Benton—their first stint of such duty. A violent storm broke shortly before they began their watch, and that, together with the wild tales of Indian attacks they had heard at the evening meal, made things a bit difficult for them. Their posts were far apart, and Frémont records that he could hear the boys calling out about "some imaginary alarm." However, says Frémont, "they stood it out, and took their turn regularly afterward."

Henry Brant figured in another Indian scare the next morning. He came galloping up from the rear of the column to report that he had seen several Indians on the other side of the Little Blue River, along which the expedition was now traveling. Kit jumped on a fresh horse, forded the river, and raced off across the plains to investigate. Frémont describes the scene in his *Report:* "Mounted on a fine horse, without a saddle, and scouring bareheaded over the prairies, Kit was one of the finest pictures of a horseman I have ever seen." Kit was back in a short time. The party turned out to be six elk!

The expedition marched on until they reached a fork of the Blue River at a high dividing ridge and from there traveled another twenty-three miles to the Platte River. They found a good place to camp near Grand Island, close to what is now Kearny, Nebraska. They had now traveled 328 miles from the mouth of the Kansas River.

Still another Indian scare occurred on June 28 as the men were eating lunch. To the cry "Indians!" each of them was on his feet with rifle ready. In the distance was a group of men on foot. As they came closer, Frémont could see they were not Indians, but a group of fourteen weary, forlorn men, their only possessions strapped on their backs. Their leader, John Lee, said that they had been on a trapping expedition for the American Fur Company, had had a series of bad breaks, and were now on their way to St. Louis, utterly impoverished. Among the fourteen Frémont recognized an old companion and asked him to join the expedition, which he did.[2] Frémont and John Lee exchanged some choice news before they shook hands to go their opposite ways.

That evening, just as the group was preparing to eat supper, three Cheyenne Indians, two men and a boy of thirteen, came into camp. Frémont invited them to eat with his mess, which was composed of Kit, Maxwell, Randolph Benton, Henry Brant, Charles Preuss, Basil Lajeunesse, Clément Lambert, and himself. Randolph and the Cheyenne boy struck up quite a comradeship. After supper, one of the Indians drew a crude map of the country, tracing the water courses, between Frémont's camp and the Cheyenne villages. The Indians asked to join the expedition as far as the village; Frémont welcomed them.

On the morning of June 30, the first buffalo were sighted and before noon the party came upon several small bands. Camp was

---

[2] The man was François Latulippe, whom Frémont inadvertently included, as a twenty-second man, in his list of the men he hired in St. Louis.

established at noon and preparations made for a big hunt the next day. In the afternoon, the hunters brought in three cows, one of which Kit had killed. He had just shot the animal and was in the act of pursuing the herd when his horse fell, throwing him to the ground. Lucien Maxwell, who was near by, set out after Kit's horse and finally caught it, but not before he had come close to shooting it in order to save Kit's silver-mounted Spanish bridle.

Kit, Frémont, and Maxwell went hunting the next day. Kit brought down a cow, and Frémont soon matched him with another one, Maxwell killing a third some distance away. Kit dismounted to skin his animal, but Frémont, having the advantage of good position, rode on after a second cow. He fired at fairly close range, but the ball hit too high and the cow ran wildly on. Frémont, following doggedly, was forced to give up the chase when he found himself at the edge of a large prairie dog village. The other hunters had a good day, too, and the expedition was well supplied with meat when it moved on the next day.

At the confluence of the North and South Platte rivers, Frémont split the expedition into two groups. The main party, under the direction of Clément Lambert and Kit Carson, was to proceed up the North Platte to Fort Laramie and there await Frémont's arrival. Frémont and five men (Preuss, Maxwell, Lajeunesse, Bernier, and Ayot), plus the three Cheyennes, whose village was upstream, set out to explore the South Platte. The size of the group was reduced the day after it left when Preuss and Bernier were sent back to the Lambert-Carson party, which they joined a day later.

On July 8, Kit saw horsemen in the distance. The men sprang into action, checking their weapons, making sure of the priming, forting up. As the mounted men came closer, they were identified, first as whites, then as a large party of trappers and traders. Kit recognized their leader: it was none other than Jim Bridger, the sage of the mountain men.

The two parties camped together that night. Old Gabe had much to tell, and it was all bad news. The Sioux were on the warpath, and they didn't care whether it was a white or an Indian enemy they scalped. And they had help: the Cheyennes and some Gros Ventres.

The Sioux and their Cheyenne allies had been out looking for trouble the year before, had found plenty of it when they engaged a brigade of trappers under Henry Fraeb. Although they killed Fraeb and three of his men, the Indians came out of the fray with heavier losses, a fact which served to enrage them all the more. They had been brooding about it ever since; now they were at the height of fury and would slaughter anyone who got in their way.

The survivors of Fraeb's party had made their way to Bridger's camp, and some of them were with him now. Their testimony, combined with Bridger's, stirred things up. Most of the men wanted to turn back and go with Bridger, who was bound for St. Louis; the others were willing to go on, at least to Fort Laramie, where there would be some measure of protection. Lambert and Kit, after a great deal of persuasive argument, finally settled things: all would continue to the fort. Old Gabe offered to accompany the expedition to the head of the Sweetwater, which was beyond Fort Laramie, but Lambert had no authority to accept his bid and was thus compelled to turn it down.

The two groups parted the next morning, Bridger and his men going downstream and the Carson-Lambert party continuing up the river. Kit and Lambert expected trouble—and so did their men. Each was alert for the slightest sign of danger, although Bridger had indicated that the uproar was much farther west. Henry Brant and Randolph Benton may well have been secretly hoping for an encounter with the Indians, a normal wish for boys who did not realize—had not seen with their own eyes—the possible consequences of any fight with Indians. If Henry and Randolph were so hoping, they were sorely disappointed because the party arrived at Fort Laramie on July 13 without having seen a single Indian. Two days later, they were joined by Frémont and his companions.

The main topic of conversation at the fort was the Indian uprising, and Kit and Frémont met with the people of the fort to discuss the situation. They learned that two small parties "had been cut off by the Sioux" that spring and that a group of Oregon-bound emigrants led by Tom Fitzpatrick was being trailed by 350 Sioux warriors. (They had left the fort only a few days before the Carson-

Lambert camp arrived.) In still another quarter, some 800 lodges of Sioux, Cheyennes, and Gros Ventres were on their way to the valley of the Sweetwater, their avowed purpose being to attack a meeting of about 100 whites (probably traders and trappers) and an undetermined number of Snake and Crow Indians. In sum, all reports (Frémont discounted them as wild rumors) indicated that anyone traveling west of Fort Laramie was courting disaster. The Frémont expedition was scheduled to go well beyond it.

Fear and apprehension were widespread in Frémont's camp. Charles Preuss records in his diary entry of July 20:

> Tomorrow we'll start, straight toward the Indians. Nothing can be done about it, my dear Trautchen [a German diminutive of Gertrude, his wife, for whom Preuss was writing the diary]. To be sure, I could stay here like Monsieur Brant—but what a disgrace, what a disgrace! I am comforted at the thought that you will have an assured haven with your mother if I should not see you again. But I hope that I shall again embrace you and our dear little girl. Of course if I had known it, I should not have come along. I see no honor in being murdered by this rabble. But all that is too late now.

Nor was Preuss the only one who felt that way. Kit himself was fearful of what would happen if they went on. Frémont notes in his official report:

> Carson, one of the best and most experienced mountaineers, fully supported the opinion given by Bridger of the dangerous state of the country, and openly expressed his conviction that we could not escape without some sharp encounters with the Indians. In addition to this, he made his will; and among the circumstances which were constantly occurring to increase their [the men in the expedition] alarm, this was the most unfortunate. . . .

Kit Carson was a brave man, but he was human, too, and practical. Like Jim Bridger, or any other experienced mountain man for that matter, he was knowledgeable in the ways of the Indian. He had fought against them, in fact had very nearly been killed by one of them, and he well knew what it was to fight against superior numbers. With no less than three tribes on the warpath and with hesitant men, like Frémont's, most of whom had probably never fought Indians before—*and this was the Indians' own country*—it was sheer folly to risk engaging an enemy who might easily outnumber you by fifteen or twenty to one. In the strongest terms he knew, Kit advised Frémont to break off the expedition and return to the States.

Lieutenant John Charles Frémont was determined to carry out his orders. He assembled his men, told them that the expedition would head for South Pass on the twenty-first, and invited those who did not want to go with him to draw their pay. Only one man refused. Frémont says he "asked him some few questions, in order to expose him to the ridicule of the men, and let him go." Kit, of course, stayed on. He was against the idea, but his loyalty and a strong sense of duty left him no other choice. He had made an agreement with Frémont and he would fulfill it, even though he feared that it would cost him his life.

The expedition, minus Henry Bent and Randolph Benton, who were to remain at the fort until Frémont returned, was preparing to leave when a delegation of Sioux chiefs arrived. They warned Frémont that their warriors were out and would surely attack his party. They did not want this to happen, they said, because they loved the white man and wanted peace. They demanded that he remain at the fort until their warriors came in. When they had spoken, Frémont told them that they were liars and proceeded to deliver a long harangue, which he concluded with a warning of his own:

> We have thrown away our bodies, and will not turn back. When you told us that your young men would kill us, you did not know that our hearts were strong, and you did not see the rifles which my young men carry in their hands. We are few, and you are many, and may kill us all; but there will be much crying in your villages, for many of your young men will stay behind, and forget to return with your warriors from the mountains. Do you think that our great chief will let his soldiers die, and forget to cover their graves? Before the snows melt again, his warriors will sweep away your villages as the fire does the prairie in the autumn. See! I have pulled down my *white houses*, and

my people are ready: when the sun is ten paces higher, we shall be on the march. If you have any thing to tell us, you will say it soon.

The die had been cast.

Frémont led his men to the fork of the North Platte and Laramie rivers, which he wanted to visit. From here they traveled upstream along the North Platte, fully expecting to be attacked at any moment. They did meet several bands of Indians during the next few days, but nothing happened. The Indians were hostile, but wary, and soon went their way. On the twenty-eighth, soon after the expedition had forded the river, a rather large band of Sioux was detected in the distance. They were not very hostile, however, and from them Frémont gained a great deal of information about the country he was heading for, most of which turned out to be false. At this point, Joseph Bissonette, whom Frémont had engaged as interpreter at Fort Laramie, left the party, telling Frémont that "the best advice I can give you, is to turn back at once." Bissonette apparently rode back toward the fort with the Indians, and Frémont used the opportunity thus presented him to send one of his men, J. B. Dumés, back to the fort. According to Frémont, "an old wound in the leg rendered [him] incapable of continuing the journey on foot, and his horse seemed on the point of giving out."

After the Indians had gone, Frémont turned back toward the river to cache all but the most necessary equipment. On the following morning, the party set out once more. Frémont's plans called for following the valley of the North Platte to the mouth of the Sweetwater. They rode on, making observations along the way, and crossed over to the Sweetwater on the morning of July 31. They had seen no more Indians along the way and were thus in a more relaxed mood when they reached Independence Rock the next day.

The Carson men were waiting for Kit when he arrived at Fort Laramie. They were delighted to see him again, and one may be sure that Kit was relieved at the prospect of having such men as Sol and Blue with him on the next leg of the journey. Like Kit, they were opposed to looking for trouble when they were almost certain to find it, but they were ready and willing to accompany Kit wherever he went. They had brought their own food and equipment and were thus independent of the expedition. Frémont does not mention them in the *Report*, nor does Preuss note their presence in his diary. They were certainly present, however, and Oliver Wiggins says they took a sizable number of plews in the mountains.

There were buffalo herds near Independence Rock, and the expedition's hunters and the Carson men had a field day. The men dried the meat and otherwise prepared to move on. Preuss records that they found a pair of bloody trousers in a recently abandoned camp, an incident which Frémont does not mention. Preuss also says that Frémont tried to photograph Independence Rock with a daguerreotype camera, another event which is not included in the *Report* but which is of historical significance because it was the first attempt to use photography in American exploration.

On the evening of August 7, they camped a few miles from South Pass, at the foot of the Wind River Mountains, in whose streams Kit had trapped many a beaver. In this range rose the main tributaries of four great rivers: the Columbia, the Colorado, the Platte, and the Missouri. Here, too, was part of the Continental Divide, the parting of the waters, with the Colorado and the Columbia emptying into the Pacific and the Platte and the Missouri flowing to the Atlantic by way of the Mississippi. East of the chain of mountains was the Louisiana Purchase; beyond it lay Oregon, a bone of contention between Great Britain and the United States.

At noon on August 10, the party camped on the shore of a beautiful mountain lake and on the morning of the twelfth, a party of fifteen men, including Preuss, Frémont, Kit, and Auguste Janisse (who was the only Negro to accompany the expedition), began to ascend the mountains in earnest. It was a difficult climb. Preuss writes that Kit went too fast and "this caused some exchange of words. Frémont got excited . . . and designated a young chap to take the lead." They stopped for the day about eleven o'clock because Frémont had a headache. "In the course of the afternoon," Preuss writes, "the quarrel was smoothed over. One claimed he had not meant it as the other had assumed, and the headache was relieved." They spent a cold, supperless night in the open, and at dawn, with no breakfast, they hurried on. The horses and equipment were left behind to await the return of the daring few whom Frémont had chosen to accompany him to the dizzying heights of what he thought was "the highest peak of the Rocky Mountains."[3]

It was Kit who made the highest climb on the fourteenth. Two of the men had become ill, and Frémont himself was attacked by giddiness and vomiting. Preuss had fallen, tumbling head over heels a couple of times before he landed safely on a rock. When Kit succeeded in reaching one of the snow-covered ridges, he could see the summit toward which they were climbing still looming several hundred feet above him.

In the afternoon, Basil Lajeunesse and four men were sent to the camp by the lake for mules, food, and blankets. Basil returned late that evening with the supplies and the four men who had been in charge of the lower camp, those he took down with him having been "too much fatigued to return." Frémont then asked Kit to accompany "all but four or five men, who were to stay with me and bring back the mules and instruments," down to the lower camp on the following morning. "Accordingly," wrote Frémont, "at the break of day they set out." Remaining with Frémont were Preuss, Janisse, Lambert, Lajeunesse, and Descoteaux, whose name does not appear in the list of men hired in St. Louis.

On the morning of August 15, after what Frémont describes as "a hearty breakfast," they mounted the mules and set out. They rode to the foot of the peak, turned the animals loose to graze, and continued the ascent on foot. They climbed far above the timber line, and the rarefied air made their breath come short and hard, compelling them to stop and rest frequently. Frémont's heart must have pounded with pride as well as from the altitude when at last he planted the American flag on the summit. And what a view! In the blue distance he could see the Tetons, while on every side were huge jagged rocks and peaks. Far below him he could see valleys where the mountain streams began their winding, varied routes,

[3] It was not "the highest peak of the Rocky Mountains." Gannett Peak is the highest mountain in the Wind River Range, and Colorado has several peaks which are higher than Gannett.

some of them converging to form broad rivers. Frémont drank in the sight, then descended to permit his companions, one at a time, to stand on the summit.

Frémont longed to stay and explore this interesting range of mountains, but his government contract had ended when he crossed South Pass. Moreover, his men were grumbling, for hunger and hardship were not part of their working agreement and they did not share Frémont's enthusiasm for going beyond South Pass. Even Basil Lajeunesse, whom Frémont calls his "favorite man," had had his fill of the extreme hardships of this trip.

The little party spent the night at the spot where they had break-fasted and rode on to the camp by the lake the following morning. Kit and the other men had returned to the main camp at the foot of the mountains, whence Frémont's group now followed them. The expedition's best barometer was broken beyond repair in crossing one of the swift mountain streams along the way, and this loss decided Frémont to return to Fort Laramie "instead of rounding the mountains" as he had planned.

On the journey back to Fort Laramie, they used the same route by which they had come. The trip was uneventful until August 24, when Frémont decided to negotiate a stretch of the North Platte in the rubber boat. He loaded it with supplies, instruments, and six men besides himself and cast off just after dawn. They had passed several dangerous places and were feeling quite successful when they suddenly hit a concealed rock. The boat was wrecked, and her crew barely escaped drowning. Much equipment—including guns and ammunition—was lost, but at least they were able to recover some of the journals in which Frémont kept the various scientific observations. They gathered up the things that had been saved and walked the rest of the way to Goat Island, where the others were waiting for them.

Inconveniences were the order of the day until they reached the place where they had cached the carts and other supplies. From here they moved on toward the fort as rapidly as possible. Kit shot an antelope on the twenty-seventh, and on the twenty-eighth he rode in with buffalo meat, which pleased Charles Preuss immensely. They had skunk for breakfast on the thirtieth (it had scored a bull's-eye on Badeau's face the night before), and on the last day of August they arrived at the fort.

On September 3, 1842, two groups of men left Fort Laramie. The Frémont expedition rode southeast along the North Platte; on October 10, exactly four months after leaving it, they arrived at the mouth of the Kansas River. Kit and the Carson men rode south, trapping their way along the eastern slopes of the Rockies, toward Taos. Beaver prices were up somewhat that fall, and Kit was able to show a profit on the plews they had taken on the way back. He spent the rest of the winter in Taos preparing for a very important event.

On February 6, 1843, Christopher Carson and Josefa Jaramillo were united in marriage by Padre Antonio Martínez at Guadalupe Catholic Church in Taos. The official witnesses were George Bent, Cruz Padillo, Manuel Lucero, and José María Valdez. The village echoed with the sound of church bells, and after the ceremony there was a large *baile* for the many guests, some of whom had traveled great distances for the wedding of the beautiful Spanish girl and the blond American. The happy couple finally escaped the crowd and the merrymaking, and Kit led his fifteen-year-old bride to their new home east of the town plaza.

For three months Kit stayed in Taos with his bride. He then took employment as hunter for a Bent caravan going to the States.

8 ★ Frémont's Second Expedition

THE REPUBLIC OF TEXAS was established at Washington-on-the-Brazos on March 2, 1836, and although the United States and several European countries recognized the new nation, Mexico, from whom the Texans had separated themselves, did not. There had been fighting before the Texans declared their independence, and there was a great deal more of it afterwards. It was a bitter struggle, as the Battle of the Alamo and the Goliad Massacre testify, but short lived after the republic was established, and in the end the Texans prevailed. On April 21, 1836, Sam Houston defeated and captured Antonio López de Santa Anna at the Battle of San Jacinto; for all intents and purposes, the war between Texas and Mexico was over. The peace which followed was uneasy, however, and sporadic clashes between Texans and Mexicans occurred for a number of years.

Many Texans aspired to annex all of New Mexico to their republic. One of these, George S. Park, wrote from Santa Fe in 1837: "Texas could easily secure control of Santa Fé if it would open a route to [the] town . . . and authority could be extended from there to California!" What Texas needed was trade, not territory—she had plenty of that. The Panic of 1837 hit her hard, and by 1840 she was in desperate financial straits. Perhaps it might be best to do something about New Mexico, especially Santa Fe. Charles Coan describes the situation in *A History of New Mexico*:

> In 1840 there was a discussion in the Texas legislature in regard to informing the citizens of Santa Fé that they were citizens of the Texas

Republic. On January 28, 1841, the House of Representatives of the Texas Congress authorized the raising of volunteers to be sent to Santa Fé, but the Texas Senate failed to agree to this proposal, and the Congress adjourned without sanctioning the Santa Fé expedition. President Lamar proceeded, however, with the organization of the expedition and spent $80,000 in equipping the 300 soldiers and officers established in a camp near Austin in May of that same year.

Manuel Armijo, considered a cruel tyrant and a coward by most *anglos* and many Mexicans, was then governor of New Mexico. He feared that many of the people in New Mexico would assist in the establishment of Texan control in his province, so he sent a report to Mexico stating that he would have to flee unless aid was furnished him because, he said, the Mexicans and Indians were generally favorable to the Texans. In general, he stirred up his subjects by spreading rumors of what the Texans would do to them if they, the Texans, came to New Mexico. And he got plenty of help from Mexico.

The ill-fated Texas Santa Fe Expedition, as it has come to be called, set out for Santa Fe in 1841. Ostensibly, it was a trade caravan with more than three hundred armed men to guard it from hostile Indians and Mexican bandits, and its primary mission was to set up trade between Texas and Mexico via Santa Fe. It did not reach its destination. Through treachery and intrigue, all of the expedition's members were eventually captured and "were marched to the City of Mexico, a journey of some two thousand miles, by order of General Armijo."[1]

News of the brutality accorded the prisoners along the line of march by some of the Mexican commanders aroused Texans and Americans alike. The Texans were more direct in dealing with the situation, however, and roving bands of them began to attack Mexican trade caravans (some of which carried goods belonging to Armijo himself), killing, robbing, burning. Most of the attacks were confined to the Santa Fe Trail, the normal trade route between Santa

---

[1] For specific details concerning the mistreatment of the Texan prisoners, see George W. Kendall, *Narrative of the Texan Santa Fé Expedition*, and Noel M. Loomis, *The Texan–Santa Fé Pioneers*.

Fe and Independence, though some occurred elsewhere, and might have continued indefinitely if the Texans had not ventured beyond the Republic's boundary (in this case the Arkansas River) to conduct some of their raids. As it was, the United States government learned of the border violations and sent troops to escort the Mexicans through U. S. territory, thereby putting a stop to Texan raids north of the Arkansas.

This, then, was the state of affairs when the Bent caravan which Kit had joined met a Mexican wagon train escorted by U. S. troops at Walnut Creek on June 14, 1843. The trade goods in the wagons belonged to Governor Armijo, and the four companies of dragoons guarding them were under the command of Captain Philip St. George Cooke, who, says Kit, "had received intelligence that a large party of Texans were at the crossing of the Arkansas, awaiting the arrival of the train for the purpose of capturing the same and [killing] and [making] prisoners of as many of the Mexicans as they could, in revenge [for] the treatment Armijo had given the Texans when [they were] in his power." Captain Cooke would accompany the Mexicans to the river; when they crossed it, they would be on their own.

The Mexican in charge of the wagon train offered Kit three hundred dollars to take a message to Armijo asking him to send a military escort to accompany the caravan the rest of the way to Santa Fe. Charles Bent urged Kit to accept the offer, so Kit and Dick Owens set out for Santa Fe by way of Bent's Fort. They encountered no Texans or Indians along the way and arrived at the fort in record time. Owens remained at the fort, while Kit, leading one of William Bent's fastest horses, rode on toward Taos alone. To avoid a party of Utes who were on the warpath, Kit left the main trail and made a wide circle of their encampment. He eluded them and arrived safely in Taos, where he sent the message on to Armijo by an express.

Meanwhile, Armijo had become concerned about his investment and had sent a party of one hundred men to meet the caravan at the Arkansas. He himself was following them with six hundred more. As things turned out, his fears were well grounded, for Colonel

Jacob Snively and a party of Texans cut the trail of Armijo's advance guard, followed it up, killed eighteen Mexicans and wounded as many more, and captured all but two of the others. The pair who escaped rode hard for Armijo's camp. When he learned of the defeat, Armijo ordered an immediate retreat to Santa Fe.[2]

Kit remained in Taos to await a reply from Armijo. He heard bitter complaints against the Governor, and because of the obvious unrest among the native population, he concluded to leave Josefa with her sister, Mrs. Charles Bent. He insisted on this arrangement whenever he had occasion to be away from Taos.

Kit had been home four days when he received dispatches from Armijo. He and Sol Silver set out at once to deliver them by way of Bent's Fort. Two days out of Taos, they saw a band of Utes riding toward them. Sol suggested that Kit ride on and leave him to fight the Indians, but Kit, true to the mountain code, refused, telling Sol that if it came to that, they would die together.

One of the Indians dismounted, left his weapons, and came forward with a great display of friendship. He pretended to be very much at ease, approaching Kit with a genial air, offering his hand, which Kit took. The moment this happened, the Indian grabbed Kit's rifle in an attempt to wrench it from him. Kit maintained his grip on the rifle and with his free hand gave the Indian such a blow between the eyes that the latter tumbled to the ground at Kit's feet. The Indian sprang to his feet, and with the fleetness of an antelope bounded across the prairie to rejoin his companions.

Sol caught Kit's horse and tied the bridle to his belt, his own horse having bolted when Kit struck the Indian. Kit and Sol stood back to back, their rifles aimed at the Indians, who were slowly advancing. When the Indians were within speaking distance, Kit hailed them in their own tongue and told them that if they came an inch closer, two of them would die. He assured them that since he and Sol had pistols, four warriors might join their ancestors. The Utes kept their distance, circling the two men for what must have seemed to them an eternity. The warriors blustered and talked among themselves,

[2] Armijo was tried in Mexico City on charges of cowardice and desertion in the face of the enemy. He was acquitted.

examining their weapons and making defiant gestures, but made no move to come closer. Kit's horse restlessly pawed the earth when the Indians rode fast in a circle, but Kit and Sol calmed him down. Sol's own horse had joined the riders and was now following them, but there was nothing to do about that. Finally, the Indians tired of trying to frighten the white men, and after much yelling and shaking of fists, they turned and rode away. With them went Sol's horse and some of the pack equipment.

When the Indians were out of sight, Kit and Sol mounted William Bent's horse, which Kit had brought instead of his own, and started on toward the fort. They kept off the main trail and walked much of the time to rest the horse from the burden of double weight. They stopped that afternoon to kill a deer for food, but they dared not build a fire to cook it for fear of attracting the Indians. Sol slept three hours while Kit stood watch, then Kit slept. Long before daybreak, they were on the trail again.

When they arrived at the fort, Kit learned that the Mexicans had proceeded to Santa Fe, but not before they had persuaded Captain Cooke to teach the Texans a lesson. Cooke and his dragoons met the Texans, disarmed them, and took forty men back to the States as prisoners. The action caused an international squabble, and Captain Cooke was accused of violating a friendly flag. A thorough investigation of the incident was made by the U. S. Army, and Cooke was cleared of all charges against him.

Kit also learned something else of importance to him: Frémont's second expedition was about three days' ride beyond the fort. Kit bought a horse and set out in search of his friend; he says in his autobiography: "I only thought that I would ride to his camp, have a talk and then return. But, when Frémont saw me again and requested me to join him, I could not refuse and again entered his employ as guide and hunter."

Frémont was pleased to see Kit ride into his camp on July 14, and the two men chatted for some time before Kit made the rounds to renew acquaintances. Charles Preuss was again Frémont's cartographer, and Tom Fitzpatrick had been hired as guide. Among others in camp who had been with the first expedition were Basil

Lajeunesse, Baptiste Bernier, and François Badeau. There were some new faces, too, among them two Delaware Indians, whom Frémont had engaged as hunters; Theodore Talbot, a young draftsman; Jacob Dodson, a free Negro in the service of Senator Benton; William Gilpin, then editor of the *Missouri Argus* (a newspaper owned by Senator Benton) and later governor of Colorado; and Frederick Dwight, "a gentleman from Springfield, Massachusetts," who was on his way to Fort Vancouver.

Kit's first job was to secure mules and other supplies from Bent's Fort. Frémont had arranged for Lucien Maxwell to bring them from Taos, but with the Armijo-Texan affair, the Utes on the warpath, and an uprising among the Indians at Taos Pueblo, this was now out of the question. So Kit rode back to the fort, bought ten mules and other necessary provisions, and rejoined Frémont at Fort St. Vrain on the twenty-third.

Before leaving the fort, Frémont divided the expedition into two forces. The main body of men, under Fitzpatrick, was to take the heavy baggage and proceed to Fort Laramie, thence to Fort Hall, where Frémont would meet them. The second party, made up of fifteen hand-picked men (including Kit, who would act as guide) under the direction of Frémont himself, would explore its way northwestward toward South Pass. Both groups departed on the afternoon of the twenty-sixth.

Frémont followed the Thompson River west for some miles, then turned north to the Cache la Poudre River, which was forded "for the last time" (the party had crossed and recrossed it several times in exploring its course) on July 30. Traveling in a northwesterly direction, the group reached the foot of the Medicine Bow Range on August 1. Here they met a war party of thirty Sioux and Cheyenne braves. Perhaps the twelve-pounder brass cannon which Frémont had brought along (he got it from the arsenal in St. Louis) commanded the Indians' respect as "big medicine." Or maybe it was the Hall carbines with which the men were armed. Whatever the reason, there was no fighting.

Frémont records a more serious brush with Indians under the date of August 5 on the North Platte. This time it was a party of Cheyennes and Arapahoes on the prowl for Snake enemies, and they halted just in time, Frémont says, "to save themselves from a howitzer shot, which would undoubtedly have been very effective in such a compact body." The pipe of peace was passed, and Frémont gave the Indians some tobacco and cotton cloth. They rode on late that evening.

On August 13, the expedition crossed South Pass at a point several miles south of Frémont's 1842 route and dropped into the valley of the Green. The morning of the eighteenth found them a few miles from Fort Bridger, which had been completed only a few days before. That evening, they "encamped on a salt creek, about fifteen feet wide," and on the following morning, Kit was dispatched to Fort Hall for supplies.

Charles Preuss recorded the following incident in his diary entry for August 23:

> Today I am right among the Snake Indians. We left our path and went to their camp to purchase horses if possible. Our flag and our cannon caused unnecessary alarm. They believed the Sioux were coming, and the warriors met us, armed and in full war splendor. The error was soon straightened out, and now we are sitting right in the midst of the crowd. Our intention has just been announced by a great orator, so it seems, for the words flow from his lips like water.
>
> Last night we traveled in the darkness until ten o'clock. What exploration! What monkey business!

Two days later he was tasting the waters of Beer Springs, which, says Frémont, "on account of the effervescing gas and acid taste, have received their name from the voyageurs and trappers of the country, who, in the midst of their rude and hard lives, are fond of finding some fancied resemblance to the luxuries they rarely have the fortune to enjoy."

Frémont became concerned about the dwindling supply of food on the twenty-sixth and sent Henry Lee to Fort Hall "with a note to Carson . . . directing him to load a pack horse with whatever could be obtained there in the way of provisions, and endeavor to overtake me on the [Bear] river." Kit and Lee rode into camp on the morning of September 4 with some flour, but little else. The fort was in short supply of nearly everything because of the many Oregon-bound emigrants who were stopping there.

The expedition journeyed on down the Bear and on September 6 sighted the Great Salt Lake. Frémont decided to descend the river and explore the lake in the rubber boat he had brought along. Accordingly, the seventh was spent in building a camp and fort and in preparing the boat—which was not as well constructed as the one used in 1842—for the trip. And since their provisions were exhausted, Frémont sent seven men to Fort Hall for more (if, indeed, they could get anything at all). This left eight men, three of whom were detailed to guard the camp while Frémont, Kit, Preuss, Bernier, and Lajeunesse explored the lake and some of its islands.

It was a well-known fact that the brave Kit Carson had little use for travel by water, especially in small boats, but no word of complaint came from him on the morning of September 8 when the crew of five set out for the lake and the nearest island. They spent most of the morning descending Bear River and were at last compelled to get out of the boat and tow it, the river having become too shallow to navigate. They camped for the night near a marsh and launched out into the lake next day after dragging the boat for some distance across mud flats. Kit said that at this point he felt like one of the mariners he and Mary Ann had read about in a book of sea stories when they were children.

They reached the island safely, although the boat leaked air out of its chambers and had to be pumped up again with a bellows, and decided to camp there for the night. Frémont called the place Disappointment Island (because he had expected it to be fertile and it was not), the Mormons later christened it Castle Island, and it was finally renamed after Frémont by Captain Howard Stansbury, who passed the lake in 1849 with a government expedition.

As soon as breakfast was finished, the group started to explore the island. Although the water around the island was crystal clear, it was thoroughly saturated with salt, and their clothing had a saline crust where spray from the lake had dried. They climbed a peak which rose about eight hundred feet above the lake. Frémont "accidentally left on the summit the brass cover to the object end of my spyglass." As he looked over the vast expanse of water below, he felt a strong desire to remain there for further exploration, but the spreading snows on mountain peaks to the south gave warning that winter was advancing. They terminated the survey with the satisfaction that they were probably the first to have broken the island's solitude with the sound of human voices.

The boat leaked on the return trip also, and it was with great difficulty that the men supplied the air chambers with enough air to keep them afloat. A strong wind arose, blowing directly against them, and the boat was tossed about by the waves. They were in imminent danger of capsizing, but at length they effected a landing on marshy ground some miles from the main camp. Two of the men were dispatched to bring horses for carrying the boat and the expedition's scientific instruments. The wind was blowing such a gale when the horses arrived that the men could scarcely pack the baggage upon them. The lake was rising rapidly, and they had scarcely left the shore when it became entirely submerged. Back at camp, it rained most of the night, but the next morning dawned bright and clear.

They boiled down five gallons of lake water, which yielded fourteen pints of very fine salt. This they packed in skins and took with them. In the evening they dined on some gulls which Kit had shot. As they traveled, ascending the Bear River, game disappeared completely. At length they met some Snake Indians with many horses, and Frémont purchased one of the fat young colts. As the men feasted upon savory steaks, their customary good humor and gaiety were restored. Frémont and Preuss, not yet having overcome the prejudice of eating horse meat, preferred to retire supperless. The next day, September 15, Frémont purchased an antelope from one of the Indians; as they were having supper a messenger rode into camp with the news that Tom Fitzpatrick and his group were within a few miles of them with an ample supply of provisions.

The following morning before sunrise, they were on the road to join Fitzpatrick. It was a joyful meeting, and Jacob Dodson immediately checked the provisions: flour, sugar, coffee, peas, rice, dried meat—and even butter! Leaving the valley of the Bear, they continued their journey to the northward and crossed over to the Snake River, thence on toward Fort Hall. They met many Indians gathering berries and from them purchased a bushel of dried berries.

At Fort Hall the expedition halted for supplies and rest. Kit tried to dissuade Frémont from any attempt to cross the mountains with so much snow already on them and more to come, but the impetuous Frémont thought they could make it through the passes before snow blocked them. So it was that on September 22 they set out along the Oregon Trail, crossed Raft River, then forded the Snake, which they followed generally until they reached Fort Boise on October 9. From here they traveled almost directly northwest to Dr. Marcus Whitman's mission at Waiilatpu, thence to Fort Walla Walla, which was several miles west of the mission. They remained at the fort for two days before continuing their journey along the south bank of the Columbia River.

By November 4, they were at The Dalles, a point almost due east of Fort Vancouver. Here Frémont split his party once more, arranging for himself and three men (Preuss, Dodson, and Bernier) to travel on to the fort with three members of an Indian family in an Indian canoe. Kit was left behind "with instructions to occupy the people in making pack saddles and refitting their equipage." Frémont's group left on the sixth and arrived at Fort Vancouver, the Hudson's Bay Company's headquarters in the Northwest, late the following evening. Frémont had now traveled a thousand miles since leaving South Pass and was nearly two thousand miles from his starting point. He had stopped along the way at various forts, had visited several tribes of Indians, and no fights with roving war parties had occurred. There had been a couple of serious errors on the part of the Indians, but no shots were exchanged. The "wild and woolly West" was beginning to tame down—at least for a while.

At Fort Vancouver, Frémont obtained supplies from Dr. John McLoughlin, commander of the fort, who reigned supreme in Oregon. Although the Hudson's Bay Company frowned upon the coming of Americans to Oregon and hoped (and tried, of course) to discourage them in every possible way, it must have realized that it was fighting a losing and quite hopeless battle. Not only did Frémont obtain needed supplies, but he was also given letters of recommendation to use at other trading posts. He aptly described the graciousness of his host in his official report when he said that "every hospitable attention was extended to me, and I accepted an invitation to take a room in the fort, *'and to make myself at home while I staid.'* "

Frémont left "near sunset" on the tenth and camped a few miles up the Columbia. He took time to make scientific observations and sketches on the way back and thus did not reach The Dalles until the eighteenth. Kit had moved the camp to obtain more grass for the horses, and this, together with the fact that he "arrived just in time to partake of a roast of California beef," pleased Frémont very much. His *Report* is sprinkled with such mentions of Kit's deeds as this, some of which are so insignificant and commonplace that one wonders why he bothered to include them. Taken together, however, they constitute affectionate testimony to Frémont's personal feelings toward Kit.

"The camp was now occupied," wrote Frémont, "in making the necessary preparations for our homeward journey, which, though homeward, contemplated a new route, and a great circuit to the south and southeast, and the exploration of the Great Basin between the Rocky mountains and the *Sierra Nevada*." Kit was in agreement with the plan, which meant traveling through new territory, but he spoke with doubt of the necessity of traveling in any range of the Sierra Nevada Mountains in the dead of winter. He wondered if it could be done.

It is surprising that the other members of the expedition did not rebel at the idea of making a wide detour on the way home, but according to Frémont:

> All knew that a strange country was to be explored, and dangers and hardships to be encountered; but no one blanched at the prospect. On the contrary, courage and confidence animated the whole party. Cheerfulness, readiness, subordination, prompt obedience, characterized all; nor did any extremity of peril and privation, to which we were afterwards exposed, ever belie, or derogate from, the fine spirit of this brave and generous commencement. . . .

If Frémont's statement is accurate, the reaction of the men is certainly a tribute to his leadership.

On November 21, Tom Fitzpatrick, who had been left behind on September 25 to bring up the carts and baggage, rode into camp. Four days later the expedition set out for Klamath Lake, far to the south, by way of the roaring Deschutes River. The weather was cold, but bright and sunny, and they made good time the first day. (Frémont records that "the howitzer was the only wheeled carriage now remaining." Not having to bother with carts or wagons would speed them up considerably.) They met several Indians, who promptly fell in with them, and that night they were compelled to tie up and guard two of them who had been caught stealing.

If Kit and Frémont expected to fight with the fierce and treacherous Klamath Indians, they were disappointed. One of the Klamaths told Kit that his tribe was at war with the Modocs to the south; this might have been the reason for their peaceful relations with the white men, or it could have been the magic of the cannon, which was fired when they reached a marsh about twenty-five miles north of the lake on December 10.

Frémont did not visit the lake proper, apparently believing that the marsh, with its many ponds of water, was the Klamath Lake he sought. After a short rest, the party struck eastward. Some of the Klamaths, thinly clad, offered to journey with the white men for a day or two; one of them said there was much snow ahead. The Indians suffered so much from the cold that they were forced to decline Frémont's request that they act as guides. He gave them presents and they returned to their village at the lake.

On the sixteenth of December, in snow up to their knees, the party pushed through a forest of pine trees to the edge of a rocky cliff. A thousand feet below them on the green, completely snow-free plains lay a picturesque little lake. They named it "Summer Lake" and called the precipice on which they stood "Winter Ridge." After a long and difficult descent, they pitched their tents on the shore of the lake, where they remained until the eighteenth.

On Christmas Day the cannon was fired, but there was little else to celebrate, for they were a discouraged lot of men. When they

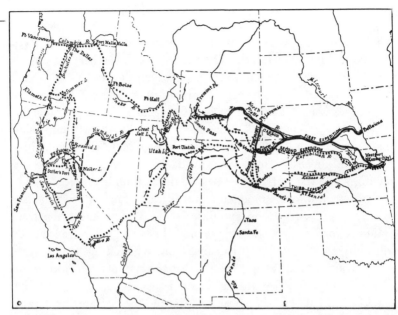

EXPLORING WITH FRÉMONT, 1842, 1843–44, 1845–46

had traversed the sparsely timbered highlands, they were cold and impeded by snow; when they descended to the sage-covered plains, they often went hungry. By now all traveled on foot in order to save their weakened horses and mules. Discerning the gloom, Frémont broke out some brandy, coffee, and sugar which he had carefully hoarded. It was, he says, "sufficient to make them a feast."

Early January, 1844, found the expedition in the Great Basin. Progress was hampered by a dense fog from January 3 through January 7 and by a lack of grass, water, and any sort of game until they camped on the shore of Pyramid Lake on January 14. Here they obtained a supply of salmon trout from some Indians, and in a few minutes, Frémont reports, "such a salmon-trout feast as is seldom seen was going on in our camp; and every variety of manner in which fish could be prepared—boiled, fried, and roasted in the ashes—was put into requisition." Preuss says of their meal: "I gorged myself until I almost choked."

On January 16, they headed south once more, following the Truckee River (they called it "Salmon Trout River") to the point

113

where it curves in from the west to flow into the south end of Pyramid Lake. Here they left the Truckee and continued bearing slightly east of south until the eighteenth, on which day Frémont made a momentous decision. He had originally intended, not to cross the Sierra Nevadas, but to skirt their eastern slopes, perhaps traversing some of their spur ranges. Now, since it was "evidently impossible that [our animals] could cross the country to the Rocky mountains," he decided to "cross the Sierra Nevada into the valley of the Sacramento, wherever a practicable pass could be found."

The ascent into the mountains was made in fairly good time, but by January 29, they had encountered deep snow and steep trails and were forced to abandon the cannon. They slogged on, encountering daily small groups of Indians, from whom they bought bags of pine nuts and all of whom said that the mountains could not be crossed—snow too deep. Finally, on February 6, Frémont, Fitzpatrick, and Kit climbed a peak and sighted the Sacramento Valley. Kit identified it by the range of mountains on its west side, which he had seen some fifteen years before on his California trip with Ewing Young. Now they were faced with the problem of finding a way to get through to the valley.

For two weeks the expedition picked its way through deep snow and across extremely rough country. The men were often required to beat a road through the snow with hand-fashioned mallets (Frémont calls them "mauls"), only to bog down again farther along, necessitating a repetition of their labor. They began to weaken from hunger, too, and both Preuss and Frémont comment on the lack of salt in their diet, which was now a steady fare of horse or mule meat. "It is lucky I have some tobacco," wrote Preuss on February 22, "bad as it is." Small consolation in starvin' times, but it was a consolation nonetheless.

February 23, Frémont wrote, was their most difficult day. They could not travel through the timber on the ridges because of deep snow and thus had to find places to scramble over rocks on southern exposures. Even these were slippery with ice, and Frémont and others who were wearing moccasins continually slipped and fell. Kit took the lead, with Frémont following closely behind, to find a path by a mountain stream. As Frémont attempted to jump "across a place where the stream was compressed among the rocks," he slipped and was thrown into the freezing water below. At once Kit leaped in after him. The water was fairly shallow, and both men searched for Frémont's lost rifle, but the frigid water soon drove them to the bank. (They eventually found the gun; it had been swept under some ice along the bank.) They built a large fire to dry their clothing and some time later made their way to camp.

The men were up at three o'clock the following morning in order to set out before the sun softened the snow crusts. They were soon descending from the mountains and by nightfall had left the snow behind them. The next day, Frémont decided to take seven men—Kit, Preuss, Talbot, Dodson, Towns, Proue, and Derosier—and press on to Sutter's Fort on the Sacramento River. There they would procure food and horses and retrace their steps to meet the rest of the expedition, which Frémont placed under Fitzpatrick's leadership. Accordingly, the advance party "took . . . some of the best animals" and set out.

February 28 brought them ill luck. Three horses, including Proveau, Frémont's favorite mount, were lost that day. (Proveau and another horse simply "gave out," and the third, a pack animal, strayed but was found the next day.) Charles Towns "became light-headed, wandering off into the woods without knowing where he was going, and Jacob [Dodson] brought him back." Baptiste Derosier, who had volunteered to bring up Proveau, got lost the next day (February 29) but finally wandered into camp on the evening of March 1. Frémont describes his appearance in the *Report*:

He imagined he had been gone several days, and thought we were still at the camp where he had left us; and we were pained to see that his mind was deranged. It appeared that he had been lost in the mountain, and hunger and fatigue, joined to weakness of body, and fear of perishing in the mountains, had crazed him. The times were severe when stout men lost their minds from extremity of suffering—when horses died—and when mules and horses, ready to die of starvation, were killed for food. Yet there was no murmuring or hesitation.

The hardships of exploration were taking their toll.

On March 2, Preuss rode ahead of the others and therefore did not know of Frémont's decision to make an early camp. When he did not come in by dark, Kit realized that he must be lost and so rode one of the horses down the trail, shouting and calling Preuss' name. There was no reply. There was still no sign of Preuss by noon the next day, but in early afternoon they came to the place where Preuss had camped the night before. Kit and the others shouted and fired their weapons, but again there was no answer. They concluded that Preuss had gone on down the stream they were following.

Late in the day, the group crossed the stream and found two huts; near by were heaps of acorn hulls. They sat down in the shade of the oak trees to let the horses rest and feed. Hearing a noise by the stream, Kit jumped up and shouted for Preuss. He received an answer from across the stream—but it was from some stray Indian who had mistaken Frémont's camp for that of his fellows. Now was added the extra worry about Preuss' not having a gun, being unprotected from hostile Indians—if they were hostile.

At this point, the lost Preuss was becoming alarmed about his position. Although he did not fear the Indians, he felt that his not finding the others was beginning to get serious. He had had nothing to eat except a portion of an ant's nest which he "bit off and swallowed" and some wild sweet onions which he dug from the rocks with his pocket knife. At length he came upon some Indians. "I walked straight up to them," he said, "sat down among them, and gave them to understand that I was hungry. They immediately served me acorns, some of which I ate, and others I put in my pocket. When they saw this, they themselves filled both my pockets to capacity. I took my leave and was much relieved that my pockets were filled; this would surely bring me into the valley."

About two o'clock on March 5, the same day he met the Indians, Preuss found the place where Frémont and the others had nooned. He pushed on, nibbling acorns along the way, and late that evening found the camp. "We were all rejoiced at his return," said Kit, "for the old man was much respected by the party."

They rode on the next day and in the afternoon discovered a large

Indian village in the broad valley of the American River. A well-dressed Indian explained in Spanish that the fort was ten miles downstream where the river emptied into the Sacramento and that the people of his village worked for Captain Sutter. The little group thanked him and hurried on toward the fort, arriving there late that evening.

Genial, German-born Captain John Sutter had seen some gruesome sights since his arrival in California in 1839, but he must have looked with wonder upon the emaciated, ragged men he rode out to meet. They had just accomplished something which he and Joe Walker would have sworn could not be done, crossing the Sierra Nevada Range in the depths of winter, but that they had done so without loss of human life must have astonished him even more. He welcomed them, made them as comfortable as he could, and supplied plenty of food and fresh horses for Frémont to take with him the next day when he rode back to meet Fitzpatrick's group. They were in worse shape than Frémont's party and had to camp overnight before coming into the fort on the eighth.

The explorers refreshed themselves at the fort until March 22, when they moved up the American River a few miles and camped on its left bank. Here Derosier ran wildly out of camp looking for his mule, which was tied close by, and disappeared before anyone could stop him. (He was later found by Captain Sutter, who nursed him back to health and sent him back to the States.) On the twenty-fourth, they continued their trip home in earnest, Frémont riding Sacramento, a gray horse which Captain Sutter had given him to replace Proveau.

Frémont led the expedition down the valley of the San Joaquin River, forded that stream at its southern bend, and continued southeastward. They crossed the Sierras through Oak Creek Pass and on April 19 cut the Old Spanish Trail, which Frémont planned to follow. That they were making fast time is indicated by Preuss' diary entries for March 27 and April 7. They traveled forty-five and fifty miles, respectively, on those two days. They were forced to halt a couple of times, however, to recover strayed pack animals, one of them a horse loaded with flour.

On the afternoon of April 24, a Mexican man named Andreas Fuentes, accompanied by eleven-year-old Pablo Hernandez, rode into camp. The pair related that their party of six—which included Pablo's parents, Fuentes' wife, and Santiago Giacome, who was from New Mexico—had started from Los Angeles with thirty head of horses in advance of a larger caravan. At a place they called the Archilette, they made camp to await the others. Several Indians visited them, making signs of friendship, and after two or three days departed. Several days later—Fuentes and the boy were on guard at the time—the camp was attacked by some one hundred warriors, who immediately attempted to drive off the horses. At Giacome's command, Pablo and Fuentes drove the animals out of camp with all possible speed, finally stopping some sixty miles away at a place Frémont calls Agua de Tomaso. Here they left the horses and set out to find the caravan, meeting Frémont along the way. Fuentes asked Frémont's help in finding his companions, who, he feared, had met with disaster. Frémont "received them kindly, taking them into my own mess, and promised them such aid as circumstances might put it in my power to give."

The expedition reached Agua de Tomaso that evening, only to find that the Indians had discovered and taken the horses. Kit and Alex Godey volunteered to help Fuentes recover the horses, and all three set out immediately. "In the evening," Frémont records, "Fuentes returned, his horse having failed; but Carson and Godey had continued the pursuit." They were back the next day. Frémont's account of their return and their meeting with the Indians is worth quoting here because it gives an excellent insight into the character of both men:

> In the afternoon of the next day [April 26], a war-whoop was heard, such as the Indians make when returning from a victorious enterprise; and soon Carson and Godey appeared, driving before them a band of horses, recognized by Fuentes to be part of those they had lost. Two bloody scalps, dangling from the end of Godey's gun, announced that they had overtaken the Indians as well as the horses. They informed us, that after Fuentes left them, from the failure of his horse, they continued the pursuit alone, and towards nightfall en-

tered the mountains, into which the trail led. After sunset the moon gave light, and they followed the trail by moonshine until late in the night, when it entered a narrow defile, and was difficult to follow. Afraid of losing it in the darkness of the defile, they tied up their horses, struck no fire, and lay down to sleep in silence and in darkness. Here they lay from midnight till morning. At daylight they resumed the pursuit, and about sunrise discovered the horses; and, immediately dismounting and tying up their own, they crept cautiously to a rising ground which intervened, from the crest of which they perceived the encampment of four lodges close by. They proceeded quietly, and had got within thirty or forty yards of their object, when a movement among the horses discovered them to the Indians; giving the war shout, they instantly charged into the camp, regardless of the number which the *four* lodges would imply. The Indians received them with a flight of arrows shot from their long bows, one of which passed through Godey's shirt collar, barely missing his neck; our men fired their rifles upon a steady aim, and rushed in. Two Indians were stretched on the ground, fatally pierced with bullets; the rest fled, except a lad that was captured. The scalps of the fallen were instantly stripped off; but in the process, one of them, who had two balls through his body, sprung [*sic*] to his feet, the blood streaming from his skinned head, and uttering a hideous howl. An old squaw, possibly his mother, stopped and looked back from the mountain side she was climbing, threatening and lamenting. The frightful spectacle appalled the stout hearts of our men; but they did what humanity required, and quickly terminated the agonies of the gory savage. They were now masters of the camp, which was a pretty little recess in the mountain, with a fine spring, and apparently safe from all invasion. Great preparations had been made to feast a large party, for it was a very proper place for a rendezvous, and for the celebration of such orgies as robbers of the desert would delight in. Several of the best horses had been killed, skinned, and cut up; for the Indians living in mountains, and only coming into the plains to rob and murder, make no other use of horses than to eat them. Large earthen vessels were on the fire, boiling and stewing the horse beef; and several baskets, containing fifty or sixty pairs of moccasins, indicated the presence, or expectation, of a considerable party. They released the boy, who had given strong evidence of the stoicism, or something else, of the savage character, in commencing his breakfast upon a horse's head as soon as he found he was not to be killed, but only tied as a prisoner. Their object accomplished, our men gathered up all the surviving horses, fifteen in number, returned upon their trail, and rejoined us at our camp in the afternoon of the same day. They had rode [*sic*] about one hundred miles in the pursuit and return, and all in thirty hours. The time, place, object, and numbers, considered, this expedition of Carson and Godey may be considered among the boldest and most disinterested which the annals of western adventure, so full of daring deeds, can present. Two men, in a savage desert, pursue day and night an unknown body of Indians into the defiles of an unknown mountain—attack them on sight, without counting numbers—and defeat them in an instant—and for what? To punish the robbers of the desert, and to avenge the wrongs of Mexicans whom they did not know. I repeat: it was Carson and Godey who did this— the former an *American*, born in the Boonslick county [*sic*] of Missouri [an obvious error]; the latter a Frenchman, born in St. Louis—and both trained to western enterprise from early life.

Perhaps Frémont did not know that when someone asked a mountain man for help, especially if it involved fighting Indians, it was freely given, even at the risk of life and limb. Kit and Godey were simply following their code.

On April 29, they reached the place where the Mexicans had camped. Here they found the mutilated bodies of the two men; the women had been taken captive. Kit says that "a party travelling in our rear [the main caravan of the Mexicans] found their bodies very much mutilated and staked to the ground." After burying the dead, they hurried on down the trail. They encountered hostile Indians on May 5 but managed to avoid conflict with them. One old chief was particularly insulting and Kit wanted to do something about it, but Frémont restrained him. The Indians were Diggers, an extremely poor tribe, and made nuisances of themselves for several days thereafter.

By May 8, the expedition was twenty-eight miles up the Virgin River, a tributary of the Colorado. They saw Indians, but these remained at a safe distance and did not venture into camp that night. On the following day, however, the Diggers got the opportunity they were looking for when Baptiste Tabeau separated from the others and rode back along the trail to search for a lame mule. The Indians fell upon him and after a brief struggle succeeded in killing him. They then threw his body into the river, took his horse, and shot the mule, which Frémont, Kit, Fitzpatrick, and several others found dying when they set out to look for Tabeau. They deduced what had happened from the blood and other signs about the scene. Kit wanted to go after the Indians and avenge Tabeau's death, but again Frémont prevailed. It was just as well, for after that they saw only one Digger, he at a great distance, who rode quickly away when he saw them.

The grassy meadows of the Vegas de Santa Clara were a refreshing sight to the members of the expedition when they arrived there on May 12. On this day they were joined by Joe Walker and eight men, a meeting which delighted Frémont because it would add strength to his party and because Walker, who knew the country through which they would pass as if it were his own back yard, would accompany them all the way to Bent's Fort. Joe and his men had been traveling with the Mexican caravan from Los Angeles and had split off when they cut Frémont's trail. After some hard riding and a brush with the Indians (in which they killed two warriors), they had finally caught up.

On May 23, they reached the Sevier River, where they were compelled to construct bulrush rafts to ferry their supplies and instruments across. And here, too, another tragedy befell them. François Badeau was accidentally killed when he pulled a rifle toward himself muzzle first. Death came instantly, the ball passing through his head.

Frémont completed his circuit of the Great Basin when he arrived at Utah Lake on the twenty-fifth, a fact upon which he comments at length in his report. From here the expedition marched rapidly northeastward to Fort Uintah, which they reached on June 6, thence to Green River and Brown's Hole. The eleventh found them within a few miles of the place where Henry Fraeb and three of his men were killed in 1841, and under the same date Frémont remarks that they "passed . . . a place where Carson had been fired upon so close that one of the men had five bullets through his body."

"Buffalo are being killed every day now," wrote Charles Preuss on June 15. "Today we arrived at the New Park." They were heading south now, and three days later they met a huge war party of Arapahoes. A parley was arranged, the outcome of which was that Frémont reluctantly agreed to accompany them to their village at the Old Park, where the expedition spent the night.

The Arapahoes were at war with the Utes, hence Frémont's difficulty with them (he had just come from Ute country and was accused of helping them against the Arapahoes). He hurried away on the nineteenth and on succeeding days learned more about the seriousness of the situation. A party of six trappers joined the expedition on the twenty-second and reported that two of their companions had been killed by Arapahoes, one only a few days before, and when Frémont arrived at the Bayou Salade, or South Park, on June 23, a village of Utes was engaged in hot battle with the Arapahoes. The Utes also requested aid, but Frémont told them that this was impossible and ordered his men to move on at a gallop.

On the twenty-ninth, they met another Arapaho war party, which, Frémont says, "had recently been committing some outrages at Bent's fort, killing stock and driving off horses." The Indians passed on, however, and that evening Frémont's party camped "at the Pueblo . . . where we had the pleasure to find a number of our old acquaintances." They moved on down the Arkansas the next day and arrived at Bent's Fort on July 1.

It is July 4, 1844, and the scene is Bent's Fort on the Arkansas. Kit Carson is the narrator:

> Mr. [George] Bent gave Fremont and party a splendid dinner. The day was celebrated as well, if not better, than in many of the towns of the States.

Another tribute to the Bents' generous board.

Frémont and his men rode off down the Arkansas on July 5. A few days later, Kit and Joe Walker took leave of the fort and headed for Taos.

EARLY PORTRAIT OF KIT CARSON

ARRIVAL OF THE CARAVAN AT SANTA FE

Courtesy Missouri Historical Society

WILLIAM BENT, ONE OF THE OWNERS OF BENT'S FORT

Bent's Fort, Which Kit Carson Helped to Build

CÉRAN ST. VRAIN, BUSINESS PARTNER OF THE BENTS

LUCIEN B. MAXWELL
With Whom Kit Carson Was Associated at Rayado

Kit Carson and John C. Frémont, the Pathfinder

SCENE IN THE SIERRA NEVADAS
Where Frémont's Second Expedition Passed

Sagundai, the Delaware Chief Who Saved Kit Carson's Life

GENERAL STEPHEN WATTS KEARNEY
Whom Carson Served as Guide

KIT CARSON'S HOME IN TAOS

Courtesy Edwin L. Sabin

INDIAN AGENT CARSON'S OFFICE IN TAOS

RUINS OF TAOS PUEBLO CHURCH
Stormed by General Price's Troops in 1847

LIEUTENANT GEORGE H. PETTIS
Commander of the Howitzers at the Battle of Adobe Walls

Teresina Bent Scheurich
Kit Carson's Niece, Who Supplied Much Information
about the Scout

LAST PHOTOGRAPH OF KIT CARSON
Taken in Boston in March, 1868, Two Months before His Death

9 ★ Third Expedition with Frémont

Taos was bustling with trade and alive with rumors of a general uprising throughout the northern New Mexico area when Kit and Walker arrived there in July, 1844. Kit and Josefa moved back into their adobe house at the east end of the plaza, and Kit talked of plans to build a house at Rayado, to start farming and raising stock. Spring would be time enough to begin this project, he thought as he sat in the warm August sun and listened to Charles Bent's account of the trade situation. A Mexican law passed in March allowed Americans to bring merchandise into Santa Fe, but they could not retail it there, so many of the American merchants and traders had decided to travel farther south. Charles and William were bringing their trade goods directly to Bent's Fort from Missouri.

Charles Bent and Padre Antonio José Martinez were at swords' points. In his "Exposition of Things in Mexico," Martinez made a scathing attack on the American traders who had built forts near the Arkansas River, blaming them for the scarcity of buffalo meat. Martinez also accused the traders of selling liquor to the Indians and buying stolen cattle from these same Indians in order to resell them at higher prices.

Padre Martinez' remarkable career began at a seminary in Durango in 1817 when he came in contact with the "new spirit of Catholic Enlightenment and National Liberalism." He was ordained in 1822 and in 1823 returned to his parental home in Taos to "rest from a chest affliction." While recuperating, he occasionally assisted Padre Sebastian Alvarez at Guadalupe Church. The following year he was well enough to assist at Tomé; then he was appointed pastor for a short time at Abiquiu, his birthplace. When Kit arrived in Taos, he was pastor of Guadalupe Church.

During his pastorate in Taos, Martinez became a powerful political boss and a semifeudal, landowning *patrón,* and throughout his years as a Catholic priest he never lost an opportunity to chastise and belittle his ecclesiastical superiors concerning church taxation and other issues which he criticized as a self-appointed champion of the common people. He vigorously resented Bishop Lamy's admonishment concerning his morals, but according to Martinez' housekeeper, who was a widow, while in the Padre's service she had five children. They were all acknowledged and provided for in Martinez' will.

Martinez served in the first legislature in 1831, and in 1846 was a member of the last departmental council.[1] He used a small Ramage printing press, which was reputed to have been brought from Spain, or possibly Mexico, by the Abreu family, to print literature, as well as to print lesson sheets in 1836 for his boys' school at Taos. The press had been used in 1835 to print four issues of the first newspaper published west of the Mississippi, *El Crepúsculo de la Libertad* (*The Dawn of Liberty*), and it was also used to reproduce propaganda material for Mexican President Santa Anna, copies of which were distributed throughout New Mexico.

Kit declined an invitation to accompany Charles Bent to Santa Fe in November because he did not want to leave Josefa alone. When Charles returned a few weeks later, he warned Mexican traders in Taos that the Texans were again riding the Santa Fe Trail to raid Mexican caravans. Most of the Mexican traders would not risk the trail that coming spring of 1845.

On Christmas Eve, 1844, Josefa and her sister, Mrs. Bent, gave a large party to celebrate Kit's thirty-fifth birthday. According to Spanish custom, *luminarias,* bright cedar fires, burned in each yard to light the way for the little Christ Child. At Taos Pueblo, Padre

[1] Hubert H. Bancroft notes that "under the new constitution of December 1836 the Territory [New Mexico] became a 'department' and was so called to the end of the Mexican rule."

Martinez led an Indian procession whose members carried blazing faggots, *anchones*, as they wended their way around the plaza with a statue of the Holy Virgin. After dinner at the Bent home there was dancing at Céran St. Vrain's in a long, low room lighted by hundreds of handmade candles burning in beautifully wrought candelabra. Kit was wearing a dress suit Charles had brought him from St. Louis. The women were petite and graceful in their long, sweeping gowns, but none of them was more beautiful than dark-eyed Josefa Carson. Together, she and Kit made a handsome couple. Kit was only five and a half feet tall, which was short by trappers' standards, and Josefa came just above his shoulders.[2] After they circled the dance floor, laughing at Kit's awkwardness—for he had never stayed home long enough to learn how to waltz—Kit joined the men in the parlor.

Politics, war, and trade were the subjects discussed when the men of Taos got together. Charles Bent prophesied war between the United States and Mexico over Texas. Jolly, bewhiskered Céran St. Vrain hoped that Governor Armijo would soon be replaced by someone who was not competing in the merchandising business. Carlos Beaubien summarized the war situation by saying that the Oregon and California migration would continue, with the disputed Oregon boundary to be settled soon; California, he hoped, would be annexed to the United States without bloodshed, as he believed Texas would be annexed soon. He ended his appraisal of the situation by saying that Brigham Young was considering a mass exodus to establish a settlement in the West.

Of all the parties given in and around Taos that year, Kit's birthday party was the most memorable. According to family tradition, Josefa admired Kit so much in his dress suit that she made him sit for an oil portrait, which turned out to be a very good likeness of him. The name of the artist is unknown, and only a reproduction of the painting can be found.

[2] It has been mistakenly stated that Josefa Carson was a head taller than her husband, but the best authorities (her son Charles and her niece Teresina, among others) have been quoted by Blanche Grant as saying that Mrs. Carson was "almost a head shorter than Kit." Spanish women were notably short and small, and if Josefa had been a head taller than Kit, she would have been at least five feet ten!

Winter thawed into an early spring. In March, Kit and Dick Owens went to Rayado, some fifty miles east of Taos, to build a house and start their farming venture. In midsummer, Kit took Josefa to the acreage, where she spent long hours watching him till, plant, build corrals, and round up his sheep and cattle. They settled down to make the most of this fertile land, but their newly found joy in a quiet life of farming and stock raising did not last long. The first week in August, 1845, an express rode in from Bent's Fort to inform Kit that Frémont was there with recruits for his third expedition.

Remembering his promise to accompany Frémont on the latter's next expedition, Kit sold his farm and stock at a loss and moved Josefa back to the Bent household. Dick Owens accompanied him to Bent's Fort, where both prepared to go with the explorers. Frémont says of Kit in his *Memoirs*:

> He sold everything at a sacrifice, farm and cattle; and not only came himself but brought his friend Owens to join the party. This was like Carson, prompt, self-sacrificing, and true. I received them both with great satisfaction.

Of the ninety men on this expedition, there were many veterans of the previous expeditions, all well known to Kit. Basil Lajeunesse was along, of course, as were Alex Godey, Lucien Maxwell, Joe Walker, Theodore Talbot, and Jacob Dodson. Edward M. Kern of Philadelphia had succeeded Charles Preuss as cartographer, and Tom Fitzpatrick had been engaged as guide again. Frémont had also hired twelve Delaware Indians as hunters, among them two chiefs, Swanok and Sagundai. Lieutenants J. W. Abert and G. W. Peck had joined him in St. Louis, and he now dispatched them, together with Tom Fitzpatrick, John L. Hatcher (who would act as guide part of the way), and thirty men to explore Canadian River country, northern Texas, and the lower Arkansas before turning north to St. Louis.

Frémont was riding his favorite horse, Sacramento, when, on August 16, 1845, his party of sixty men left Bent's Fort. They were a well-appointed group, most of them being experienced men equal to any emergency. They set out along the Arkansas and on September 2 were encamped on its headwaters. "The weather now was delightful," wrote Frémont, "and the country beautiful. Fresh and green, aspen groves and pine woods and clear rushing waters, cool streams sparkling over rocky beds."

They crossed the Continental Divide and pushed on to the Great Basin. The valley of the Great Salt Lake was the first object for observation, and they pitched their tents at a point well south of their encampment of 1843. The water of the lake was so low that Kit, Frémont, and a few others could ride their horses through the shallows to Antelope Island, as Frémont named it. They killed some of the antelope they found on the island, and when they got back to shore an old Indian came up to Frémont and told him that he was the sole owner of all the antelope on the island. He was very serious and reproached Frémont for trespassing. Frémont presented him with "some red cloth, a knife, and tobacco" as payment for the game they had killed. The Indian left, quite satisfied with his bargain.

The visit made two years previously had given the lake a somewhat familiar aspect, but systematic observations were repeated. On the eastern shore they saw a large band of Indians. On the south shore they observed an Indian drinking salt water because there was no fresh water in the neighborhood. Here Kit looked out over the sun-baked plain which was to be their route of travel; it offered scant encouragement of what might lie beyond. In the distance, about sixty miles in their line of travel, rose black, dry-looking mountains, and beyond them a higher peak held some promise of water and the possibility of firewood.

Having learned caution on his previous trips, Frémont did not care to risk his entire party on a desert trek that might end in disaster. Four men, including Kit, Maxwell, and Archambeau, were sent ahead to locate water and grass. They were to go to the high peak, where, if he found water, Kit was to build a fire as a signal for Frémont and the others to proceed. On the evening of the second day, Kit's group reached the foot of the mountain[3] and found grass

[3] Frémont bestowed upon it the name "Pilot Peak" because it had guided the party to grass and water.

and fresh water. Archambeau rode back to meet the others, who by now were well into the desert. The Indians with whom Frémont had talked had told him that this was "a country of no life," and now he could well believe it.

On November 1, they left the water hole and proceeded westward until November 5, when, at the east end of the Humboldt Mountains, the party divided to cross the Great Basin at different angles and meet on the eastern shore of Walker's Lake. There were ten in Frémont's group, including Kit, Maxwell, Owens, and some of the Delawares. The second group, under the leadership of Edward Kern, with Joe Walker as guide, was to "follow down and survey the Humboldt River and its valley to their termination in what was called 'the Sink.'" They would then follow the eastern slopes of the Sierras to the lake.

Frémont's section set out at a rapid pace, but they were soon slowed by the rugged nature of the country, which compelled them to cross mountains and rocky hills wherever they could and to camp at such place as would afford them grass and water for their animals. There were Indians about, too, but singly and in small groups, and the party seldom saw them. Frémont records several occasions on which they met Indians, two of which are worth quoting here:

We had made our supper on the antelope [which Kit had killed in the afternoon] and were lying around the fire, and the men taking their great comfort in smoking. A good supper and a pipe make for them a comfortable ending no matter how hard the day has been. Carson who was lying on his back with his pipe in his mouth, his hands under his head and his feet to the fire, suddenly exclaimed, half rising and pointing to the other side of the fire, "Good God! look there!" In the blaze of the fire, peering over her skinny, crooked hands, which shaded her eyes from the glare, was standing an old woman apparently eighty years of age, nearly naked, her grizzly hair hanging down over her face and shoulders. She had thought it a camp of her people and had already begun to talk and gesticulate, when her open mouth was paralyzed with fright, as she saw the faces of the whites. She turned to escape, but the men had gathered about her and brought her around to the fire. Hunger and cold soon dispelled fear and she made us understand that she had been left by her people at the spring to die, because she was very old and could gather no more seeds and was no longer good for anything. She told us she had nothing to eat and was very hungry. We gave her immediately about a quarter of the antelope, thinking she would roast it by our fire, but no sooner did she get it in her hand than she darted off into the darkness. Some one ran after her with a brand of fire, but calling after her brought no answer. In the morning, her fresh tracks at the spring showed that she had been there for water during the night. Starvation had driven her to us, but her natural fear drove her away as quickly, so soon as she had secured something to eat. Before we started we left for her at the spring a little supply from what food we had. This, with what she could gather from the nut-pine trees on the mountain, together with our fire which she could easily keep up, would probably prolong her life even after the snows came. . . .

Several days later they had another curious experience:

Making our way along the foot of the mountain towards our rendezvous we had reached one of the lakes where at this season the scattered Indians of the neighborhood were gathering to fish. Turning a point on the lake shore the party of Indians some twelve or fourteen in number came abruptly into view. They were advancing along in Indian file, one following the other, their heads bent forward and eyes fixed on the ground. As our party met them the Indians did not turn their heads nor raise their eyes from the ground. Their conduct indicated unfriendliness, but, habituated to the uncertainties of savage life, we too fell readily into their humor, and passed on our way without a word or halt. Even to us it was a strange meeting.

Indian stoicism? No, Frémont says, it was "an instance of sullen and defiant hostility among Indians and where they neither sought nor avoided conflict."

Frémont camped on the shore of Walker's Lake on November 24, and three days later the Walker division rode in. Frémont decided to split the expedition again in order to make faster time through the Sierras, the Kern-Walker party skirting the range to the San Joaquin Valley and Frémont's group making a more direct effort across the mountains by way of the pass at the head of the Truckee River. They were to meet "at a little lake in the valley of a river called the Lake Fork of the Tularé Lake."

On December 1, Frémont and his men were pressing forward to reach the pass before a heavy fall of snow could block their passage. On the fourth, they were on the headwaters of the Truckee, and the next sunrise found them on the dividing ridge. The weather was clear, and the only snow to be seen was on higher ridges and the peaks of the mountains. They turned south to avoid a rough descent and were soon descending rapidly over an easy trail.

They moved more slowly when they reached the Sacramento Valley so that Frémont could make "the usual astronomical observations and notes of the country." On December 9, they were at Sutter's Fort (Sutter had named his settlement Nueva Helvetia). Frémont describes their arrival in the *Memoirs*:

> Captain Sutter received me with the same friendly hospitality which had been so delightful to us the year before. I found that our previous visit had created some excitement among the Mexican authorities. But to their inquiries he had explained that I had been engaged in a geographical survey of the interior and had been driven to force my way through the snow of the mountains simply to obtain a refuge and food where I knew it could be had at his place, which was by common report known to me.

They remained at the fort long enough to rest and buy supplies, then headed for San Joaquin Valley to rendezvous with the rest of the expedition.

On December 19, as they were riding in the foothills of the Sierras, they discovered a fresh Indian trail. The signs indicated that a large number of horses were being driven toward the mountains from the direction of the San Joaquin. Frémont dispatched four men—Maxwell, Owens, and two of the Delawares—to scout the situation and prepared to set up camp. They had scarcely started to unsaddle when they heard shots. They quickly mounted again, leaving four men to guard the camp, and rushed toward the sound of the firing. There they discovered the scouts atop a small knoll, completely surrounded by more than a hundred Indians. Frémont and his men charged, thereby diverting the Indians' attention for the moment, whereupon the Delawares recovered the four horses (the men had dismounted to take cover and defend themselves). Owens and Maxwell cut down an Indian apiece, and the whole party retreated to their camp, firing intermittently to cover the move. The Indians harassed them for a few hours but were gone by midnight. Frémont posted a strong guard, but the only incident to occur was that one of the Delawares fired at a wolf, mistaking it for an Indian.

In order to avoid further conflict with the Indians, Frémont led his men away from the mountains in a southeasterly direction. On December 22, they arrived at the appointed rendezvous but did not find the Walker party. Indeed, contact with Walker was not established until February, 1846, when Kit and Dick Owens, who had been dispatched to look for him, met him on the San Joaquin. By then, Frémont had been to Yerba Buena (San Francisco) and Monterey, where, with the American consul, Thomas O. Larkin, he called on the Mexican authorities: General José Castro, the commanding general; former Governor Juan Alvarado, and other officials. Governor Pio Pico was in Los Angeles at the time. Frémont asked that his party be allowed to purchase food, clothing, and other supplies in Monterey. "The permission asked for was readily granted," wrote Frémont, "and during the two days I stayed I was treated with every courtesy by the general and other officers."

Kit, Owens, and the Walker section—who had misunderstood the site of the rendezvous, stopping some eighty miles south of it to await Frémont—joined Frémont about thirteen miles south of San José. Instead of going on to Oregon, Frémont gave orders to start south. On March 3, while they were camped near the Salinas River, the quiet of the afternoon was disturbed by the sudden appearance of an officer with two assistants. He introduced himself to Frémont as Lieutenant Chavez and announced that he had orders from the Mexican government to ask the Americans to leave Mexican territory by the quickest route. Frémont records his reaction: "I desired him to say in reply to General Castro that I peremptorily refused compliance to an order insulting to my government and myself."[4]

The next day, Frémont moved his camp a few miles to the crest of a hill between the Salinas and San Joaquin rivers, about thirty miles from Monterey. On March 6, on Gavilan Peak, which overlooked the mission at San Juan and the valley of the Salinas, the Frémont men built a log fort and, amid cheers, raised the American flag. Soon it would wave over the entire territory of California and Oregon.

Mexican cavalry watched the American camp but did not attack. Twice that number of Mexican soldiers might well have considered the odds before attacking a "fortified hill patrolled and garrisoned by American sharpshooters." Kit says they grew tired of waiting for the Mexicans to attack. Frémont states that he thought he had "remained as long as the occasion required," but Hubert Bancroft asserts that Frémont was induced to leave Gavilan Peak by Consul Larkin, who wrote to him as follows:

> It is not for me to point out to you your line of conduct, you have your instruction from the government; my knowledge of your character obliges me to believe you will follow them; you are of course taking every care and safeguard to protect your men, but not knowing your actual situation and the people who surround you, your care may prove insufficient. . . . . Your encamping so near town has caused much excitement. The natives are firm in belief that they will break you up, and that you can be entirely destroyed by their power. In all probability they will attack you; the result either way may cause trouble hereafter to resident Americans. . . . Should it be impossible or inconvenient for you to leave California at present, I think, in a proper representation to the general and prefecto, an arrangement could be made for your camp to be continued, but at some greater distance; which arrangement I should advise if you can offer it.

With this message Larkin enclosed a letter from General Castro in which the General warned Larkin to impress upon Frémont the necessity of complying with his orders at once if he were to avert

[4] Consul Larkin explained Castro's change of feeling in a letter to the Secretary of State: "Within twenty days the general says he had received direct and specific orders from Mexico not to allow Captain Frémont to enter California."

the consequences of his illegal entry into this area. Larkin had previously warned Frémont that Castro would soon have two hundred men in arms against him. Kit told Colonel Peters: "General Castro came with several hundred men and established his headquarters near us. He would frequently fire his big guns to frighten us."

Consul Larkin's communications to Frémont were intercepted by Castro, but copies succeeded in reaching Frémont. Frémont's answer, written in pencil and dated March 9, was the only communication sent from the camp on Gavilan Peak:

> I this moment received your letters, and, without waiting to read them, acknowledge the receipt which the courier requires immediately. I am making myself as strong as possible, in the intention that if we are unjustly attacked we will fight to extremity and refuse quarter, trusting to our country to avenge us. No one has reached our camp, and from the heights we are able to see with the glass troops mustering at San Juan and preparing cannon.
>
> I thank you for your kindness and good wishes, and would write more at length as to my intentions did I not fear that my letter would be intercepted. We have in nowise done wrong to the people or the authorities of the country, and if we are hemmed in and assaulted here we will die every man of us under the flag of our country.

That evening, however, the Frémont party left their fort.

Descending into the San Joaquin Valley on March 11, they crossed the river, reached the Stanislaus the sixteenth, and arrived at Sutter's Fort on the twenty-first, making camp just across the American River. Three days later they moved on, visiting Keyser's Ranch on Bear River, Cordua's on the Yuba, and Neal's on Butte Creek (Neal was a blacksmith with Frémont's second expedition), and on March 30 arrived at Lassen's Ranch on Deer Creek, where they remained until April 5. After a week's trip up the Sacramento Valley to Cow Creek and back, they again camped at Lassen's Ranch from April 11 to April 14 (Frémont says April 24). From here, Frémont sent Talbot down the river to Yerba Buena to obtain supplies, while some of the other men—Godey, Martin, and probably Kit—were sent out to purchase horses from the Indians. The animals had been stolen from California residents, and in a letter to Frémont, Sutter urged him to leave them behind.

Martin and Carson both relate that at Lassen's Ranch they were called upon by the settlers for aid against the Indians, who were threatening a general attack. The result was a raid by the Frémont group in which the Indians were defeated, a large number being slain in their village.

While at Lassen's, Frémont's men gave a two-day barbecue for a party of emigrants who were encamped near by. An Indian from San José Mission (he was called Antolino) employed by Francis Day carried a sensational report that the emigrants were part of two hundred armed foreigners whose purpose was to attack Monterey as soon as Indian reinforcements could be obtained from Oregon. The only basis on which the Indian could make the charge was the emigrants' offer to join Frémont's group for a movement against the Californians, but according to Bancroft, this offer was turned down. Lucien Maxwell reportedly told Charles Bent that it was Kit who had advised Frémont not to make any appearance of aggression, at least until war was formally declared.[5]

Meanwhile, on March 11, General Zachary Taylor had "crossed the Rubicon by marching from Nueces for the Río Grande, carrying the American flag into 119 miles of unsurrendered Mexican territory." But Kit and Frémont had no way of knowing about this, or they would certainly have remained in California to make aggressive moves of their own.

On May 6, 1846, the Frémont expedition arrived in Oregon and made camp on the shore of Klamath Lake. Two evenings later, Frémont was alone by the fire, listening to night noises and mentally penetrating undiscovered mysteries of new trails and lofty summits. He was in his chosen area of wooded wilderness where he loved to believe that he was the first white man. He writes in his *Memoirs*:

By unexplored, I wish to be understood to say that it had never been

[5] In Volume XX of his *History of California*, Hubert Bancroft gives his own interpretation of these events. It is somewhat different from the reports of Frémont, Carson, and Larkin.

explored or mapped, or in any way brought to common knowledge, or rarely visited except by strong parties of trappers, and by those at remote intervals, doubtless never by trappers singly. . . . It would have been dull work if it had been to plod over a safe country and here and there to correct some old error. . . .

How fate pursues a man! Thinking and ruminating over these things, I was standing alone by my camp-fire, enjoying its warmth, for the night air of early spring is chill under the shadows of the high mountains. Suddenly my ear caught the faint sound of horses' feet, and while I was watching and listening as the sounds, so strange hereabout, came nearer, there emerged from the darkness—into the circle of the firelight—two horsemen, riding slowly as though horse and man were fatigued by long travelling. In the foremost I recognized the familiar face of Neal, with a companion [Sigler], whom also I knew. They had ridden nearly a hundred miles in the last two days, having been sent forward by a United States officer who was on my trail with despatches for me; but Neal doubted if he would get through. After their horses had been turned into the band and they were seated by my fire, refreshing themselves with good coffee while more solid food was being prepared, Neal told me his story. . . .

Sigler and Neal had been sent by Marine Lieutenant Archibald Gillespie, who, with three men, was camped some fifty miles away in hostile Indian country. Gillespie had been sent to California by the government and had letters of dispatch for Frémont. In Neal's opinion, Frémont could not reach Gillespie in time to save him.

Frémont knew that it would be foolhardy to ride the trail at night, so, the following morning, a relief squad set out. It consisted of Kit, Frémont, Owens, Stepp, Godey, Maxwell, Lajeunesse, Denny, and the four Delaware Indians. After a hard day's ride, they arrived at Gillespie's camp, which was located by a small stream, and were greeted by the Lieutenant and his men. Here was news from home, the first in eleven long months.

The men around the main campfire (there were two other fires) listened to Lieutenant Gillespie tell of his dangerous trip from Washington, which he had begun in October of the previous year. He had made the journey across Mexican territory into Old Mexico in the guise of an invalid traveler. On the west coast of Mexico, he and his men had taken passage on a ship for Monterey. Arriving in California, they had traveled up the Sacramento. Then they had gone northward in search of Frémont when they met Neal and Sigler, who knew the location of the Frémont camp. Lieutenant Gillespie told of the grave danger of an attack by unfriendly Indians, thus sending Neal and Sigler ahead to tell Frémont of their peril while he and three men stayed behind to feed and rest the horses.

The dispatches had now been delivered to Frémont, and among them was a letter from Senator Benton which Frémont interpreted to indicate that he was to find out about any "foreign schemes in relation to California, and so far as might be in my power to counteract them." Lieutenant Gillespie told Frémont that he had been directed by the Secretary of State to acquaint him with his instructions, which were to ascertain the feelings of the California people toward the United States and to find out what designs the British had on California.

Gillespie brought tidings of war, for Frémont writes in his *Memoirs*:

> Now it was officially known to me that my country was at war, and it was so made known expressly to guide my conduct. I had learned with certainty from the Secretary of the Navy that the President's plan of war included the taking possession of California, and under his confidential instructions I had my warrant. Mr. Gillespie was directed to act in concert with me. Great vigilance and activity were expected of us both, for it was desired that possession should be had of California before the presence in her ports of any foreign vessel of war might make it inconvenient.

As an officer of the U.S. Army, Frémont felt that he must do all in his power to prevent California from coming under British or French control. He had known for some time of Senator Benton's ambition to annex California to the United States. Thinking and pondering on this sudden turn of events, Frémont, sitting alone by the fire long after the others had retired, heard a movement among the animals. Without notifying his men, who were exhausted and asleep, Frémont, pistol in hand, walked through the moonlight to investigate. It was a plucky and reckless act. Finding nothing, he returned to camp and retired. He had scarcely settled in his blanket when an attack by the Klamath Indians took the camp completely by surprise. Had Kit been the one to hear the uneasiness among the animals, it would have been a different fight, for he would have given an alarm.

The attack came so suddenly that for a moment everything seemed to happen at once. Kit and Owens, who were sleeping near each other, were awakened at the same time by the sound of Indian tomahawks as they struck the heads of Denny and Basil. Kit jumped up, calling to Basil. Basil didn't answer, but Kit heard Denny groan a little as he died. The four Delaware Indians, who were sleeping by the fire, sprang up to defend the camp as the Klamaths charged them. There were no orders given; things went too fast. As Kit later said, "the Colonel had men with him that did not need to be told their duty."

Crane, one of the Delawares, had caught up an empty gun as the Klamaths charged, fighting them off until he was shot full of arrows, three entering his heart. Frémont, Owens, Maxwell, Godey, Stepp, and Kit ran to the assistance of their faithful Delawares. They all must have fired at once; Kit said he thought it was Stepp's gun which killed the chief, for it was at the crack of his gun that the Klamath chief fell. When the other Indians saw their chief cut down, they ran out of the camp, leaving his body where it had slumped. They stayed back in the shadows of the woods and continued to shoot arrows into the camp, making repeated efforts to recover the body of their chief. The Frémont men were determined that they should not have it, and each movement in the shadows brought a volley of rifle shots. In the thick of all this, Frémont heard Kit's voice ring out: "Look at the fool. Look at him, will you?" This was said of Godey, who had stepped up to the light of the fire to examine some part of his gun which had gone wrong, there making a perfect target for a poisoned arrow. Turning resentfully to Carson, Godey walked slowly out of the circle of light.

Three of the Frémont group lay dead—Basil Lajeunesse, Denny, and Crane—and another of the Delawares had been wounded. For the rest of the night, no one slept; everyone was on guard. However, the Indians did not return.

At dawn Kit examined the dead chief. He had an English half-ax slung to his wrist by a cord, and there were forty of the "most beautiful and warlike arrows" Kit had ever seen. Kit remarked that "he must have been the bravest man among them, from the way he was armed, and judging from his cap." The arrows Kit admired so much were all headed with a lancet-like piece of iron and poisoned for six inches at the point. Lieutenant Gillespie recognized the chief as one of the Indians with whom he and his men had shared their scanty supply of meat in exchange for a salmon. Frémont and his party undoubtedly saved Gillespie and his men from annihilation, for the Klamaths had been on Gillespie's trail all along.

By examining tracks, Kit estimated that the attackers numbered some fifteen or twenty. He knew that the Indians would return with more warriors, so he suggested that the party move on down the trail. The three dead were carried on pack mules for about ten miles, but the trail became so thick with heavy timber and the Indians were so close that Frémont ordered the men buried. Of this Frémont wrote:

> With our knives we dug a shallow grave, and wrapping their blankets round them, left them among the laurels. There are men above whom the laurels bloom who did not better deserve them than my brave Delaware and Basil. I left Denny's name on the creek where he died.

The three remaining Delawares blackened their faces and grieved silently. When the group mounted their horses and rode on, they followed a short distance, then dismounted, tethered their horses, and stole back to camp. They hid in the bushes, knowing the Klamaths would be stealing up to the place to rob the bodies. The others were not surprised to hear a volley of shots. Soon the Delawares rejoined them—with two scalps. Sagundai, one of the Delaware chiefs said: "Better now. Very sick before. Better now." Their primitive belief required them to exact immediate reprisals for a life lost among them.

Frémont and Gillespie thought it expedient to return to California. In the morning, Kit was sent ahead with Owens and nine others with orders from Frémont to send back word if any large Indian villages were discovered; if the Indians saw Kit first, he was to act as he thought best. They had gone about ten miles when they came upon a large Klamath village of about fifty lodges. The agitated movements of the Indians indicated that they were preparing for battle. Kit decided to attack at once in a surprise move. To do so, they had to cross a river. "Here is a good place," said Kit, and he leaped his horse into the river. The others followed, and all went in over their heads, wetting their powder and rendering their guns useless. Just at that moment, Frémont and the main party came up, and the fight with the Indians began.

Kit states that the Indians were severely punished and that the Frémont party camped about two miles from the site of the village after the battle. Owens was sent back to it with twenty men to watch for returning warriors. He soon sent word to Frémont and Carson that some fifty Indians had returned to the place, presumably to bury their dead. As soon as Frémont heard this, he, Carson, and five others set out to join Owens. They took a different route from the one Owens had taken, Kit said, in order to remain concealed. Frémont describes the encounter in his *Memoirs*:

> About a mile from the village I made my camp on a *clairière* in the midst of woods, where were oaks intermingled with pines, and built a strong corral. Meantime I kept out scouts on every side and horses were kept ready saddled. In the afternoon Indians were reported advancing through the timber; and taking with me Carson, Sagundai, Swanok, Stepp, and Archambeau, I rode out to see what they were intending. Sacramento knew how to jump and liked it. Going through the wood at a hand-gallop we came upon an oak tree which had been blown down; its summit covered quite a space, and being crowded by the others so that I was brought squarely in front of it, I let Sacramento go and he cleared the whole green mass in a beautiful leap. Looking back, Carson called out, "Captain, that horse will break your

neck some day." It never happened to Sacramento to hurt his rider, but afterward, on the Salinas plain, he brought out from fight and back to his camp his rider who had been shot dead in the saddle.

In the heart of the wood we came suddenly upon an Indian scout. He was drawing his arrow to the head as we came upon him, and Carson attempted to fire, but his rifle snapped, and as he swerved away the Indian was about to let his arrow go into him; I fired, and in my haste to save Carson, failed to kill the Indian, but Sacramento, as I have said, was not afraid of anything, and I jumped him directly upon the Indian and threw him to the ground. His arrow went wild. Sagundai was right behind me, and as I passed over the Indian he threw himself from his horse and killed him with a blow on the head from his war-club. It was the work of a moment, but it was a narrow chance for Carson. The poisoned arrow would have gone through his body.

Giving Sacramento into the care of Jacob, I went into the lodge and laid down on my blanket to rest from the excitement of which the day had been so full. I had now kept the promise I made to myself and had punished these people well for their treachery; and now I turned my thought to the work which they had delayed. I was lost in conjectures over this new field when Gillespie came in, all roused into new emotion. "By Heaven, this is rough work," he exclaimed. "I'll take care to let them know in Washington about it." "Heaven don't come in for much about here, just now," I said; "and as for Washington, it will be long enough before we see it again; time enough to forget about this."

He had been introduced into an unfamiliar life in joining me and had been surprised into continued excitements by the strange scenes which were going on around him. My surroundings were very much unlike the narrow space and placid uniformity of a man-of-war's deck, and to him the country seemed alive with unexpected occurrences. Though himself was not, his ideas were, very much at sea. He was full of admiration for my men and their singular fitness for the life they were leading. He shared my lodge, but this night his excitement would not let him sleep, and we remained long awake; talking over the incidents of the day and speculating over what was to come in the events that seemed near at hand. Nor was there much sleeping in the camp that night, but nothing disturbed its quiet. No attack was made.

The trail for Sacramento was resumed, with the Frémont-Gillespie group on guard day and night against Indian attacks. Once when Maxwell and Archambeau were riding ahead on the path, they encountered a lone Indian who immediately let an arrow fly at Maxwell. But Maxwell flung himself from his saddle just in time and the arrow sped over him. Archambeau killed the Indian and placed his scalp on the trail as notice to friend or foe.

As the group pressed on, the Klamaths dogged their path, watching for an opportunity to take them by surprise. Upon Kit's suggestion, Frémont bypassed a canyon and thereby escaped a clever ambush. The Indians boldly rushed out to fight but retreated as Kit and his men charged. One warrior in a rocky shelter kept the white men at bay until Kit crept around to where he could get a good view of him and shot him. The Indian had a fine bow and a full quiver of arrows, which Kit presented to Lieutenant Gillespie. Of the Indian, Kit said: "He was a brave Indian, deserved a better fate, but he had placed himself on the wrong path."

After a weary journey, with Indians watching them all the way, the party at last reached Lassen's Ranch on the Sacramento River. Here they "tarried for a few days to recruit." Following the river some distance to a well-known camping spot called "The Buttes," they established camp on May 24, 1846. It was a beautiful spot near the junction of the Bear and Feather rivers, below the present town of Marysville. From here Frémont sent Gillespie to obtain supplies from the American warship *Portsmouth*, which was lying at anchor in the Bay of San Francisco.

The Frémont camp became a rallying place for Americans, and the fiery Frémont took it upon himself to protect his fellow countrymen by striking a blow before the enemy could burn the fields. "I judged it expedient," said Frémont, "to take such precautionary measures so this forward movement would leave no enemy behind to destroy the strength of my position by cutting off my supplies."

After the supplies arrived from San Francisco (on June 8), Frémont moved his camp to the vicinity of Sutter's Landing. Kit and the men must have been glad to see the genial Captain Sutter again on June 13 and to unite forces with him. Using the fort as their base, Kit, Maxwell, and ten others from the Frémont camp joined

Ezekiel Merritt in capturing 170 horses—reinforcements on the way to General Castro. Lieutenant Francisco Arce, who was in charge of the horses, was released to tell Castro that if he, Castro, wanted his horses, he might very well try to come and take them. As soon as the horses had been safely corralled at the fort, Ezekiel Merritt, Dr. Robert Semple, John Grigsby, and some thirty followers rode westward to the old mission of San Francisco Salano, "the garrison of Sonoma." On the morning of June 14, they captured the fortress, taking as prisoners the commandant, General Mariano Guadalupe Vallejo; his brother, Don Salvador Vallejo; the General's secretary, Victor Prudon; and the General's son-in-law, an American named Jacob P. Leese. With the Mexicans' munitions, horses, and food supplies safely in hand, they declared California "a free and independent government."

The next day, the group devised a flag, which they called "the Bear Flag," to fly over the rude fortress of Sonoma. It was about five feet long and three wide and was designed by William L. Todd, a settler from Illinois. The material used was cotton, with a lower border of red flannel. The flag depicted a brown bear facing a large star of red flannel. Below this was written "California Republic."

Basil Lajeunesse had been killed May 9, 1846, the same day General Taylor had fought and won the Battle of Resaca de la Palma, and two days before he had won at Palo Alto. On June 15, 1846, other frontiers were being opened, other battles won. The Oregon Treaty was signed in Washington, D.C., by the American secretary of state and the British foreign minister; the forty-ninth parallel was to be an international boundary from the Rockies to the Pacific. General Taylor was achieving brilliant successes on the lower Río Grande; at Fort Leavenworth the celebrated "Army of the West" had assembled under General Stephen Watts Kearny; and sixteen thousand Mormons had crossed the Mississippi River on their journey westward.

In California, the new commander, William B. Ide, had prepared a proclamation bidding the people to "repair to my camp at Sonoma without delay to assist us in establishing and perpetuating a republican government." At Sutter's Fort, Frémont had placed Edward

Kern, his topographer, in command. The captives Vallejos, Prudon, and Leese had been jailed at the fort, where Leese records poignantly: "We pass'd the next day in the most aughful manner reflecting on the cituation of our familys and property in the hands of such a desperate set of men." Harsh words from a fellow American!

To release the United States government from responsibility, Frémont drew up his resignation. However, this did not save him from court-martial or his government from responsibility. Kit Carson, Lucien Maxwell, Alex Godey, Dick Owens, and the Delawares were as yet not in the regular army and were therefore not subject to any government orders—except from Frémont. It would take many months for his resignation to reach Washington and then more months for it to be acted upon.

The war with Mexico was accelerated. From Sonoma, Frémont recruited 160 men to march to San Rafael Mission for the purpose of attacking forces under the command of the Mexican Captain Joachim de la Torre, who had just violated all ethics of war by butchering ("with knives") two of Commander Ide's scouts, Fowler and Cowie. Frémont, Gillespie, Kit, and the men were infuriated at the atrocities committed by Captain Torre, and on May 28 they were at San Rafael, waiting upon revenge, with Frémont's orders that no quarter should be given and no prisoners taken. Irving B. Richman describes the scene:

> While the Frémont group waited a boat was seen approaching from San Pablo. This boat Kit Carson with a squad was sent to intercept. It landed at Point San Pedro, and three strangers having embarked, Carson and his men left their horses, advanced, took careful aim and shot them down. The victims proved to be Francisco and Ramon de Haro of San Francisco, and José de los Berreyesa, an aged ranchero of Santa Clara. An eye witness of the affair, Jasper O'Farrell, stated in 1856 that Carson asked Frémont whether he should make prisoners of the strangers, and that the lieutenant, waving his hand, replied, "I have no room for prisoners."

When the affair came up for discussion in the Senate of the United States, Senator Benton, Frémont's father-in-law, tried to excuse the act by saying: "In return for the murder of Cowie and Fowler, three of the de la Torre's men being taken, were shot."

The brunt of the hostile criticism for this tragic affair was directed at Kit and Frémont, as well it might be. Edwin L. Sabin sums up the situation by saying: "This was not like Carson, trained though he had been in the exigencies of frontier warfare where no quarter was given nor expected. Frémont glosses over the circumstances, laying it at the door of 'my scouts, mainly Delawares.' . . . But Frémont's company were supposed to be aiding the cause of civilization, of 'liberty, virtue, and literature,' under 'favor of Heaven' (as appealed the Bear flag proclamation), and this wanton killing, without accusation or any trial, never can be justified."

Frémont, Kit, and eleven others "crossed the Golden Gate straits for the Castillo of San Joachim" in a boat borrowed from the American ship *Moscow*. They reached Fort Point just in time to see a group of horsemen escaping toward Yerba Buena. Stepp, the gunsmith, spiked some of the fourteen guns, long brass Spanish cannons, and took shots at the horsemen, all of whom escaped into the hills.

On July 4, they arrived once more at Sonoma, where they celebrated Independence Day with salutes and a dance in the evening. Part of the celebration was to solemnize the organization that day of the California Battalion of Mounted Riflemen, boasting 225 men, John C. Frémont, commanding. Among the members were Kit Carson, Lieutenant Gillespie, Henry L. Ford, Granville P. Swift, Richard Owens, John Grigsby, John Sears, and William B. Ide, who had been the commander of the Sonoma garrison.

The conquest of California, in which Frémont and Kit were destined to play a major part, had begun. The ships *Portsmouth*, out of San Francisco, and *Savannah*, lying below Monterey, were standing by with orders to defend the Americans in case of hostilities. Commodore John D. Sloat, commander of the *Savannah*, had orders from Secretary of the Navy George Bancroft to watch the course of events in California and at the proper time to raise the American flag. But Commodore Sloat was much better at watching than he was at acting. "Your anxiety not to do wrong has led you into a most unfortunate and unwarranted activity," Secretary

Bancroft wrote to Sloat when he learned of the Commodore's hesitation. But Sloat still hesitated, although he had learned of General Taylor's victories and the blockade of Vera Cruz. If Sloat, "knowing that princes and republics alike are liable to ingratitude," seemed overly cautious, Frémont must have seemed impetuous indeed, raising the American flag so prematurely and taking such a bold stand by land.

The growing evidence of British designs in California might have been a factor in regard to the action which Commodore Sloat decided to take on July 7 when he landed 250 men from the various vessels of his squadron. The landing took place at Monterey, and at ten o'clock "the flag, in charge of Lieutenant Edward Higgins, was raised on the flagstaff of the Custom House, and the Proclamation of Occupation was read by Purser Rodman M. Price in Spanish and in English, before our own force and the assembled citizens of the place, from the porch of the Custom House."

Although on July 7, 1846, California was formally annexed to the United States, there was much fighting to be done and the battle was far from being won. Two days later, on July 9, the Stars and Stripes were raised at San Francisco by Lieutenant J. W. Revere of the *Portsmouth* and on the same date superseded the Bear Flag at Sonoma. At sunrise of July 11, at Sutter's Fort, to a salute of twenty-one guns, Frémont raised the American flag given to him by Captain J. B. Montgomery of the *Portsmouth*. Then the Frémont group started for Monterey.

Kit learned much later that on July 3, while he was so busy in California, his wife Josefa was in real danger. The demonstrations in Taos were alarming enough to cause George Bent and Tom Boggs to move their families to the protection of Bent's Fort. In addition, they took with them Josefa and her sister, Ignacia Bent, with the three Bent children, the youngest a girl of two or three years, Estafina. John Hatcher accompanied them, his wife being at the fort. As soon as things quieted down, John took Josefa, Ignacia, and his own wife back to Taos.

Lieutenant Revere of the *Portsmouth* gives a lively account of California events in *A Tour of Duty in Calfornia*:

On the tenth day of July, the whole northern district including the Bay of San Francisco, was in possession of the United States, and the principal points garrisoned by our troops. All the Americans, and most of the foreigners took up arms and volunteered *en masse* to defend the American flag which they regarded as the symbol of liberty, emancipation, and regeneration. Proceeding to the principal posts they offered themselves to the American officers as volunteers, without pay or emolument, each man taking with him his trusty rifle and accoutrements. It was a touching evidence of the influence of our free democratic institutions to see these rough old trappers, whose lives had been passed with the Indians and wild beasts, rally around the flag of their native land. . . .

On July 16, the British flagship *Collingwood*, under command of Rear Admiral Sir George Seymour, sailed into port at Monterey. If the American flag had not been flying there, Seymour would have raised the British flag, for he said to Commodore Sloat: "Sloat, if your flag was not flying on shore I should have hoisted mine there."

In the meantime, Frémont and his men made a conspicuous return to Monterey, where their deeds had preceded them. The British were still there and viewed the entry of the buckskin-clad fighters with wonder. Purser Rodman M. Price of the *Cyane* describes the scene:

It was indeed a novel sight—the command, numbering two or three hundred men marching in a square within which was the cattle which they were driving for their subsistence. They were mostly clothed in buckskin and armed with Hawkins [*sic*] rifles. The individuality of each man was very remarkable. When they dismounted, their first care was their rifles. Frémont was the conspicuous figure. Kit Carson and the Indians accompanying him were the objects of much attention.

The Reverend Walter Colton, chaplain of the *Congress*, was more dramatic in his description.

They were two hundred strong all well armed, and have some three hundred extra head of horses in their train. They defiled two abreast, through the principal street of the town. The ground seemed to tremble under their heavy tramp. Their rifles, revolving pistols, and long knives, glittered over the dusky buckskin which enveloped their sinewy limbs, while their untrimmed locks, flowing out from under their foraging caps, and their black beards, with white teeth glittering through, gave them a wild savage aspect. They encamped in the skirts of the woods which overhung the town. The blaze of their campfires, as night came on threw its quivering light into the forest glades and far out at sea. Their sentinels were posted at every exposed point; they sleep in their blankets under the trees, with their arms in their side, ready for the signal shot or stir of the crackling leaf.

Anchored at Monterey were the American ships *Congress*, commanded by Commodore Robert Field Stockton, and the sloop of war *Cyane*, under Captain Samuel F. Du Pont. The Frémont battalion marked time on shore while Commodore Stockton and Frémont discussed the situation. General Castro and his men had escaped to Los Angeles, where they were reported to be organizing men and artillery for an attack on Frémont's group. Frémont told Stockton that he and his men had been too late to catch General Castro by land, so it was agreed that Frémont and his army should travel by sea to San Diego and from there launch an attack on the Mexican general.

While Stockton and Frémont were discussing the proposed attack, rifle shots echoed from the shore. Kit and the other men were astonishing the British officers by shooting Mexican pesos at 150 paces. Their remarkable accuracy kept the Britishers busy replacing coins, and soon most of their coins were shot to pieces.

When Frémont returned from the *Congress*, he felt much better about the escape of General Castro. Stockton had agreed that Frémont had been justified in acting defensively and that there were good grounds for pushing an offensive by land and sea. He assured Frémont that if Commodore Sloat would yield command—which was probable—he, Stockton, would be in accord with Frémont's plans. Sloat, who would have none of Frémont and his ideas (and had said so in plain English when Frémont visited him on the *Sa-*

vannah), did resign on July 21, transferring his broad pennant to the *Levant*, and sailed for Panama on the first lap of his return journey to Washington.

Commodore Stockton, a Princeton man, gladly assumed the responsibility of command and appointed Frémont a major, Lieutenant Gillespie a captain, and enrolled the rest of the mountain men in a unique organization: the Navy Battalion of Mounted Riflemen! Du Pont was impressed by the fighting qualities of Kit, Owens, Godey, the Delawares, and the rest of the Frémont men who came aboard his ship for the journey down the coast.

On July 25, in their new service as a navy battalion attached to the squadron, the Frémont men set sail for San Diego on the *Cyane*. It was a billowy trip by sea, and Kit, who had never been known to be ill, was seasick all the way and vowed that thereafter he would travel only on the back of a horse or mule. The Reverend Colton, who had watched with amusement as the mountain men boarded the ship, now made this accurate statement: "The wind is fresh, they are by this time cleverly sea-sick, and lying about the deck in a spirit of resignation that would satisfy the non-resistant principles of a Quaker. Two or three resolute old women might tumble the whole lot of them into the sea."

San Diego gave the battalion a friendly reception and assisted them in finding horses. At the end of a week, the riflemen were outfitted and ready to ride on to Los Angeles, where General Castro and Governor Pio Pico were camped on the outskirts with more than five hundred men. Before leaving, Frémont detached some eighty Marines and forty volunteers to garrison San Diego.

In constant expectation of an attack, Frémont and his battalion rode on, but they met with no demonstration of any kind. Outside Los Angeles they were joined by Stockton and his Marines, who had been waiting on the *Congress* off Los Angeles. The road was empty. General Castro and Governor Pio Pico had rapidly retreated toward Mexico when they learned that U. S. Marines had landed near Los Angeles and that Frémont and Kit Carson were on their way to occupy Los Angeles.

On August 13, the combined forces of Frémont and Stockton

entered the town and took possession without firing a shot; it was more like an Army-Navy parade than a conquest. In four days, California was declared a territory of the United States. Commodore Stockton issued the proclamation on August 17, appointed himself governor of California, Frémont military governor, and Gillespie "Commandant of the Southern District with headquarters at Los Angeles." Then the Commodore sailed away.

Late in June, 1846, unknown to Kit and Frémont, the third division of the United States Army, designated as the Army of the West, had left Fort Leavenworth under the command of General Stephen Watts Kearny with 300 men of the regular army and a cavalry regiment under Colonel Alexander W. Doniphan, who had with him in addition to the regiment some 500 volunteers, making a total of 1,700 men. Colonel Sterling Price followed with another division of 1,800 men. New Mexico and Arizona, except that they were part of the territory to be acquired, figured very little in the preliminaries of the proposed conquest. (New Mexico, first to be conquered, retained a smoldering resentment in regard to American rule which eventually resulted in the 1847 Taos revolt.)

General Kearny's original instructions of June 3, 1846, from the Secretary of War advised him, in the event he took possession of New Mexico and California, to continue in employment all officers friendly to the United States. "All officers," said the Secretary of War, "would be required to take the oath of allegiance to the United States, and any arbitrary restrictions existing should be abolished." General Kearny was given full authority to establish temporary civil governments in acquired territories and was further ordered to assure the people that they would be protected, if loyal, and that it was the wish of the United States to provide them with a free government with the least possible delay.

When the Army of the West reached Bent's Fort and started on the long, dry march to Las Vegas on August 2, Governor Armijo's spies relayed to him at Santa Fe exaggerated accounts of the American army. Armijo called a meeting of Mexican officials to discuss plans for defense; it resulted in a bombastic proclamation, issued by Armijo, to the effect that all citizens were required to render "reserveless sacrifices to protect our country," and so forth. Governor Armijo pointed out that the trouble with the United States, which had been managed with "dignity and decorum by the Supreme Magistrate of our Republic," had not been satisfactorily concluded as demanded by the "unquestionable rights of Mexico over the usurped territory of Texas, and for that reason, it has been indispensably necessary to suspend the diplomatic relations with the rejected minister and envoy extraordinary from the North American government."

And now the Army of the West was marching toward New Mexico. Already diplomatic representatives had been sent out ahead of it to ascertain how the Mexicans and those Americans living in New Mexico felt about American rule. From Bent's Fort, Lieutenant Decourcy and twenty men were sent to Taos to "feel the pulse of Pueblos and the Mexican citizens"; Captain Cooke, with twelve men, was dispatched in advance as "a sort of ambassador" to treat with Governor Armijo for the peaceful submission of eastern New Mexico and to escort James Magoffin, who had been given a secret mission in Santa Fe.

With General Kearny was Antoine Robidoux as interpreter and William Bent, who commanded a company of spies; Tom Fitzpatrick (who later took over Kit's dispatches at Socorro) was the guide. On August 14, General Kearny reached Las Vegas (New Mexico), where he made a speech from a housetop, absolving the people from their allegiance to Armijo and promising protection to the life, property, and religion of all who submitted peacefully to the new order. The alcalde and others were induced to take an oath of allegiance to the United States and were continued in office.

From Las Vegas, Kearny went to Tecolote, San Miguel del Vado, and then, on the seventeenth, to Santa Fe, where he was met most cordially by Acting Governor Juan Bautista Vigil y Alared. Armijo had fled to the south.

The Stars and Stripes were raised on the Santa Fe plaza at sunset and saluted with thirteen guns. That night, General Kearny slept in the old Palace of the Governors while his army camped near by. On the following days, the General assembled the people on the plaza, where he made his proclamation through an interpreter, and the Mexican officers took the required oath of allegiance. The program was much the same as the earlier ones at Las Vegas and San Miguel, when the people were assured of protection for "their lives, property and religion, not only against American depredators, but against the Mexican nation, Governor Armijo, and their Indian foes."

On August 19, Lieutenant Emory selected a site for a fort; four days later work began on Fort Marcy, an adobe structure overlooking the city from an adjoining hill. The next few days were given over to the organization of a civil government and a tour of Tomé to investigate unfounded rumors of troops marching from Mexico.

Three days later, on August 22, General Kearny issued the "Kearny Code of Laws." The laws were compiled by Willard P. Hall under the direction of Colonel Doniphan (who was a lawyer) and translated into Spanish by Dr. David Waldo. They were based on the statutes of Missouri and Texas and on the Livingston Code. The Kearny Code, arranged alphabetically, "covered such subjects as: attachments, courts and judicial powers, costs, crime, and punishments, executions, fees, guardians, jurors, laws and practice at law, records, revenue, sheriffs, treasury, and witness." The Code was put into effect immediately and was used until 1886.

General Kearny appointed Kit Carson's brother-in-law, Charles Bent, as civil governor of the territory; Mrs. Bent's cousin, Donciano Vigil, was secretary of state, and Richard Dallam was appointed marshal. Francis P. Blair, Jr., served as U.S. attorney, Charles Blummer as treasurer, and Eugene Leitzendorfer as auditor. The Superior Court judges were Carlos Beaubien, Santiago Abreu, Joab Houghton, and Antonio José Otero.

On the twenty-fifth of September, the Army of the West set out by the Gila route for California with three hundred dragoons. On the eve of its departure, General Kearny gave a grand ball for the new officers and the civilians of Santa Fe and vicinity.

IO ★ Guide to Kearny

ON SEPTEMBER 5, 1846, with fifteen men (among whom was his old trail partner, Lucien Maxwell), Kit set out from Los Angeles with dispatches. His destination was Washington, and he promised to return in 120 days—60 days' travel each way! Kit held high hopes of seeing his wife in Taos, if only for a day, or even a few hours. He would be proud to tell her that he had been appointed lieutenant on special courier duty.

The trail was not entirely new to Kit, for it was the same one he had taken with Ewing Young: via the Mohave Desert and the Gila country and on to Taos. Kit and his men rode hard through the pass and down to the desert in a cloud of dust, stopping only for brief rests. The Gila was reached and ascended, and within ten miles of the copper mines where Kit once worked under Robert McKnight, an Apache village was sighted about ten o'clock one morning. Kit consulted with Maxwell and decided to make camp and ask for a parley. He told the Apaches that they, the whites, were friends and wished to trade animals. The Apaches agreed to trade, and Kit and his men made camp near by, in an advantageous place, to be sure, in case of sudden attack by the Indians. All that day they traded with the Apaches and early the next morning started toward Taos. From the Apaches, Kit learned that an American officer known to the Indians as "Horse Chief of the Long Knives" had taken New Mexico from the Mexicans. This meant that Kit's trail through New Mexico was open, with no Mexicans to fight on the way.

On October 6, 1846, below Socorro on the Río Grande del Norte, the Carson party met General Stephen Watts Kearny and the Army of the West. The dragoons under the Horse Chief were eleven days out of Santa Fe and had covered 150 miles, while Kit and his men were nearly thirty days out of Los Angeles and had covered 800 miles, wearing out 34 mules in the process! Thomas Fitzpatrick, Kearny's guide, did not know the Gila route to California. Kit, who did know it, had thus appeared at an opportune time. Captain Abraham R. Johnston, who later rode to his death at San Pasqual, described the meeting in his journal:

> October 6, marched at 9, having great trouble in getting some of the ox carts from the Mexicans; after marching about three miles we met Kit Carson, direct on express from California with a mail of public letters for Washington; he informs us that Colonel Frémont is probably civil and military governor of California.

This message must have greatly surprised General Kearny. After questioning Carson at length, the General told him that inasmuch as he had just traversed the country through which the Army of the West was to pass, he wanted Kit to lead the way to California. Kit's quick reply was that he was pledged to go to Washington with mail and dispatches and that he wouldn't think of not fulfilling his promise. General Kearny, of course, told him that he would relieve him of his duties and send Fitzpatrick instead. Reluctantly, Carson considered this order from Kearny.

Kit was relieved of his dispatch duty by Fitzpatrick, and although Kit objected, Kearny remained firm in his decision: Carson would guide the dragoons to California. The General's argument was that Fitzpatrick could take the dispatches for safe delivery within the prescribed time limit, and the good of the service demanded that Kit guide the column through this country where Fitzpatrick was unfamiliar with the devious route. Later, Kit confided to Senator Benton: "I let him take me and I guided him through, but went with great hesitation, and had prepared everything to escape the night before we started, and made my intention known to Maxwell who urged me not to do so."

There was sympathy for Kit in the camp below Socorro because of his disappointment at not being able to go on to Taos to see his family. General Kearny and his officers and men were disappointed, too, but for another reason: there were no battles to be fought in California, no laurels to be won; the government had already been established, and the long desert march offered nothing but hardship—or so they thought. So Kearny detached three of his five companies, about two hundred men, and sent them back to Santa Fe.

General Kearny had another reason for sending the troops back, for just about a week after he had left Santa Fe, he had been overtaken by a messenger bearing the disconcerting news that the Navahos were raiding again. Kearny had promised the New Mexicans that under the American flag the Navahos would not be allowed or permitted to make raids. A return message to Colonel Doniphan consisted of orders to settle the trouble with the Navahos before marching south to join General John E. Wool, who was supposedly advancing on Chihuahua from Texas. Kearny sent other messages by Tom Boggs, who had left Santa Fe with the dragoons as one of the Kearny scouts. Maxwell, who was to go to Washington with Kit, continued on to Taos to see his wife, Luz. He delivered news of Kit to Josefa.

The next morning, Tom Fitzpatrick rode east with the dispatches, and the occasion was one of much perplexity for Lieutenant Carson. The immediate conflict of authority and the conflict yet to come— between Kearny and Frémont—were things that Kit, with his simple, straightforward ideas of honesty and square dealings, was never able to understand.

On October 18, Kit was leading the Army of the West, now consisting of some one hundred enlisted men, two howitzers, and six large, eight-mule wagons, as it proceeded from the Río Grande toward California. For the march westward, General Kearny had retained the artist John Mix Stanley (of beaver-day fame), Antoine Robidoux, François Menard, and some twenty-one officers and civilians. All of the enlisted men were mounted on mules, the officers and General Kearny on horses, and the baggage was packed in the mule-drawn wagons. The two howitzers, in command of Lieutenant John W. Davidson, found hard going in the sand and rocks. After a week on the road, Kit had told Kearny that with all the excess baggage, it would take them four months to reach California. The General asked Kit's advice, got it, and followed it. He abandoned the carts and wagons; the essential baggage was packed on the mules.

A day's march from the copper mines in New Mexico, Lieutenant William H. Emory records, they met Mangas Coloradas, or Red Sleeves, the Apache chief. Red Sleeves brought twenty of his warriors and some women to visit the Army of the West. The Indians were dressed in the manner of the Mexicans, wearing wide drawers, moccasins turned up at the toes, and leggings to the knees, with sharp knives inserted in the outside folds of the leggings, ready for quick use. They were armed with fusils, lances, and bows and arrows. Their long hair floated in the wind.

Red Sleeves spoke to General Kearny at length, assuring him of friendship, and the General gave the Apache chief a paper stating that he had talked to him and that the Apaches under Red Sleeves had pledged perpetual friendship for the Americans. Other chiefs came into camp, and some of them petitioned the General to make raids in Mexico and let them join the Americans for the plunder. One chief said: "You fight for the soul, we fight for plunder; so we will agree perfectly; their people [the Mexicans] are bad Christians; let us chastise them as they deserve." General Kearny, of course, rejected their proposals, and they all went away.

Kit led the column through the Mimbres River country toward the head of the Gila. They followed the Gila to its mouth and crossed the Colorado River below that point on November 22.

Lieutenant Emory, one of two topographical engineers with Kearny, describes a tense moment on the march:

The day was warm, the dust oppressive, and the march [of] twenty-two miles [was] very long for our jaded and ill-fed brutes. The general's horse gave out and he was obliged to mount his mule. Most of the men were on foot, and a small party, composed chiefly of the general and staff, were a long way ahead of the struggling column, when

155

as we approached the end of our day's journey, every man was straightened in his saddle by our suddenly falling on a camp, which from the trail, we estimated at 1,000 men. . . .

Kit scouted ahead and found fresh signs of mess fires and loose horses in large numbers. He reported that it was not a military camp; some of the officers had thought that perhaps General Castro, having recruited in Mexico, was on his way back to California. Since the camp itself had not been sighted yet, it was decided that Lieutenant Emory and Kit should take fifteen men and, under cover of darkness, ascertain who the men in the camp were and what they were doing in this part of the country.

Reporting back after the operation, Lieutenant Emory told General Kearny that they were humble horse traders on their way from California to the Sonora (Mexico) market with five hundred animals. The chief of the party, as Emory described him, was "a tall, venerable-looking man [who] represented himself to be a poor employee of several rich men engaged in supplying the Sonora market with horses." The Lieutenant later learned, regretfully, that this man was "no less a personage than José María Leguna, a colonel in the Mexican army."

The next day, November 23, before the Kearny column moved out, Lieutenant Emory brought a Mexican to General Kearny for questioning. He proved to be a carrier of mail bound for Mexico, and the letters revealed the fact that there had been a counter-revolution in California on October 15. Americans in Los Angeles, Santa Barbara, and a few other places had been driven out. Antoine Robidoux learned from the letters that his brother, Louis, who had been appointed alcalde by the Americans, had been jailed by the Mexicans.

Here was news indeed for an invading army with only a third of its members present, and those in a deplorable condition for fighting. That night there was much discussion in camp about what had happened in California during the past month—since October 15. Where were Frémont and Gillespie? Where was Commodore Stockton? On November 25, the Army of the West moved on toward the dry-wash desert of southeastern California, where, ninety miles away, were the mountains whose western slopes faced the Pacific. The wild horses they had obtained from the Mexicans were not of desert breed; they soon failed and died. The enlisted men, unaccustomed to the rough life of the desert, were sunburned and some of them barefooted—a sorry-looking lot to try to retake California.

On November 30, they arrived in the rough and arid foothills of the eastern part of what is now San Diego County. This route was lower than the one Kit took across the Mohave when he started with the dispatches, but his idea was to cut down to San Diego and miss Los Angeles and its Mexican troops. At that time he did not know that San Diego had not been taken by the Mexicans, and his choice was the Carson luck again. It was the trail traveled by couriers, traders, and soldiers between Los Angeles and Sonora of northern Mexico, the trail taken by Davy Jackson and his party in 1831, convoying their pack loads of silver, and it became the trail for the Butterfield Southern Overland and the Banning stages between Fort Yuma and the California Divide.

Oppressed by the burning sun and the stinging wind that cracked and blistered their skin, the men climbed on through the hills with but one horse and a few mules. On December 2, they arrived at the ranch of the pioneer settler, Jonathan T. Warner, in the valley of Agua Caliente; sixty miles to the southwest was San Diego, and Los Angeles lay some one hundred miles to the northwest.

Warner was in San Diego and unable to get back through enemy lines to the ranch, Kit was informed by the ranch hands, who also told him that the Mexicans held all of California except San Diego, Monterey, and San Francisco. Kearny asked about horses and was told that there were not enough horses on the ranch to mount the column, but an Indian *vaquero* volunteered information that about fifteen miles farther along the road to Los Angeles were horses herded for the use of Mexican General José María Flores.

Kit and Lieutenant Davidson were ordered to mount twenty-five men on ranch horses and capture as many of the Mexican's horses as they could without loss to themselves. They set out at dark that same day and rode hard for a place called Aguanga. In a surprise attack they captured most of the herd, but many of the horses were wild and had never been broken to the bridle, making them undesirable as cavalry mounts. About noon the next day, Kit and Davidson returned to the Kearny camp with the captured animals.

While Kit and Lieutenant Davidson were away, Edward Stokes, an Englishman who had a ranch at Santa Isabel, about fifteen miles out of San Diego, rode into General Kearny's camp. He said that he was "neutral in this war" but offered to take a message to Commodore Stockton the next morning when he went to San Diego. In a letter General Kearny informed Stockton of his position and asked the latter to open communication with him; he also told Stockton—and this was the big thing—that he had orders from the Secretary of War to make himself governor and that he was the commander-in-chief of California as soon as he had conquered it!

Shortly after Kit left California in September, Lieutenant Gillespie was ousted at Los Angeles. He and his group fled to San Pedro and boarded the merchantman *Vandalia*. When the *Savannah* arrived from San Francisco, Gillespie and his men joined 350 sailors and marines in an attempt to retake Los Angeles, but Colonel José Antonio Carrillo and General Flores, with 100 cavalrymen, so harassed the trudging Americans that they were forced to retreat with a dozen casualties, killed and wounded. The letters intercepted by General Kearny had not all been Mexican exaggeration.

At the time, Colonel Frémont was in the valley of the Sacramento recruiting volunteers. A hasty message brought by Midshipman Edward Fitzgerald Beale sought out Frémont at the Suisun Bay. With his California Battalion augmented by three companies of newly arrived emigrants and two pieces of artillery, Frémont set out for Los Angeles on November 30. Meanwhile, Theodore Talbot and nine men escaped to the mountains, where they hid out for a month before slipping off to Monterey. At San Diego, Ezekiel Merritt and his men, having fled from Los Angeles, found protection on a whaler in the bay. Stockton was in San Francisco at the time of the uprising, but as soon as he heard what was happening, he boarded the *Congress* and picked up the Gillespie party on the way. They had been kept in Los Angeles Bay by Mexican lancers in the hills.

On December 3, Commodore Stockton was astonished to learn from the letter delivered by Edward Stokes that the Army of the West, under Brigadier General Stephen Watts Kearny, was at Warner's Ranch:

> Dec. 2, 1846. Sir: I this afternoon reached here, escorted by a party of the 1st regiment of dragoons. I came by order of the pres. of the U. S. . . . Your express by Mr. Carson was met on the Del Norte, and your mail must have reached Washington ten days since.

A deferred surprise was in store for Stockton when he learned that Carson was with General Kearny. Stating that Mr. Stokes would guide the contacting party from San Diego, Kearny asked for information about the affairs in California as quickly as possible.

The Commodore's answer to Kearny was that he was sending a detachment of mounted riflemen and field pieces under command of Captain Gillespie and that there was a "rebel camp" of 150 men not far away. He suggested a surprise attack and added that a deserter from this camp would give Kearny the correct location.

On the cold rainy morning of December 4, Kearny's dragoons resumed the march to San Diego. The last entry in Captain Johnston's Journal was made that night, two days before he was killed:

> Marched at 9, and took the route for San Diego, to communicate with the naval forces and to establish our dept., not knowing yet in what state we would find the country. Marched fifteen miles in a rain, cold and disagreeable, and camped at St. Isabelle, a former ranch of San Diego mission, now, by hook or by crook in the possession of an Englishman named Stokes; here hospitality was held out to us—Stokes having gone to San Diego. We ate heartily of stewed and roast mutton and tortillas. We heard of a party of Californians of 80 men encamped at a distance from this; but the informant varied 16 to 30 miles in his accounts, rendering it too uncertain to make a dash in a dark stormy night; so we slept till morning.

Captain Gillespie's command consisted of a navy squad under Lieutenant Beale (he was now acting lieutenant) and Midshipman James M. Duncan and twenty-six mounted riflemen of the California Battalion under command of Captain Samuel Gibson, who had been a sergeant in the Sonoma campaign. Beale's lieutenant was Alex Godey, Kit's long-time friend. Gillespie had ten men from the *Congress*, along with a brass cannon which had been brought down the coast from Sutter's Fort.

Gillespie was burning with revenge to take Los Angeles. It was still raining on the morning of December 5 when he and his group marched to meet Kearny, who was on his way from one Stokes *rancheria* at San Ysabel to another one at Santa Maria. The two groups made contact and marched on toward Santa Maria. Lieutenant Emory says they "arrived at the *rancheria* after dark, when we heard that the enemy was in force nine miles distance, and not finding any grass about the *rancheria* we pushed on and encamped in a canon two miles below."

General Kearny resolved to continue along the main road to San Diego, arguing that he was not about to sit and wait for the enemy in the hills to gather forces, cut him off, and starve him out. Lieutenant Tom Hammond, with a small party, was sent to reconnoiter the enemy's position. He reported that the Mexicans were encamped "about three leagues further on" at an Indian village called San Pasqual and that they would have to be dealt with if the General wished to march to San Diego by the main road. Kearny decided to attack early the next morning.

Captain Johnston and twelve dragoons, mounted on the best of the horses and guided by Kit Carson, were to lead the advance guard for the attack on Captain Andrés Pico and his eighty horsemen. Captain Pico, brother of former Mexican Governor Don Pio Pico, had arrived the day before for the purpose of trying to cut off the advance of Captain Gillespie, who, he had heard, was in the hills near San Diego looking for horses. Captain Pico paid scant attention to the rumors that a large body of Americans was advancing along the road; he therefore did not expect when he went to San Pasqual, to meet any men except Gillespie's.

General Kearny, escorted by Lieutenant Emory and Lieutenant William H. Warner and four of his topographical-service men, followed the advance guard. Behind Kearny was the main body of fifty dragoons commanded by Captain Ben Moore and Lieutenant Hammand, many of them mounted on mules. Following the dragoons were the Gillespie-Gibson riflemen, and after them, in charge of Lieutenant John Davidson, came the two howitzers and their crews. Major Swords brought up the rear with sixty men—a force of dragoons, riflemen, and civilians—guarding the baggage train with the four-pounder.

The march to San Pasqual was a slow one; the air was cold and heavy with moisture. Within a mile of the Mexican camp, the column was discovered by Pico's spies. The advance guard had now been joined by General Kearny and his staff. The General ordered the men to trot their horses, then charge when the enemy camp was sighted.

Thundering down the hill came Captain Johnston's advance guard, the remaining companies following. Suddenly Kit's horse stumbled and threw him headlong, breaking his rifle. The Pico group stood their ground after Pico's sharp command to hold fast and fight when he saw only twenty men charge down the hill. The Mexicans, shouting "Viva California!" drew their muskets to send a volley of shots into the American ranks. Captain Johnston, shot through the center of the forehead, fell dead, and a dragoon, badly wounded, pitched forward from his saddle. Kit Carson, lying still while his companions passed over him, finally saved himself by crawling from under the horses. He grabbed a dead dragoon's carbine and seeing an unmounted horse near by, caught it and remounted to join the battle.

Captains Gillespie and Moore, followed by their men, raced in to join the fight. The Californians, having inflicted their worst upon the advance guard, quickly fled. After running a half-mile, they suddenly wheeled, lances poised, to meet the Americans. The ensuing battle was terrible. General Kearny was lanced in two places and would have been killed had not Lieutenant Emory shot his assailant. Lieutenant Warner was lanced three times, and François

Menard was killed. Conspicuous on his white horse, Captain Moore had been stalked to death by Leandro Osuna, and Lieutenant Tom Hammond died that day from sword wounds he received trying to save Captain Moore. Captains Gibson and Gillespie both received lance wounds, as did Antoine Robidoux and ten others.

It was a battle in which it was proved that the lance, wielded from horseback by men of agility, was a highly effective weapon. Of Kearny's enlisted men, ten dragoons were killed, including two sergeants, two corporals, a private of the Gibson company of volunteers, and an employee in the topographical service; wounded were one sergeant, one bugler, and nine privates of the dragoons. (Dr. A. J. Griffin gave eighteen as the total killed and fifteen or seventeen wounded.) Many who survived had received from two to ten lance wounds. Kit, with his usual luck, came out unscathed; so did Alex Godey. The American army had fought with desperate valor against heavy odds.

When the howitzers arrived, the enemy again fled. One of the mules, hitched to a cannon, ran into the Mexican lines, dragging the cannon along, but, fortunately, the Pico force did not know how to use it. Technically, one might say that this was a victory for the Americans, who remained in possession of the field, but practically, it was also a victory for the Mexicans, who had inflicted more damage.

The Army of the West camped on the battlefield a short distance beyond San Pasqual. Here Dr. Griffin spent the day dressing wounds. General Kearny, whose wounds had bled profusely, fainted, and the command devolved to Captain Henry S. Turner. Of the dead, all had been lanced to death with the exception of Captain Johnston and a dragoon, both of whom were killed by bullets.

Captain Turner immediately sent Lieutenant Godey, Private Burgess, and two other volunteer riflemen to San Diego to ask for wheeled vehicles for the wounded, as well as for supplies and reinforcements. Stokes was already on his way to see Stockton and report the battle, or what he had heard of it.

After nightfall the Americans buried their dead, and with the sunrise of another morning the column moved on, with General Kearny again commanding. On the hills hovered the California lancers, waiting for an opportunity to attack. After a nine-mile march, the Kearny men reached the San Bernardo Ranch, where they watered their animals and fed on chicken. There was no grass, however, so the column turned south toward the San Bernardo River bottoms. Its makeshift ambulances, constructed of poles and blankets, grated along on the ground, the jolting adding to the sufferings of the wounded.

They had scarcely gone a mile when the Mexican cavalry unit dashed in at full speed to attack their rear. The Americans were on a hill, and the Mexicans made a desperate effort to drive them from it but were forced to retire in face of heavy fire from Gibson's volunteers. The Americans moved up, losing some cattle they had brought along. They had to occupy the hill and cease their advance or be flanked again and again as they marched, thereby inviting the loss of their packs and their wounded. They would have to stay on the hill until the wounded could care for themselves and help could come. The little water they could find was obtained by digging, and there was no forage for the animals. The next morning, the temperature was one degree above freezing, and there was a heavy frost to add to the discomfort of the wounded men.

Kearny was now concerned about Godey and his men, doubting that they had reached San Diego yet. On the ninth, Captain Pico sent up a flag of truce with the announcement that he had captured the four Americans, whom he would exchange for four of his own men. But the Americans had only one prisoner to exchange.

Lieutenant Beale was sent down to arrange the exchange, with instructions to get Godey back if possible. Captain Pico told Beale that Godey was too valuable; another man would have to do—Burgess perhaps. Beale showed no emotion; Burgess was the least intelligent of them all. Lieutenant Emory was sent with the one prisoner to make the exchange.

Burgess related to Kearny that they had reached San Diego and that Godey had received dispatches from Commodore Stockton to bring to Kearny but that he did not know what was in them. On their way back to camp, they were captured by Captain Pico's men, but before the capture, Godey had managed to cache the dispatches under a tree. That was all Burgess could tell Kearny.

The hours dragged on; some of the wounded men were better. The thirsty mules and horses continued to bolt to find water and grass, and the Pico men would rope them as soon as they came within range. Again Kearny decided to send to San Diego for help. This time Lieutenant Beale offered to take his Indian servant and make the trip, but General Kearny told him he should also take another man. Beale requested Kit Carson. Kearny refused to let Carson go on the plea that he was needed there. Beale then said that he would try it with only his Indian boy. Kearny replied: "In that case you may have Carson."

A brief preparation for the trip was made. Each took a rifle, a revolver, a sharp knife, a canteen of water. General Kearny asked what was in the supply tent and was told "a handful of flour." The General ordered the flour be baked into a loaf for the Lieutenant, but Beale refused to take the food, saying he would find his own food, which he did. He went to a burned-out fire pit and scraped from the ashes some peas and grains of corn and put these in his pockets. Kit and the Indian provided some "dried mule beef," which the latter had found in one of the officer's tents.

At dusk the three started on their thirty-mile journey to San Diego. Pico had learned from Godey that Kit Carson was with the Americans and had thrown a triple guard around the hill where the Americans camped. He also kept a patrol moving, warning his men that the Americans had better not escape.

In order not to outline themselves against the night sky as they descended the hill, Kit, Beale, and the Indian crawled on their stomachs past the first row of guards. Kit and Beale removed their shoes and discarded their canteens in order to crawl more quietly past the next row of sentries. They tucked their shoes in their belts, but long before they were safe beyond the sentries they had lost them. Their feet were burning with cactus spines. They crept over the ground so close to their enemies that at times they could have reached out and touched them. When they were almost out of danger, one of the roving sentinels rode up, dismounted, and lighted a cigarette. Kit, who was ahead of Beale, reached back and softly kicked his companion as a warning to lie perfectly still and flat on the ground. After what must have seemed hours, the Mexican remounted and rode away. It was during an interval such as this one that Lieutenant Beale, worn by mental and physical torture, said to Kit, "We are done. Let's jump and fight it out!" But the courageous and more experienced Kit answered, "No! I have been in worse places than this."

At last they were beyond the guards and in open country, with trees here and there. They walked as rapidly as possible, and morning found them well on their way to San Diego. They left the high ground and took to the canyons. Their feet became swollen and cut and their throats parched, but they plodded on toward their goal. The Mexican patrols encircling San Diego had to be evaded before they could reach Commodore Stockton.

Back at the camp on the hill, the Americans passed another miserable night with their wounded. The one who seemed most likely not to survive the night was Robidoux, but early in the morning he awakened Lieutenant Emory to ask if he smelled coffee, expressing his belief that "if he had a cup of that wonderful beverage it might save his life." Knowing that there had been no coffee in camp for many days, Emory thought Robidoux was out of his head, or dreaming. It was thus with great surprise that the Lieutenant also began to smell coffee and discovered that his servant had obtained some coffee somewhere and was brewing it over a small fire. It was with great pleasure that he gave Robidoux a cup of coffee. Robidoux always claimed that with that cup of hot coffee, his hope for life returned.

Near San Diego on the evening of December 9, Kit, Beale, and the Indian boy separated to take three different routes—to assure that at least one of them would arrive safely. In San Diego at nine o'clock that evening, Commodore Stockton had just started the relief force on its night march to Kearny's rescue when a sentry challenged a lone Indian boy. It was Beale's servant. He had barely finished telling his story (in Spanish) to Commodore Stockton when

Lieutenant Beale was carried in, partially delirious. Beale's uniform was in tatters and his feet were cut and badly swollen. Kit arrived at three o'clock the next morning; in order to assure success, he had taken the longest route. His feet were so badly torn and swollen that he could not walk for many days. The Indian boy died, and Beale did not fully recover his health for two years. He lay in sick bay on the *Congress* for a month before he was able to hold a pen to write.

On December 10, in Kearny's camp on the hill, Sergeant Cox died and was buried in a deep grave piled with stones to proof it against coyotes and wolves. That same day, the Mexicans drove a herd of wild horses through Kearny's camp, hoping to stampede Kearny's animals. The charge was turned aside, and two or three of the wild horses were shot. They proved to be good food for the hungry Americans, who had been eating their own mounts.

When Dr. Griffin announced that all except two of the wounded could ride a horse, General Kearny decided to cut his way through to the coast, regardless of the cost. All excess baggage was burned, and while they were waiting for daybreak, they heard horses approaching. It was the 180 men, under Lieutenant Gray, sent by Stockton on the night Carson and Beale arrived in San Diego. They marched all night on the ninth, hid during the day, and resumed their march that night. The reinforcements spent the remainder of the night distributing provisions and clothing to Kearny's men.

Captain Pico left his cattle in the field and hastily retreated. The Americans gathered the stray horses and cattle and marched for San Diego, where, upon their arrival, they found Beale in a bad way and Kit threatened with the loss of his feet.

The village of San Diego consisted of a few adobe houses, many with adobe floors and only a few with plank floors. Kearny was impressed by the comforts of the *Congress*, where he visited Kit and discussed affairs with Commodore Stockton. It was impossible to convince General Kearny that California had been conquered long before he arrived, especially after the battles he had just fought. He questioned Stockton's right to the governorship, but Stockton insisted upon conserving his titular rank of commander-in-chief and civil governor in this province, which he himself claimed by conquest.

Kearny's wounded were taken to sick bay on the *Congress* while Kearny and Stockton made plans to gather their forces in preparation for the march on Los Angeles. Kit was in sick bay on his birthday, and during the nineteen days he spent in San Diego (December 10–29, 1846), Lieutenant Beale remained very ill.

Frémont's position was unknown to Commodore Stockton, who said: "During the entire period, I have not received any intelligence of the movements of Major Frémont." Nor was Frémont any wiser about the movements of Commodore Stockton, and he certainly had no idea that General Kearny was on the scene, and of course he had not yet learned that Kit Carson was in San Diego instead of Washington. On Christmas Day, Frémont and his four hundred riflemen, marching south to retake Los Angeles, lost a hundred horses and mules among the ravines during a rainstorm. It was a worse blow than General Flores' small army could have dealt them.

On December 29, Kit, as chief of scouts, left San Diego with the Kearny-Stockton force of four battalions—about 600 men. There were 57 dragoons of the original 110, all afoot; 60 of Gillespie's riflemen; 433 sailors and marines from the three ships in the harbor; 25 Indians and Californians, serving as teamsters and commanded by Captain Henry S. Turner of the dragoons; three engineers; and three medical officers. Captain Archibald H. Gillespie of the Volunteers, Lieutenant William B. Renshaw of the Navy, and Captain J. Zielin of the Marines also joined the effort to retake Los Angeles.

A battery of six field pieces was commanded by Lieutenant Richard L. Tilghman of the Navy. Quartermaster Lieutenant George Minor of the Navy had charge of the wagon train, which consisted of one carriage and ten oxcarts. The wheels of the carts were cross-sections of ties (*carreta* fashion) two inches in diameter. With the men dragging at these awkward vehicles, filled with baggage, and the dragoons walking, it took eight days to advance the 125 miles to Los Angeles—a slow undignified march which did nothing to mitigate the increasingly bad temper of General Kearny.

On the afternoon of January 8, 1847, the little army arrived at "the Paso del Bartolo of the Río San Gabriel," some fifteen miles south of Los Angeles. The Mexicans, under General Flores, assisted by Colonels Andrés Pico and José Carrillo, had chosen a good position on a hill opposite the point where the Americans would have to cross the river. General Kearny ordered a halt while he looked the situation over, remarking about the possibility of quicksand. "Quicksand or no quicksand the guns shall pass over," retorted Stockton, whereupon he gave the order to cross the river.

Inspired by Stockton's courage, Kit and some of the men plunged into the lead. They dragged two field pieces through the knee-deep water to a counterbattery position; a third, commanded by Commodore Stockton, covered the crossing of the column and its "Yankee corral." The five hundred Mexicans fired briskly, then suddenly charged the rear of the column as it crossed the river. Flores' purpose was to cut out the pack and lead horses, but Gillespie and his rear guards turned the Mexicans aside. Another furious charge by the enemy, a countercharge by the Americans, answering with artillery which cleared the hill, and the Battle of San Gabriel was won.

The Mexicans withdrew their forces and the Americans camped for a few hours on the battlefield. Expert horsemen, the Mexicans had, without dismounting, stripped their fallen animals of bridles and saddles and had carried off their dead and wounded. The American casualties were three killed and twelve wounded.

On the morning of the ninth, the Stockton-Kearny forces marched on toward Los Angeles, into the mesa angle between the rivers San Gabriel and San Fernando. Flanking the road to Los Angeles at the Cañada de los Alisos, they found the enemy awaiting them. General Flores opened fire with his two nine-pounders at long range, to which the Americans gave no reply. Flores deployed from higher ground, making a crescent in front of the Americans, who marched into it to silence the Mexican nine-pounders. Kit and his group repulsed the attack on the left flank and Gillespie again protected the rear. Thinking that this was the beginning of a good fight, the Stockton-Kearny group discovered that it was the end, for the enemy had vanished from the battlefield. Thus was won the final battle in the reconquest of California.

It was now three o'clock in the afternoon and the Americans had three men severely wounded; Lieutenant Rowan and Captain Gillespie were slightly bruised by spent bullets. Stockton sized up the situation by saying that "the town is known to have large quantities of wine and *aguardiente*. From previous experience with sailors and dragoons, a night of close contact with such ready pleasures does not promise well for our cause."

The group crossed the Los Angeles River and camped on the right bank some three miles below the town. The next morning, January 10, a flag of truce "was brought into camp by Célis, Avila, and Workman" (one of the brothers to whom Kit was apprenticed in Missouri), who came to intercede in behalf of the Los Angelinos. They told Stockton that no resistance would be made to the Americans and in turn were promised kind treatment and protection.

About noon, the American army entered Los Angeles, directing its march to the plaza with colors flying and a band (of sorts) playing. Captain Gillespie again raised over his quarters the flag which he had been forced to lower four months previously.

The next morning, unknown to Kearny and Stockton, Frémont and his group stopped some twenty miles from Los Angeles, and on January 13, Pico and Carrillo surrendered to Frémont their artillery and arms "to assist and aid in placing the country in a state of peace and tranquility." In return, Frémont guaranteed them "protection of life and property and permission to leave the country without let or hindrance." This was the Treaty of Cahuenga.

On January 14, much to the astonishment of Stockton and Kearny, Frémont and his battalion marched into Los Angeles. In his turn, Frémont must have been doubly surprised to see Kit, whom he had supposed to be in Washington, or even back in Taos by this time.

As soon as Frémont arrived, Kit left General Kearny and joined his former commander. Stockton and his men marched for San

Pedro, where all embarked on a man-of-war for San Diego. Commissions to Frémont as governor and Colonel William H. Russell as secretary of state were issued by Stockton on January 16, but their terms of office actually began on the nineteenth when Commodore Stockton turned over his command upon his departure from Los Angeles. He also suspended General Kearny from the command of the troops conferred on him at San Diego:

> Sir: In answer to your note received this afternoon, I need say but little more than that which I communicated to you in conversation at S. Diego: that Cal. was conquered and a govt put into successful operation; that a copy of the laws made for me for the govt of the territory, and the names of the officers selected to see them faithfully executed, were transmitted to the pres. of the U. S. before your arrival in the territory. I will only add that I cannot do anything, nor desist from doing anything, or alter anything on your demand; which I will submit to the president and ask for your recall. In the mean time you consider yourself suspended from the command of the U. S. forces in this place. Faithfully, your obed, serv. R. F. Stockton, com-in-chief.

Realizing that his authority from the Secretary of War was being ignored by both Frémont and Stockton, Kearny wrote to the Commodore:

> I must for the purpose of preventing collision between us, and possibly a civil war in consequence of it, remain silent for the present, leaving with you the great responsibility of doing that for which you have no authority, and preventing me from complying with the president's orders.

Frémont had been under the command of Stockton before Kearny came to California; naturally, he thought he should continue taking orders from Stockton. On January 17, 1847, he wrote to General Kearny:

> I feel myself, therefore, with great deference to your professional and personal character, constrained to say that, until you and Commodore Stockton adjust between yourselves the question of rank, where I

respectfully think the difficulty belongs, I shall have to report and receive orders, as heretofore, from the Commodore.

To Kit this sounded like logic, reasonable and just. To Kearny it
sounded like a crime punishable by death, and he reported Frémont
to the War Department for mutiny.

At this time the new commander-in-chief of naval forces, Commodore W. B. Shubrick, was approaching Monterey with dispatches
which would break the deadlock and proclaim Kearny supreme in
command in California. These orders directed Kearny to use Frémont in the best way for the public interest if Frémont wished to
remain in California, but if he preferred to leave the territory, he
was to be permitted to do so.

Meanwhile, on January 19, in Taos and its environs, the bloody
revolt which killed Kit's brother-in-law and endangered his wife
broke out, but Kit was not to know of this horror for at least another
sixty days. He remained in Los Angeles with Frémont, who had
taken up his governorship (it lasted less than two troubled months).
At Frémont's request, Lieutenant Beale, still very ill, was brought
to Los Angeles on the *Cyane*, and here he remained until February
25, when he asked permission to accompany Kit east when he took
Frémont's dispatches.

It was fortunate for Kit that at this time of conflict between army
and navy authorities in California he was again detached on express
duty to Washington. Lieutenant Emory was going by way of Panama with Kearny's dispatches, and Lieutenant Gray, with Stockton's
dispatches, was also headed for Washington.

II ★ Revolt in Taos

ARRIVING IN SANTA FE after forty days of travel, Kit was deeply shocked to learn of Governor Bent's death at the hands of insurrectionists. With all haste he turned north to Taos to learn that Josefa and her sister, Mrs. Bent, and her children were safe. The village was still in a state of shock when Kit and Lieutenant Beale rode in from Santa Fe.

On January 14, 1847, Charles Bent, governor for less than three months, had started from Santa Fe to Taos in order to bring his family to the capital. Accompanied by five persons, including Sheriff Stephen Louis Lee, Prefect Cornelio Vigil, and Circuit Attorney J. W. Leal, he reached home on the eighteenth.

A revolt had been planned for December 19, 1846, then postponed until midnight, December 24, but the timely discovery of the plot by American officials had prevented the Mexicans from carrying it out. Governor Bent reported that he had first received information concerning the revolt from Donciano Vigil, secretary of the civil government, on December 17; that seven of the minor leaders of this plan had been arrested and later released; and that Tomás Ortiz and Diego Archuleta, two other leaders, were being pursued. Bent also said that informants had told him that the revolt was to occur in the four northern counties: Santa Fe, San Miguel, Taos, and Río Arriba. The plot seemed so slight that no convictions were rendered and thus no one was punished; government officials "felt that the conspiracy had failed." The thwarting of their efforts did not, however, allay the Mexicans' determination to overthrow

American rule, and their planning continued, this time with the utmost secrecy.

Supposing all danger past, Governor Bent and his party left the capital, but when they arrived in Taos, Charles told his wife to be prepared for any emergency. On the outskirts of Taos they had encountered a group of drunken Taos Indians who demanded that he release some of their fellows from the Taos jail. He explained to the Indians that the matter would have to be handled through the usual process of law, whereupon the Indians disbanded and went their way. But, Governor Bent told his wife, "the Indians are being incited by the Mexicans and might do anything."

Although the Governor had refused to believe that it was dangerous for him to travel to Taos at this time, he now realized the jeopardy to his family and friends. Apparently, he was unaware that the Mexican rebels had worked for many months to arouse the Indians to the point where they would help drive out of New Mexico all of the Americans—as well as the Mexicans—who had taken office in 1846. The animosity of the rebels was evidently nearing its peak at this time.

All during the night of January 18, Pablo Montoya and Tomacito Romero, the two Indian leaders, rode the trail between Taos Pueblo and the village gathering their forces for the attack. Before dawn on the morning of the nineteenth, it began snowing and was bitterly cold. The insensate mob of Indians and Mexicans had worked themselves into a state of irrational fury, and Taos Lightning, a raw, undistilled whiskey, kept them emotionally charged.

Occupying the adobe home with Charles were his wife Ignacia, and their children; Mrs. Bent's sister, Josefa Carson, Kit's wife; and Mrs. Rumalda Luna Boggs, Charles' stepdaughter, the wife of Thomas O. Boggs. Just home from college was Mrs. Bent's and Mrs. Carson's young brother, Pablo (Paul) Jaramillo, and visiting with him was Narciso (Narcisse) Beaubien, son of Judge Carlos Beaubien and brother-in-law of Lucien Maxwell. The only other person in the Bent household that fateful morning was a servant. The house was unguarded, for Governor Bent would not allow a sentinel to be placed without.

Before dawn, there were disturbances on the Taos plaza and some noise near the Bent house. Rumalda Boggs, who was fifteen at the time, had slept little that night. Twice she arose to see if Teresina, the Governor's five-year-old daughter, was covered against the cold. She found the little girl sleeping through the noise. Rumalda heard the servant stirring in the kitchen, but the rest of the household was apparently asleep.

About 7:30, loud voices, followed by a clamorous pounding on the door, awoke the Bent household. The Governor rose from his couch and started toward the door. Ignacia and Josefa begged him to go out the back door and make his escape on one of the fast horses in the stables. He refused to do so. In his quiet, gentle way, he tried to calm the family and walked toward the front door to talk to the men who were gathered outside it. He knew that he would have to take a brave stand in order to protect his family and guests from the mob.

What the Governor did not know was that the mob had already been to the jail, waving torches and demanding the release of the prisoners. They had captured Sheriff Lee, had taken him along to the jail. He was in favor of releasing the prisoners until military reinforcements could arrive from Santa Fe, but Cornelio Vigil would have none of it. He called the rebels thieves and inferiors and ordered them to leave the place. Prefect Vigil's belligerancy served to increase the mob's anger, and they literally hacked him to pieces. In the confusion, Lee broke away and climbed to the roof of a nearby house, but the maddened insurrectionists were right behind him and he suffered the same fate as Vigil. Attorney Leal was sought out in the early morning and marched naked through the icy streets; when he stumbled, his body was shot full of arrows and he was scalped alive. He was in such agony that he begged his captors to kill him. Finally, he dropped in the snow, and an arrow mercifully ended his suffering.

So it was that when the rebels pounded on Governor Bent's door, their hands and clothing were already stained with blood. Charles opened the door, the women and children standing terror stricken behind him, only partially dressed. In a quiet voice, he asked them what they wanted. "We want your head, your *gringo* head!" they screamed. "We want your scalp!"

The Governor talked calmly, for he realized that the crowd was crazed with drink. He whispered to his wife to have the women dig a hole in the wall and escape to the adjoining house while he spoke to the men. As he turned to the group, a bullet struck him in the face. Half-stunned, he staggered back; his wife rushed to his side and grasped his arm. The Governor made no outcry, but put his hand up to his face.

While these events were taking place, Mrs. Carson and Mrs. Boggs had already started digging at the adobe wall in the back room. Their only tools were a large iron spoon and the fireplace poker. Soon they had a hole large enough to crawl through. The small children were pushed in first, then some of the women crawled into the dark, cold room beyond.

Ten-year-old Alfred Bent brought his father a gun and said: "Papa, let us fight like men." The Governor motioned the boy to go back where the women were and continued to try to dissuade the Indians and Mexicans from their purpose. He suggested a meeting at which grievances could be aired; he offered to go with the mob if the Americans and his family could be spared. But the crowd was beyond reasoning. The Governor swayed again, and an Indian leaped toward him and ripped off his scalp with a long knife; arrows struck him in the face and body. He crawled slowly to the hole in the wall and the women pulled him through.

Some of the assailants followed him through the hole, and others effected an entrance through the flat, dirt-covered roof. A final shot rang out and the Governor fell dead. There was a commotion outside, and the mob left the room. The Bents' servant was pointing at the hayloft and screaming, "Kill the young ones and they will never be men to trouble us!" Pablo Jaramillo and Narcisco Beaubien had hidden in the loft, and now the blood-crazed rioters scrambled after them. The boys were hacked and mutilated until their bodies could not be distinguished from each other.

The women and children, still dressed in their night clothes, remained with the Governor's body. They had nothing to eat all that day and part of the next. The insurrectionists had left the village in a grip of terror, and for many hours no one dared venture out; trails in and out of Taos were unsafe. The following day, a Mexican friend came to the stricken family, bringing some shabby clothing for disguises. He darkened their faces with soot and took them to his home, putting them to work in the kitchen with the servants. He also buried the Governor's body where it would be safe until it could be interred according to the rites of the Church.

The revolt also extended to Mora and Arroyo Hondo. At Mora, Lawrence Waldo, younger brother of Dr. David Waldo, was brutally murdered, and Kit's old friends and fellow trappers William Howard and Markhead (for whom Carson had taken the Blackfoot bullet in his shoulder) were killed on the trail as they were bringing their fur packs to Taos.

The Mexican and Indian revolutionists dashed on to Arroyo Hondo, about ten miles north of Taos, where Simeon Turley had a prosperous mill and distillery. Turley and eight men held out against the attack for two days before the rioters gained access to the corrals and set fire to the main buildings. Turley and six of his men were killed. The two who escaped, John Albert and Charles Townes, traveled on frozen back roads to Santa Fe to obtain help for the stricken villages of northern New Mexico.

American homes and stores had been ransacked and burned. Céran St. Vrain was in Santa Fe when Colonel Sterling Price received news of the revolt on January 20. Price immediately summoned soldiers from Albuquerque and called for a volunteer company to be organized under St. Vrain. On January 23, with 353 men, Price and St. Vrain started for Taos. Four days later, at Los Luceros, they met reinforcements under the command of Captain Burgwin. Additional forces joined Colonel Price, increasing his ranks to 480 men. The insurrectionists were first encountered on the afternoon of January 24 near Santa Cruz de la Cañada, some twenty-five miles northwest of Santa Fe, where they had assembled under Ortiz and Montoya with plans to attack Santa Fe. No doubt the Indians in the group were remembering their short reign of power in New Mexico when José Gonzales, a Taos Pueblo Indian, took over as governor in 1837 after an insurrection.

The enemy at Santa Cruz numbered between 1,500 and 2,000; they were soon scattered by Colonel Price's army. The next encounter was at Embudo, where the Americans met about 600 rebels, of whom they killed 20 and wounded 60. From Embudo, Price turned eastward to Trampas and Chamisal, arriving there on January 31. Tramping through heavy snow, they reached Taos three days later and were informed that the rebels had fortified themselves in the massive adobe church at Taos Pueblo, some three miles north of the village. Price ordered an attack on the church as soon as they reached it. Nothing was accomplished toward dislodging the rebels, and as night approached, the army retreated to the village to camp.

At nine o'clock the following morning, the Americans renewed their attack with an artillery barrage on the church. Colonel Price ordered the mounted men under Captains St. Vrain and Slack to the opposite side of the Pueblo so that they could intercept any rebels who tried to escape to the mountains or to Taos. About three hundred yards from the north wall, Lieutenant Dyer and his command were stationed with a six-pounder and two howitzers, while Lieutenant Hassendaubel of Major Clark's battalion (light artillery) remained with Captain Burgwin in command of two howitzers. This arrangement provided a field of fire which could sweep the front and east sides of the church.

After two hours of steady fire, not one round of which inflicted appreciable damage on the solid, thick walls of the church, Colonel Price determined to storm the building. He gave the signal for Captains Burgwin and McMillin to head their companies and charge the western flank of the church while Captains Angney and Barber and Lieutenant Boon charged the north wall. As soon as this was accomplished and the troops had established themselves under the west wall of the church, axes were used in an attempt to breach the wall and a temporary ladder was put to the roof so that the beams could be fired.

It was at this time that Lieutenants McIlvane, Lackland, and Royall, with Captain Burgwin, headed a small party which left the protection of the church walls in an attempt to force the front door. Before Captain Burgwin reached the door, he received a severe wound which took his life three days later. The assault proved fruitless, and the men retired to a covered position behind the wall, two of them carrying the wounded Burgwin.

During the attempt to break down the front door, Colonel Price's command had succeeded in cutting small holes in the western wall, through which they now threw shells, doing some damage inside. A six-pounder was brought up to a spot within sixty yards of the church by Lieutenant Wilson, and by 3:30, after ten rounds had been fired, one of the holes was widened enough for the Americans to take possession of the church without further opposition. Lieutenants Dyer, Wilson, and Taylor led the way into the smoke-filled interior as rebels, without firing a shot, retired to the gallery, where an open door admitted air. Meanwhile, the troops on the north side were ordered to charge by Colonel Price. Being almost surrounded, the Indians and Mexicans poured out of the gallery and fled toward the mountains; some took refuge in the large houses on the east side of the Pueblo.

Captains St. Vrain and Slack, followed by their mounted commands, pursued the insurrectionists into the mountains, killing fifty-one of them. Only two or three men escaped. By this time it had grown dark, and the American army set up camp in the houses on the west side of the Pueblo. They had been completely deserted by the Indians. The next morning, the rebels sued for peace. This was granted by Colonel Price on the condition that they deliver to him Tomacito Romero and the other instigators of the rebellion.

While leaders of the revolt were in jail at Taos awaiting trial, a dragoon named Fitzgerald, whose brother had been killed by Romero, shot and killed the rebel leader. Fitzgerald was immediately placed under arrest, but he made his escape that night and was never brought to trial for his crime.

Within the next few days, Montoya, the self-styled "Santa Anna of the North," was tried by a court-martial of six officers: Captains

Angney, Barber, and Slack and Lieutenants Ingalls, White, and Eastin, who was judge advocate of the court. Montoya was found guilty and hanged on the public plaza at Taos in the presence of the American troops and some fourteen of the villagers.

In the months that followed, each of the rebels was caught, tried, and convicted. At one time there were more than eighty prisoners in the Taos jail! According to Lewis H. Garrard, the court was in session daily, and five Indians and four Mexicans were sentenced to be hanged on the last day of April. He describes the three female witnesses by saying, first, that Mrs. Bent, the late Governor's wife, was quite handsome, and must have been a beautiful woman in her youth. Mrs. Boggs was not so agreeable to him in appearance, but of Mrs. Carson he said that her style of beauty was of the "haughty, heart-breaking kind—such as would lead a man with the glance of the eye to risk his life for one smile, and he could not but desire her acquaintance." The dress and manners of the three ladies bespoke to Garrard a greater degree of refinement than usual.

When Mrs. Bent gave her testimony and pointed out the Indian who had killed her husband, she sealed his death warrant, but Garrard noted that not a muscle in the chief's face moved. Padre Martinez was designated as the elusive instigator of the rebellion. His name was first listed in connection with repeated attempts on the part of the Mexicans to rid themselves of their American conquerors.

Kit Carson arrived in Taos between the two principal trials and hangings—those of April 9 and April 30, 1847. He joined his statement in support of the Padre's guilt as expressed by the Reverend M. J. Howlett in his biography of Joseph P. Machebeuf:

> Although the U.S. Government did not find Father Martinez guilty of direct complicity in the unfortunate insurrection, it is said that he had much to do with the uprising of the Indians and the Mexicans at Taos, when Governor Bent and fifteen Americans and their Mexican sympathizers were massacred on January 19th.

Kit's statement in regard to the excommunication of Padre Martinez, which took place in 1861, is as follows:

We shall not let them do as they did then [1847] when they murdered and pillaged. I am a man of peace, and I can fight a little yet, and I know of no better cause to fight for than my family, my church and my friend Senor Vicario Machebeuf.

However badly Kit might have wanted to stay in Taos with Josefa and her bereaved sister, the fact remained that he was on government business and had to deliver dispatches in Washington. Accordingly, he set out with Lieutenant Beale, Talbot, a California Indian, and several others for Bent's Fort on the Arkansas. On April 20, they met Lewis Garrard in camp near the Purgatoire River. On May 6, at the mouth of the Purgatoire, some of Kit's men who had dropped behind the main party in order to recruit fresh horses met George Frederick Ruxton, who was on his way to the States with government wagons. The Carson men learned from Ruxton that the Pawnee Indians were attacking wagons bound for the States and relayed the information to Kit when they caught up with him. Kit and his group were attacked by the Pawnees on the trail, but they managed to escape.

Arriving in St. Louis the last of May, Kit was hospitably met by Senator Benton with an invitation to use the Benton home in Washington as his headquarters while he was in the East. He arrived in Washington in June, and the members of Benton household were charmed with his gentleness and modesty. It was the beginning of Kit's lasting friendship with the Senator and his family.

Kit's name had preceded him. Wherever he went, he was regarded as a national hero. For one thing, he had just completed a trip from California to St. Louis in far less time than such a journey had required before, and for another, Frémont's reports of the first two exploring expeditions had spread Kit's fame farther than he had any idea they would, judging by the throng greeting him at St. Louis. The story of the Bear flag and the Carson-Godey ride to avenge the Fuentes camp were the most chronicled tales of the California trip. Here was Kit Carson in St. Louis, able to tell of events in California and the recent insurrection in New Mexico. No wonder his name was in every newspaper! Kit, shy and retiring, did not enjoy the shower of attention and publicity.

After a visit with the Bentons, Kit went to Fayette to visit his first-born daughter, Adaline. He had not seen her since he brought her to Missouri to stay with Mr. and Mrs. Leander Amick, his niece and her husband, on their farm between Fayette and Glasgow. Mrs. Amick was the daughter of Kit's sister Elizabeth. Up to that time, Adaline had been attending Rock Springs School, but Kit was anxious to give her a better education than that small public school provided. After consulting with the Amicks, he enrolled Adaline as a boarding student in the old Howard-Payne Female Seminary at Fayette.

Satisfied that Adaline was in good hands, Kit left for Washington. It was late in the evening when he reached the end of his journey. When the dusty train clanked to a stop, Kit, blue eyed, stocky and desert tanned, was easily recognized by Jessie Benton Frémont, who said she knew him at once from her husband's description of him.

At the Frémont-Benton home, Kit confided to Mrs. Frémont that he was afraid the ladies would not want to meet him if they knew he had had an Indian wife. Jessie Frémont assured him that his having married an Indian would not bar him from the company of the women of Washington. With that, Kit seemed to be at ease.

On June 7, Kit delivered his dispatches and the Benton letter to President Polk; Mrs. Frémont accompanied him. The President felt that Frémont was "greatly in the wrong," as he indicated in his diary entry for June 7:

> Mr. Carson delivered to me a long letter from Col. Frémont which had been addressed to [Senator] Benton. It related in part to the recent unfortunate collision between General Kearny and Commodore Stockton, and between the former and Col. Frémont in California. Mrs. Frémont seemed anxious to elicit from me some expression of approbation of her husband's conduct, but I evaded making any. In truth I consider that Col. Frémont was greatly in the wrong when he refused to obey orders issued to him by General Kearny. I think General Kearny

was right also in his controversy with Commodore Stockton. It was unnecessary, however, that I should say so to Col. Frémont's wife, and I evaded giving her an answer.

On the back of the Benton letter, President Polk wrote, "Received from Mr. Christopher Carson," along with the date, and gave Kit an appointment for that evening to discuss more fully the California trouble between Kearny and Stockton. They talked at length about the California situation. The President gave Kit no indication of his personal feelings in the matter, but he liked Kit's loyalty to the interest of his friend and chief, Colonel Frémont. He also appreciated Kit's sincerity, and felt that Kit was the only visitor he had had for a long time who wasn't looking for personal favors.

The next day, the Cabinet agreed with the President that General Kearny was in the right. It was decided to send Kit to California with sealed dispatches which would put an end to the controversy.

The President saw a way to reward Kit for his services to the government. Although Congress was not in session to approve it, on June 9 he issued a commission to Christopher Carson, appointing him a second lieutenant in Frémont's regiment of mounted riflemen. The news was released to the press, and Kit was quite surprised to read in the *Union*:

> Since Carson's arrival, solely through the appreciation by the President of his merits and services, he has received a commission of lieutenant in the rifle regiment of which Mr. Frémont is the lieutenant-colonel. The appointment was unsolicited and unexpected—the suggestion entirely of the President's own recognition of the deserts of this man of the prairies—a fact that is most honorable to the Executive, and makes the favor the more gratifying to the friends of Carson.

Kit was well fitted for his new position, and his frontier experiences differentiated him from the scores of young lieutenants and other officers who had formal military training. According to Edwin L. Sabin, "many of the colonels spoke like border troopers." And very few colonels advanced to brevet brigadier general, as did Kit in later years.

In Washington, Kit visited Lieutenant Beale and his family. Ned Beale of the Navy, back home from the conquest of California, and Christopher Carson, Indian scout and guide in Frémont's narratives, must have made quite a pair in Washington social circles. Kit, however, was anxious to get started again, and it was with relief that he received his orders on June 14:

> Sir: You will proceed with the despatches herewith for the commanding officer in Santa Fé and California, taking the route via Fort Leavenworth. On arriving at Santa Fé, you will hand to the commanding officer at that place the communication addressed to him, and then proceed to California and deliver to General Kearny, or, should he have left the country, to the officer of the United States army highest in rank, the despatches addressed to them.
>
> You are authorized to receive from the Indian agent near Fort Leavenworth the United States mules left in his charge by Mr. Talbot, who came with you from California.
>
> You will be entitled to transportation from this place to California.
>
> > Very respectfully, your obedient servant,
> > W. L. Marcy
> > Secretary of War
>
> Lieutenant Christopher Carson,
> Washington City.

Kit had another article to deliver when he reached California: Jessie Frémont had entrusted him with an oil miniature of herself to give Colonel Frémont, who, she presumed, was still on duty in California.

Kit left Washington on June 16. Accompanying him were Lieutenant Beale, bearing navy dispatches, and Mrs. Frémont, who was going to St. Louis to join her father. In St. Louis, Lieutenant Beale fell ill again and had to be taken back to Washington.

Senator Benton was anxious to know what Kit and his daughter had to say concerning their visit to the President. Kit told him that President Polk had evaded the issue completely and had in no way revealed his feelings in the matter. Senator Benton must have thought it indeed strange that Kit, who could tell what an Indian

183

was thinking and what he would do next, couldn't even get an ink-
ling, from the President's expression, of how he stood in the matter
of Kearny *versus* Frémont.

After a day's visit in the Benton home, Kit started alone for Fort
Leavenworth. He spent a day in Howard County visiting relatives,
then boarded a Missouri River steamboat for the fort, where he
secured the army mules left by Talbot and picked up fifty recruits.
He had already sent a message to Josefa, telling her of his appointment and asking her to meet him in Santa Fe.

A hundred miles east of Pawnee Rock, Kit and his recruits camped
near a government wagon train which was also headed for Santa
Fe. At dawn, the Comanches stampeded the cattle, running them
through the Carson camp. If Kit thought he had his green recruits
properly trained to picket or hold animals in a stampede, he was
mistaken. He lost two horses in the raid.

Josefa and her sister were waiting for Kit in Santa Fe. The dispatches were delivered, and the recruits reported to the commanding officer at Fort Marcy. The next day, Kit left Josefa long enough
to round up fifteen of his men for the trip to California. They accompanied Josefa and Mrs. Bent as far as Taos, then turned northwest,
cutting across southwestern Colorado, thence into Utah, and down
through the Sevier country to the Virgin River. In southeastern
Nevada, where Kit and some of these same mountain men had
traveled with Frémont in 1844, they ran into hostile Indians. The
fight lasted until the Indian chief was killed and the Indians fled.
Soon after that, Kit and his men ran out of food and had to kill
a mule.

Arriving in Los Angeles in October, 1847, Kit learned that the
seat of government had been moved to Monterey, with Colonel
Richard B. Mason of the First Dragoons as governor of California.
The most distressing news was that some months previously Kearny
had taken Frémont back to Washington under arrest, charging him
with mutiny.

As Kit rode on to Monterey, his thoughts were probably not of
the miniature of Mrs. Frémont he had in his possession, but of his
friend Frémont. He undoubtedly recalled how Kearny had praised

Frémont to him when he was on his way to Washington with dispatches from Frémont and Stockton. Kit later told Senator Benton:

> I told him a civil government was already established. . . . General Kearny said it made no difference; that he was a friend of Colonel Frémont and he would make him governor himself. He began from the first to insist on my turning back to guide him into California. . . . He told me he was a friend to Colonel Frémont and Colonel Benton, and all the family . . . and General Kearny seemed to be such a good friend of the Colonel's, I let him take me back. . . . More than twenty times on the road, General Kearny told me about his being a friend of Colonel Benton and Colonel Frémont and all their family, and that he intended to make Colonel Frémont the governor of California, and all this of his own accord, as we were traveling along or in camp, and without my asking him a word about it.

12 ★ On Dispatch Duty

THE FIRST PERSON Kit saw when he rode into Monterey was the red-haired adjutant to Colonel Mason, Lieutenant William Tecumseh Sherman, who was anxious to meet Carson, "the man who had achieved such feats." They walked together to Colonel Mason's quarters, where Kit personally delivered the dispatches.

After a few days, Mason assigned Kit to duty with Captain Andrew Jackson Smith at Los Angeles. Lieutenant Carson's name had already appeared in the *San Francisco Californian*. On December 1, 1847, that newspaper announced his arrival in Monterey, noting that he had left Washington about June 20. His name had almost preceded him again.

Kit must have been intensely bored during the few weeks he served in Los Angeles, but his next task was more interesting. With twenty-five men, he was assigned to guard duty at Tejon Pass. Here Kit spent the winter of 1847–48 in high, wooded country where Mexican and Indian smugglers and horse thieves were known to cross the twenty-mile-wide pass. Kit and his men examined express, packs, men, and animals.

In March or April of 1848, Kit was again ordered to take dispatches to Washington. He was relieved at Tejon Pass and given an escort of twenty men. At Bridge Creek, some fifteen miles from Los Angeles, he set up camp to secure horses and prepare for the journey. In Los Angeles, Kit learned that Lieutenant George D. Brewerton was to accompany him. Kit announced his intention to stay at Bridge Creek, and Lieutenant Brewerton, having grown tired of fleas, "with which all the adobe houses in town were infested," decided to go with Kit to Bridge Creek, where he could get an insight into the life he was to lead for some months to come.

For a number of weeks the Carson camp was a busy place. Its occupants mended saddles and bridles, bought supplies and procured satisfactory horses and mules for the long overland trip. They packed their baggage carefully to insure a properly balanced load on the pack animals. On May 2, they broke camp and traveled to Los Angeles, where Kit picked up important dispatches and mail.

Since the discovery of gold at Sutter's Mill was known to Colonel Mason and Lieutenant Sherman long before Kit left Los Angeles on the trip east, it can be assumed that news of the find was in Kit's saddlebags, for the official announcement of the discovery—in President Polk's message of December 5, 1848—was written by Lieutenant Sherman. However, Kit was not the first to carry the news, for the discovery of California gold was known in the East a month before Kit arrived. Sherman's message to the President said, in part:

> It was known that mines of the precious metals existed to a considerable extent in California at the time of its acquisition. Recent discoveries render it probable that these mines are more extensive and valuable than was first anticipated. The accounts of the abundance of gold in that territory are of such an extraordinary character as would scarcely command belief were they not corroborated by the authentic reports of officers in the public service who have visited the mineral district and derived the facts which they detail from personal observation. Reluctant to credit the reports in general circulation as to the quantity of gold, the officer commanding our forces in California visited the mineral district in July last, for the purpose of obtaining accurate information on the subject. When he visited the country there were about 4,000 persons engaged in collecting gold.

The *California Star* of April 1 must have had some comment about the discovery, and copies of the *Star* arrived in Independence, Missouri, in June. Nathan Hawk of Company B, Mormon Battalion, carried letters over the Sierras, and Captain Shreve arrived in the East from California on August 10 and delivered a letter to be printed in the *American Journal of Science and Arts*, whose September issue devoted much space to "Mines of Cinnabar in Upper California," the last paragraph of which said: "Gold has been found recently on the Sacramento, near Sutter's Fort. It occurs in small masses in the sands of a new mill race, and is said to promise well." Although both Kit and Brewerton must have known something of the richness of the discovery, neither seemed to attach much importance to it, for gold in the Sacramento was known to the padres long before 1848.

The trail east would take them through Cajon Pass, across the Mohave Desert, and along the Old Spanish Trail. Jesús Garcia (only two of the dozen names he bore) had been hired as cook, muleteer, and factotum. Brewerton described him as being old and ugly, with a villainous countenance, although Garcia had given himself many virtues, among them packing a mule in the twinkling of an eye, lassoing, and riding the wildest of horses, and being completely honest. But Jesús, the paragon of virtue, allowed himself to be tempted by a pair of Brewerton's boots and some clothing and was gone when the Carson party left Los Angeles.

Just as Brewerton and Carson were ready to depart, a young Mexican named Juan appeared and asked to fill Garcia's vacancy. After questioning him, Kit turned to Brewerton and said: "A greater rascal, I don't think ever lived than that young Mexican, but he knows how to take care of a mule." Juan had crossed the desert once before with an American trader, and for just plain cussedness (or perhaps revenge) he had cut holes in the provision bags, releasing all their contents, and both the trader and Juan were reduced to the point of starvation before they finally reached a settlement. Since Brewerton could do no better, he decided to hire the erring Juan and keep a close watch on him.

Eight days out, they overtook a party of about two hundred Mexican traders dressed in every costume imaginable, from embroidered jackets with silver bell-shaped buttons to the scanty garb of animal skins worn by the Indians. They were strung out for more than a mile. The Carson group camped near them for one night, then outdistanced them.

Brewerton thought the ride through the desert monotonous. They rode from fifteen to fifty miles a day, the mileage depending upon the distance to water and the weariness of the animals. Kit rarely spoke while traveling, said Brewerton. "His keen eye was continually examining the country, and his whole manner was that of a man deeply impressed with a sense of responsibility." At night the men took turns at guard duty. Brewerton noted that a mule was always the best sentry, since it would discover the presence of Indians long before its human guard saw them. Thus alarmed, the mule would snort, extending head and ears toward the culprit.

Kit Carson's preparation for the night interested Brewerton. He felt that a braver man than Kit never lived but that in spite of this fact, Kit exercised great caution. The Lieutenant describes a typical evening in his book, *Overland with Kit Carson*:

> While arranging his bed, his saddle, which he always used as a pillow, was disposed in such a manner as to form a barricade for his head; his pistols, half-cocked, were laid above it, and his trusty rifle reposed beneath the blanket by his side, where it was not only ready for instant use, but perfectly protected from the damp. Except now and then to light his pipe, you never caught Kit exposing himself to the full glare of the camp fire. He knew too well the treacherous character of the tribes among whom we were traveling; he had seen men killed at night by an unseen foe, who, veiled in darkness, stood in perfect security while he marked and shot down the mountaineer clearly seen by the firelight. Kit would say, "No, no, boys; hang around the fire if you will, it may do for you if you like it, but I don't want to have a Digger slip an arrow into me, when I can't see him."

A rather amusing event occurred one night. Brewerton had slept soundly until about midnight, when he was suddenly awakened by an unaccountable feeling of dread. He jumped to his feet and there, coiled and ready to strike, was a rattlesnake. As he moved the *macheers* which served as his mattress, the snake made its escape into a hole beneath his bed. Brewerton explained:

I had retired early, and in arranging my couch had spread it directly near the door of his snakeship's domicile. The snake had probably been out to see a neighbor and, getting home after I was asleep, felt a gentlemanly unwillingness to disturb me, and as I had taken possession of his dwelling he took part of my sleeping place, crawling under the blanket where he must have lain quietly by my side, until I rolled over and disturbed him. I can scarcely say that I slept much that night, and even Carson admitted that it made him a little nervous. Had I been bitten, our only remedy would have been some common whisky, which we carried with us in case of such an accident. It is a fact worth knowing, that in the mountains strong liquor is considered a certain preventative to any ill effects from snakebites; to administer it properly it must be given at once, and in large quantities, until the patient is fully under its influence.

Shortly after Kit's group had passed the *jornada*, they camped by a small stream to refresh themselves and to let their horses feed on the scanty patches of grass. They were thus stretched out in the shade when Kit, who was lying near Brewerton, rose on one elbow and asked, "Do you see those Indians?" He pointed to the crest of one of the bluff-like hills near by. Brewerton, of course, saw nothing. Kit was explaining what he had seen when an old Indian rose from the rocks and began to yell and wave his arms in a declaration of friendship. Kit answered the Indian in his own tongue and advanced to meet him. When the Digger had been presented with a gift, he yelled for his companions to join him. Cautiously, the Diggers walked into camp, two or three at a time, until there were a dozen or more, as Kit had predicted. They immediately let Kit know that they were hungry, and more coffee was put on the fire. The Diggers were given some dried beef which had become wet and moldy. This they ate ravenously, but the coffee they seemed doubtful about until Kit and his men drank some of it; then they emptied the kettle, and would have eaten all the camp's provisions had they been offered. Brewerton noted that "they expressed their satisfaction by rubbing down their stomachs, and grunting in a manner which would have done credit to a herd of well-fed swine."

Just about this time Joe Walker and party rode into camp. They joined the circle which had been formed. Kit "fired up his dudheen," took a puff, and handed it to Walker, who repeated the procedure and handed it to Brewerton. He, in turn, handed it to the oldest man among the Diggers, who, after taking two or three long puffs, retained the smoke in his mouth until, as Brewerton expressed it, "his distorted face bore the resemblance of an antiquated monkey's under trying circumstances." The pipe passed from one Indian to the other until it came again to the old Indian, who placed it securely in his mouth and continued to smoke until he refilled it. He continued smoking absently, and even the reproving grunts of his fellows could not make him take the pipe from his mouth. Some of the Indians had brought lizards with them, and they now ate them —raw, with no preparation other than jerking off their tails.

Kit told the Diggers as much as he wanted them to know; they remained all day. At sunset, Kit's cry of "Catch up" set the camp in motion. The next day, a few Indians visited the camp, but their actions were so suspicious that Kit kept a young boy as hostage to assure their safe passage through the country during the night. This seemed to give great uneasiness to the tribe, and that night the Indians yowled from the hilltops. Finally, Kit answered them in Ute, and the boy yelled back to his tribe that he was all right. It was Brewerton's lot to guard the Indian, but the rest of the night passed quietly. Next morning, Kit gave the boy some presents and allowed him to depart.

Continuing east, the Carson-Brewerton group safely crossed Green River, but when in June they came to the Grand, it was running very high. Kit proposed rafts upon which they could float their baggage across the river. These completed, the men piled packs, riding saddles, and Kit's saddlebags on one of them, the mail in the safest place they could find. Brewerton recorded Kit's instructions to the men: "All you men who can't swim may hang on to the corners of the raft, but don't any of you try to get upon it except Archambeau, who has the pole to guide it with; those of you who can swim are to get hold of the tow-line, and pull it along; keep a good lookout for rocks and floating timber; and whatever you do, don't lose the mail bags." With that final warning the raft was shoved off into the swirling stream.

Archambeau and Brewerton swam out to guide the raft, or, rather, to try to pull it to the opposite shore. After fighting the swift current for what must have seemed an eon, the little group was unceremoniously tossed upon the shore a mile downstream—the same shore, that is. Brewerton, who swam out with a lariat to secure the raft to a tree, was knocked unconscious by a passing piece of timber. Archambeau grabbed him by the hair, which, luckily, hadn't been cut for months, and dragged him to shore, where he soon revived.

By four that afternoon, they were again ready to try their luck with the raft. This time they were successful, but as soon as they reached the opposite shore, Archambeau was taken with violent cramps. When he had recovered, they turned their attention to unloading the raft, being assisted by a party of Indians.

On the opposite shore, the cavvy was driven into the water to swim across, and Kit, with a few men and a small portion of the baggage, followed with another raft. They made the trip safely, but the large raft carrying most of the provisions, six rifles, three saddles, and much of the ammunition hit something and disintegrated. Everything on it was lost.

Brewerton lost his notebook, his geological and botanical specimens, and many of his sketches, but he did manage to save his deerskin suit, his rifle, and a few rounds of ammunition, which was more than most of the other men salvaged. Many of them lost their clothing, guns, ammunition, and saddles.

They had only three days' rations, and when they were gone, a horse was killed and freely eaten by all except Brewerton, who refused to partake of it for some forty-eight hours. Hunger finally won, and he ate horseflesh for more than a week. His comment was: "I can only say that it was an old animal, a tough animal, and a sore-backed animal—and, upon the whole—I prefer beef."

The food situation changed as soon as they reached the foothills of the Rocky Mountains. There they found an abundance of deer, elk, and mountain sheep. They made camp, and Kit and Brewerton set out to hunt. They soon discovered a doe with her fawn in a grassy nook. Dismounting, Kit advanced with more than ordinary care, for he knew their supper depended upon his marksmanship. Brewerton held the horses while Kit worked his way within range. Brewerton wondered why Kit didn't fire, but Kit coolly calculated his distance before he finally raised his rifle, at the same time showing himself to the doe, who raised her head and offered a better target. They made a triumphal entry into camp with the now cut-up deer tied to their saddles.

At length the Carson group, ragged and dirty, descended from the mountains onto the plains, where they were greeted by many fresh Indian signs. A large war party had passed shortly before. That night, they camped by a stream swollen by melting snow, and thousands of mosquitoes descended upon them. The men made smoky fires and stood over them until their eyes were rivers of water.

About noon the next day, they met some Mexican traders who had come to trade with the Indians. From them Kit learned that a party of mountain men, much larger than his own, had been attacked by the Indians, soundly defeated, and robbed of all their property. That night, the guards were doubled and the fires of the Indian camp shone brightly about half a mile away. Kit's order was no fires, but during the night the animals' restlessness told him of lurking Indians, and Kit decided to leave before they should attack at dawn. About midnight, Kit and his men departed silently and rode hard until dawn, when they stopped a short time to rest their animals.

Everyone was just beginning to relax when a sudden turn of the trail brought them into full view of some two hundred lodges located on a rising hill about a half-mile to the right. All hope that they might slip by unnoticed vanished when a handsome Indian rode rapidly up to Kit and Brewerton. He was in full war paint and gaudy paraphernalia. In Spanish, he inquired for the captain.

Speaking in Ute, Kit asked the Indian who he was. The latter put a finger into either ear and shook his head. Brewerton records Kit's reaction: "I knew it. It is just as I thought, and we are in for it at last. Look here, Thomas! Get the mules together, and drive them up to that little patch of chaparral while we follow with the Indian."

A few moments later, Kit leaned over as if to adjust his saddle and told Brewerton to "look back, but express no surprise." About 150 Indians in full war paint were charging down upon them, but by this time, the whites had reached the chaparral. Kit sprang from his saddle, says Brewerton, and gave orders to his men: "Now boys, dismount, tie up your riding mules; those of you who have guns, get round the *caballada*, and look out for the Indians; and you who have none, get inside, and hold some of the animals. Take care, Thomas, and shoot down the mule with mail bags on her pack, if they try to stampede the animals."

The Indians charged in, screaming, but held their fire. Kit stood in front of his men, giving orders and haranguing the Indians. "His whole demeanor," said Brewerton, "was now so entirely changed that he looked like a different man; his eyes fairly flashed, and his rifle was grasped with all the energy of an iron will." Kit spoke to the Indians. "There," he said, "is our line; cross it if you dare, and we begin to shoot. You asked us to let you in, but you won't come unless you ride over us. You say you are friends, but you don't act like it. No, you don't deceive us so, we know you too well; so stand back, or your lives are in danger." Quite a brave speech for the leader of a handful of men to deliver to 150 warriors. The Indians must have thought so, for they hesitated, and just then a runner came up to them.

Kit took quick advantage of the pause, says Brewerton, and called out: "Now, boys, we have a chance to jump into your saddles, get the loose animals before you, and then handle your rifles, and if these fellows interfere with us we'll make a running fight of it." Needless to say, the order was hastily carried out.

The Indians followed for a while but finally dropped behind. Kit and his men put as much distance as possible between themselves and the Indian village and arrived about midnight at some Mexican shepherds' huts. Here they learned that two hundred American volunteers were on their way to punish the Indians for recent outrages in that vicinity. That, Kit figured, must have been the message

the runner delivered to the would-be attackers. Call it coincidence—
or the Carson luck.

The following day, Kit and his men resumed their journey and
arrived at Taos that evening. Brewerton stayed with Kit and Josefa
for a few days, then took most of the men and went on to Santa Fe
where he was to meet Kit later.

Upon proceeding to Santa Fe, Kit learned from Colonel E. W. B.
Newby that the Senate had refused to confirm his commission. Not
understanding politics, Kit did not realize how powerful Senator
Benton's Indian-hating enemies could be, and then too, Kit was a
friend to the red man. At that time, most of the military officers
and government officials in Washington considered the Indian a
savage animal to be hunted down and exterminated.

Friends advised Kit to refuse to carry his dispatches any farther,
but Kit told them:

> I was entrusted with these dispatches, having been chosen in Cali-
> fornia, from whence I came, as the most competent person to take them
> through safely. I will fulfill the duty if the service I was performing
> was beneficial to the public. It does not matter to me whether I am
> enjoying the rank of lieutenant or only the credit of being an experi-
> enced mountaineer. I have gained both honor and credit by perform-
> ing every duty entrusted to my charge and on no account do I wish
> to forfeit the good opinion of a majority of my countrymen merely
> because the United States Senate did not deem it proper to confirm my
> appointment to an office I had never sought and one which if con-
> firmed, I would have to resign at the close of the war.

In Santa Fe, Kit got in touch with Brewerton, who was awaiting
Kit's arrival. It was June, and Brewerton had caught a severe cold,
from sleeping in a draft, he said. Kit informed the Lieutenant that
he proposed to obtain fresh animals from the quartermaster, reduce
his party to ten experienced men, and take a short cut directly to
Fort Leavenworth. Brewerton was in no condition to travel, so Kit
left Santa Fe without him. Colonel Newby warned Kit that the
Comanches were raiding along the Santa Fe Trail, supposedly in
reprisal for the loss of game, forage, and wood.

Kit's path led back to Taos, where he met his friend Lucien Maxwell and learned of the tragedy which had just befallen him on the same trail Kit was taking. Maxwell's first encounter had been with the Apaches, who surrounded him at Green Horn River. He succeeded in driving them off and was joined by General Elliott Lee and Charles Townes (the same man who had escaped the Taos Massacre). Maxwell, Lee, Townes, and their groups, consisting in all of fourteen men, had started for Taos by way of Raton Pass when they were again attacked by Indians. The fight which ensued must have been a desperate one, for Maxwell was wounded and Townes, Paschal Riviere, and José Cardenal were killed. Maxwell escaped but was robbed of eighty-two animals and everything else he possessed, even his rifle. General Lee was also wounded but escaped.

It looked as if Kit and his men were headed for disaster. In his account of the trip from Taos, Oliver Wiggins says that Kit reduced his party to five men (including Kit) on the assumption that a small and able group could get through where a larger party would fail. Blue names himself, Jim Beckwourth, and Jesse Nelson (who later married Susan Carson, daughter of Kit's brother Robert) as three of them. They left Taos on June 26.

The trail led to Pueblo, a settlement on the Upper Arkansas some seventy-five miles from Bent's Fort, then north and northeast to the Platte River, thence down to the Missouri frontier.

Seven Kiowa Indians rode into camp one noon. As they were eating, the chief told his men to kill all the whites "when the smoke starts around the third time." Kit, who understood Kiowa, told Wiggins to watch him closely and if he lifted his hand, shoot.

When the pipe started around the third time, Kit said in a pleasant but firm tone: "This is the last smoke, is it? Now you kill us." The Indians threw off their blankets to get at their weapons, and Wiggins and the other men prepared to fire as they did so. The Indians stopped short, whereupon Kit gave them a verbal lashing: "You red dogs!" he shouted. "Thought you would murder us, did you? Do you know who I am? I am Little Chief—I am Kit Carson. Take a good look at me before you die. You're a nice bunch of cowards. Shame on you and your tribe! Go! Get out! Tell your chiefs you have seen Kit Carson and he gave you your lives. Stop!" Kit ordered as the Indians sheepishly moved away. "Take your bows, so you can kill rabbits. Next time you smoke the pipe of peace with a white man, don't plan to murder him."

Kit and his men took a short cut to the South Platte, and Nelson states that the evening fires were deserted soon after supper so that the party could spend the night a mile or so beyond in a hidden place. It was a precaution of the trail to assure safe passage, and Kit was using every trick known to a mountain man to get his dispatches through Indian country.

At the confluence of the South and North Platte rivers, they met a trading company of fifteen men. Beckwourth, Nelson, Wiggins, and the other man returned to Taos with one of the company, and Kit joined the traders. They rode down the South Platte to Fort Kearny, then headed south for the emigrant trail by way of the Republican and Kansas rivers through friendly Indian country and on to Fort Leavenworth. From the fort Kit traveled by boat to St. Louis, arriving there about July 30. Although Kearny was in St. Louis at the time, there is no record of Kit's having seen him. In view of Frémont's recent court-martial and resignation from the Army, it was best that Kit did not see him, for he had not yet forgotten Kearny's hostile attitude toward his chief.

Kit left St. Louis the next day and delivered his dispatches in Washington the second week in August. There, at the spacious home of Senator Benton, he dictated his statement concerning Kearny. There, too, he saw his old friend Joe Meek, mountain man, who was inclined to become "intoxicated with the ferment of his imagination." Joe had been sent to request that Oregon be organized as a territory and to persuade the federal government to establish military posts for the protection of Oregon settlers. He also had the unpleasant duty of informing government officials of the massacre of Dr. and Mrs. Marcus Whitman and their companions at Waiilatpu. Joe's own half-Indian daughter, Helen Mar, was one of the victims. Joe Meek's story horrified the nation.

On August 15, Kit attended the baptism of Charles and Jessie Frémont's little son, Benton, born the last of July, at the Episcopal

Church of the Epiphany. Kit was sponsor. Kit did not tarry after the christening for he was anxious to return home. He stopped in Missouri to visit Adaline, then hurried on.

Kit arrived back in Taos sometime in October, 1848, and stayed there most of the winter. Upon two occasions he was called for duty with Colonel Benjamin S. Beall, the first of which came about in the following way. Colonel Beall had ordered a company of soldiers to cross the mountains in pursuit of Apaches, but the soldiers had found it "impracticable" as they reported, to proceed, whereupon the Colonel replied that there was no such word in a soldier's vocabulary. After that announcement he took charge himself and employed Kit as guide. Deep snow did not stop Kit and the Colonel, who pushed through the drifts with great difficulty, but it did slow them up. When finally located, the Indians had retreated so far as to be safe from the soldiers, and, to the wrath of the Colonel, not an Indian was taken. Since supplies were running low, he was compelled to retreat. On the return trip, they accidentally stumbled upon an Apache village, into which the Colonel ordered an immediate charge. The Indians fled, except for two chiefs, who were captured. Colonel Beall, his anger cooled, lectured the chiefs, making them promise to behave themselves, then freed them and returned to Taos.

On January 21, 1849, Céran St. Vrain stopped by Kit's house on his way to the States and found Frémont to be a visitor there. Céran tarried to hear about the fateful fourth expedition, which had started to California from Bent's Fort the previous November with Old Bill Williams as guide. By the middle of December, they were stalled by deep snow, lost, and starving. Relief parties were sent out, but it was the ninth of February before all the survivors were brought to Taos. Eleven men had died in the mountains, and the expedition's baggage and records were lost. According to family tradition, Kit's younger brother Lindsey made the trip, but his name does not appear in any of the accounts of the expedition.

While visiting Kit, Frémont learned that Ned Beale had passed through Santa Fe on his way from Washington to California with government dispatches. Beale had no way of knowing that Frémont and Carson were in Taos or he would certainly have gone out of his way to see them. Revived and rested some weeks later, Frémont continued on to California by the southern route.

In February, Kit was again employed as guide by Colonel Beall on a trip to the Arkansas, where a large force of Indians with Mexican captives were camped. The Colonel's orders were to free the Mexicans and return them to Mexico, which action was obligatory under the provisions of the Treaty of Guadalupe Hidalgo.

At length, the two companies of dragoons reached the Arkansas, where, the Colonel found to his amazement, almost two thousand Indians had gathered to meet their agent. The agent, being a sensible man, advised Colonel Beall not to try to take the captives, for the Indians were in an ugly mood and if aroused might massacre the whole command. After much persuasion from traders, officers, and the agent, Colonel Beall consented to postpone taking the captives until some later day when, perhaps, a treaty could be arranged with the Indians.

Back in Taos, Kit resolved to stay at home with his wife and niece. Both he and Maxwell were "tired of leading a roving life," as Kit expressed it. They intended to establish a settlement at Rayado, where they began to erect buildings and make other improvements. Lucien Maxwell had purchased all of the Miranda-Beaubien land-grant interests, which made him the owner of the largest tract of privately owned land in the United States. He now built an adobe mansion from which to rule it.

In October of 1849, Kit was again called for guide duty, this time on a grizzly affair. A large caravan under the command of Francis Xavier Aubrey was traveling the Santa Fe Trail (Aubrey had just won fame as a result of his ride from Independence to Santa Fe, 780 miles, in the record time of eight days). With Aubrey was a prominent merchant, James W. White, his young wife, and their baby daughter. A few days out of Santa Fe, Aubrey, thinking that danger of an Indian attack had passed, gave his permission for the White family to take a small escort and ride ahead.

What the caravan members did not know at the time was that the hated Apache chief White Wolf and his band had been following them for many days but had not attacked because they were out-numbered. When the White party left the main caravan, White Wolf was waiting. He and his warriors came to the White camp and asked for presents but were refused and ordered to leave. The Indians rode off but later attacked the White group, killing a Negro servant and a Mexican, who fell on the fire. Mr. White and the others tried to escape, but the Apaches killed all of them except Mrs. White and the child, who were made captives. A short time later, some Mexicans came by and, seeing the wagons, started to plunder. The Indians, concealed near by, fired at them and wounded a young boy, who was left for dead. He lay quietly until the Indians had gone and then, with an arrow sticking between the bones of his arm, wandered around until he found safety with a party of Americans.

The next day, Aubrey and his caravan found the remains of the White camp. They buried the dead and sent an express to Santa Fe with the news. At Taos a rescue party was organized. Major William N. Grier of the First U.S. Dragoons, then in command at Taos, employed Antonio Leroux and a man named Fisher as guides, and when the dragoons arrived at Rayado, Grier hired Kit.

White Wolf soon learned that he was being trailed and there-after used every trick he knew to mislead his pursuers. Kit, how-ever, knew that when the trail apparently led up a mountain and away from water, it was a fake trail devised by the crafty White Wolf. Another scheme to throw off the whites was effected when the Indians broke camp each day: a number of Indians separated into small groups and rode in different directions, meeting later at some appointed place.

For ten or twelve days the soldiers followed the Indians over difficult trails, finding in each camp abandoned by the Indians some article belonging to Mrs. White. Sometimes it would be only a piece of her clothing, but it spurred the rescuers on. Finally, the day came. The Indian camp was sighted, and Kit immediately rode for it at a gallop, calling the men to charge in a surprise attack, but Major Grier ordered a halt, upon the advice of Leroux, to parley with the Indians.

Just as the halt was ordered, a shot rang out, the bullet passing through Grier's coat and lodging in his gauntlets, which were in his pocket. As soon as he had recovered from the shock of the impact, he ordered his men to charge, but it was too late. The Indians had fled, leaving Mrs. White's body, shot through the heart with an arrow, behind them. The signs indicated that she was trying to run toward her rescuers when the Indians cut her down. No trace of the child was found.

On the return to Taos, near Las Vegas, one of the worst winter storms in Kit's memory struck suddenly and forced them to take refuge in the woods. One man was frozen to death. The same storm engulfed the Apaches' camp and many of them were frozen to death, but not White Wolf, who met his fate on March 5, 1854, when Lieutenant David Bell of the First Dragoons shot him and then, "so tenacious of life was he," smashed his head with a large rock.

When Mrs. White's brother, Isaac Dunn, came to Taos to investigate the murder of his sister and to see if he could locate her daughter, Kit told him that the treatment his sister had received from the Indians had been so brutal that she could not possibly have lived long. Congress had appropriated $1,500.00 to ransom the child, and Agent Calhoun sent word that if they did not deliver her, they would receive a justly deserved punishment. The child was never found, however, and after many years Isaac Dunn gave up the search.

13 ★ Indian Agent

DURING THE WINTER OF 1849–50, when a detachment of dragoons under the command of Leigh Holbrook was stationed at Rayado, the Indians were more hostile than usual. They were, they told Kit, prepared to make a desperate last stand to protect their land from the invasion of the whites.

The spring of 1849 brought an incredible surge of gold-seeking California-bound emigrants over the Santa Fe and Oregon trails. Most of them took the Santa Fe Trail to Bent's Fort, then veered in various directions to cross the mountains. The stories of gold did not excite Kit Carson, nor did gold-fever seize William Bent, now owner of Bent's Fort since the death of George Bent in October, 1847, and the murder of Charles in January of the same year.

William was occupied with Indian troubles, and he must have been perturbed about the recent cholera epidemic which had wiped out half the southern branch of his wife's people, the Cheyennes. The Indians believed the white man had brought this bad magic to them in order to kill them off; they didn't know that cholera struck in the white man's cities as well. Its ravages were seen in the hundreds of graves dotting the Oregon Trail. In vain the Indians had tried to outrun the invisible enemy, "the big cramps," as they called it.

William Bent, who lost his Cheyenne wife when their fourth child was born, married her sister, Yellow Woman, a traditional Indian custom among the Cheyennes. It was generally believed by William's many friends that the loss of his wife and the shock of the cholera epidemic temporarily deranged him. Others expressed belief that he was angry because the government had made him such a low offer for the fort, which was to be used as an army post.

On the night Yellow Woman's mother died of cholera, she took the body to a tree by the river, where she and some of the Cheyennes placed it on a scaffold in the high branches, as was their burial custom. Then she took the children back to the fort, where William sat moody and depressed. The next day, August 21, he ordered the fort stripped of every movable article of value; twenty wagons were loaded with furs, trade articles, fur presses, guns, and other valuables. He then moved his wife and children five miles down the river to a new camp. When he had settled them in their tents, he rode back to the fort alone.

A strange conflict must have raged in William's heart. Here was the largest adobe fortress ever built. It was a trading post for the Indians, not a military post from which to fight them, or even a place for the Indians to hold their dances, nor was it built for the Indians to capture and use against the whites. Perhaps all of these things were going through William's mind as he rolled kegs of powder into the rooms of the fort and set fire to the wooden *vigas* and the heavy wooden doors. Now the Indians could never move in and hold dances to mock him, nor could the United States Army ever use these walls as a fortress against his wife's people.

As William rode back to his Indian wife and his halfblood children, a tremendous explosion split the evening air—the death cry, so to speak, of the greatest trading fort in the history of the Southwest. For two days a pall of black smoke hung over the area.[1]

William Bent built another and smaller trading post at Big Timbers, which proved to be a better location for trading than the old

---

[1] This is the story of the destruction of Bent's Fort as told by Teresina Bent Scheurich and passed on to Blanche Grant. However, C. W. Hurd, in his *Bent's Stockade*, says that "the best authorities agree, and the results of recent research practically prove, that William Bent did not destroy his Fort." Mr. Hurd quotes Rufus Phillips and P. G. Scott, both of whom arrived in that part of the country about 1870, as saying that the fort was not blown up. Mr. Hurd also says that Robert Bent, William's son, made a statement at Boggsville to the same effect.

fort. Kit wondered if that could have been the real reason behind the destruction of the adobe castle on the Arkansas. William never said, and time has kept his secret well.

Sometime in March, 1849, the Indians attacked Kit's ranch at Rayado to steal horses and wounded two Mexican herders. One of the Mexicans managed to get to Rayado, about two miles away, to give the alarm. Kit, Bill New (who was later killed by some of the same Indians), Holbrook, and the dragoons hurried to the ranch and at daybreak picked up the trail. They followed it for twenty-five miles before catching up with the raiders. In a surprise attack, they killed five of the nine Indians and recaptured all of the horses except the four ridden by the Indians who escaped.

On May 5, 1850, Kit and Tim Goodale made a trip to Fort Laramie "with thirty horses and mules." They made a good trade, for travelers to California always needed fresh animals by the time they reached Fort Laramie. When Kit started home, his only companion was a Mexican boy; Goodale had gone on to California to hunt for gold. On the trail, Kit learned that the Apaches were waylaying travelers, and when he stopped at Greenhorn Settlement to recruit animals for the home journey, Charles Kinney offered to accompany him to Rayado. They traveled only at night and covered about forty miles the first night. At daybreak, they hid their horses in the brush, and Kit climbed a high tree to look for Indians. He remained there all day, at times nearly falling asleep. Near evening, he saw some Indians about half a mile away; they had not discovered the whites' trail. Kit quickly scrambled out of the tree. He and Kinney saddled their animals but kept to the brush until dark, then took the road to Red River and home.

Upon Kit's arrival at Rayado, he found that the Indians had stolen all his stock. Although troops were stationed there at the time, there were so many Indians swarming around that the troops were afraid to attack them. Kit must have reported his loss to army headquarters because in a short time Major Grier was sent to return the animals. He killed some of the Indians and returned all of the stock except that eaten by the Indians.

In the spring of 1851, Kit received a pair of silver-mounted pistols. Engraved upon them was a message of appreciation from the donors commemorating the occasion which called for the gifts. The previous fall, Samuel Weatherhead and Elias Brevoort left Santa Fe for the States with a large amount of money. A Mr. Fox and some thirty men joined forces with them, or were hired by them as escorts through Indian country. Fox developed a scheme to murder the two merchants, promising to divide the money among those who would help him. In Taos, Fox revealed his plan to an acquaintance, but the man didn't report it until the Weatherhead-Brevoort party was well on its way. He finally told the story to Lieutenant Oliver Hazard Perry Taylor, who got in touch with Kit to ask his help. Kit felt that it was too late to stop the murders, but he was willing to try. With ten dragoons, he rode out to intercept the party. The second night out, they met Captain R. S. Ewell, who added himself and his twenty-five soldiers to the pursuit. They took the shortest possible route and rode day and night until they overtook the caravan.

Weatherhead and Brevoort must have turned pale when they heard about the fate they had escaped. Kit took the would-be murderers back to Taos, where they were eventually set free because, according to the report, they had not actually committed a crime. Kit would accept no reward from the grateful gentlemen, so the pistols were sent to him in appreciation.

In March of 1851, Kit set out for St. Louis with twelve wagons to purchase merchandise for Lucien Maxwell. At Westport, Kit boarded a steamboat for St. Louis, where he bought the supplies and took them (by boat) back to Westport Landing for transfer to his wagons. Kit does not mention it in his autobiography, but he now went to Fayette to get Adaline and take her to New Mexico. With her came young Susan, daughter of Robert Carson, and Susan's husband, Jesse Nelson. They returned to Westport, rejoined the wagons at the mouth of the Kansas River, and set out for Taos along the Santa Fe Trail. Kit decided to take the Bent's Fort fork of the trail because there would be more grass and water for the animals.

About fifteen miles from the Arkansas River crossing, they encountered a village of Cheyennes. Skirting it, they camped some twenty miles beyond. Kit knew that for some reason the Cheyennes were angry with the whites; what he did not know until later was that a Cheyenne chief had been beaten by one of Colonel Edwin V. Sumner's officers. The young chief had seen a ring on an officer's wife and had taken it from her finger to look at it. The woman screamed for her husband, who came running up with a buggy whip and lashed the chief across the face. To an Indian this was the greatest of insults and was to be avenged on the next white party available. Kit's caravan happened to be the one.

The Indians came in two's and three's to visit Kit's camp. They talked among themselves as they smoked, saying that "they could easily kill [Kit] with a knife, and, as for the Mexicans . . . they could kill them as easily as buffalo." Kit was alarmed. He had only thirteen Mexicans and two Americans with him, and he knew the Mexicans would be of little use in a fight, such as this would be. Then, too, he was worried about the two girls, whom he had ordered to remain concealed in the wagons until the Indians had gone.

Kit told the Indians that he was ignorant of the cause of their seeking his scalp, that he had done them no injury. He ordered them from the camp, saying that any who refused to leave would be shot. When they had rejoined their fellows, he ordered the men to hitch up the horses and mules and move on fast and to carry their rifles in one hand and their whips in the other. The wagon train moved on in close formation, the two girls staying out of sight in one of the wagons, with Kit and Nelson riding near by. They traveled until dark, when they were forced to make camp, for their tired animals could go no farther, although Kit knew the Indians still followed.

Calling one of the Mexicans to him, Kit told him to ride hard to Rayado, where the soldiers were stationed, for help. The night passed quietly and before dawn Kit's group was on the trail. The Indians followed closely all morning, and at noon, five of them approached. Kit ordered them to halt, then let them come into camp so that he could inform them that he had sent a messenger to Rayado to bring troops. The Indians checked the trail, saw that Kit had indeed sent for help, and immediately left the vicinity.

Meanwhile, the Mexican boy whom Kit sent for help met Colonel Sumner the third day out. He delivered Kit's letter, but the Colonel refused to send aid, so the boy continued on to Rayado, where Major Grier detailed Lieutenant Robert Johnston and party to go to Carson's rescue. On the way, Lieutenant Johnston met Colonel Sumner, who now sent Major Henry Carleton and thirty men along.

Kit was annoyed about the whole affair. "To the Colonel [Sumner] I do not consider myself under any obligations," he said, "for two days previously by his conduct he showed plainly that . . . rendering aid to a few American citizens in the power of Indians, enraged by the conduct of some of his command, was not his wish." And Kit obviously considered the officer's treatment of the Indian most unfair: "I presume courage was oozing from the finger ends of the officer, and, as the Indians were in his power, he wished to be relieved of such [a] commodity."

Kit warmly thanked Majors Carleton and Grier and Lieutenant Johnston for coming to his assistance. Colonel Sumner undoubtedly wished to make amends for the shoddy way he had treated Carson, for he appointed him purchasing agent for the Utes and Cheyennes at the Rayado post. Maxwell was given the contract for supplies.

Jesse and Susan Nelson built a home on the Rayado near Kit's ranch, and Susan and Adaline often rode in the safer areas about the ranch. Adaline, slim, dark, and vivacious, with flashing black eyes, was a high-spirited girl and could ride any horse on her father's ranch, with or without a saddle. A crack shot, she also taught Susan the art of shooting from the saddle.

In the spring of 1852, Kit and Maxwell "rigged up a party of eighteen men" for a final trapping spree through their old haunts in the Rocky Mountains. They worked their way to Bayou Salade, then traveled down the South Platte to the plains. They worked hard, but they also loafed, for this was indeed enjoyment for these retired "men of the beaver." They relived the good old days of expeditions into the mountains like boys returned to the treasure islands of their childhood. They traveled for some two months, trapping, living off the land, enjoying the majestic scenery. The streams yielded beaver in abundance, and the men were soon as skilled with their traps as they had been ten or fifteen years before.

On July 4, they entertained a party of Sioux Indians with a feast of bear steaks. Some of the older Indians knew Kit, and all of the young warriors in the band had heard of him. To them, he was the bravest white man living. They talked and smoked after the meal. Some spoke of the invisible foe—cholera—and how it had frightened many of their war chiefs into peace. The Sioux and other tribes, one of the braves told Kit, felt that smallpox and cholera had been sent by the Great Spirit to punish them for their warlike ways against the whites and some of their Indian brothers.

From the Laramie Plains, the mountain men went to New Park, then trapped to Old Park and back to Bayou Salade. They ranged to the Arkansas at the mouth of Royal Gorge, trapped it to where it comes out of the mountains. From there they followed the Rayado River through Raton Range to the settlement of Rayado. They were well laden with pelts, which fact caused Oliver Wiggins to speak of the trip as "a grand trapping expedition."

After New Mexico was ceded to the United States in February, 1848, by the Treaty of Guadalupe Hidalgo, the American bishops and priests of the Seventh Council of Baltimore petitioned the ecclesiastical administration for separation from Mexico. When Kit left for Missouri to bring his daughter home, New Mexico had already become a territory (September 9, 1850), and when he returned, the legislature had begun to function, with Padre Martinez presiding and six other Catholic priests among its thirteen members from seven counties.

Sometime that year, according to family records, Kit's daughter Adaline married Louey Simond, or Simmons. She and her husband went to California, and little is known of her life after that. She later married George Stilts, and in 1861, when she was only twenty-four, she died near Mono Lake, California. Her grave, by the lake, lay neglected until 1930, when on Mark Twain Day a monument placed there by Venita McPherson was unveiled by the actor Henry B. Walthall.

In February of 1853, Kit and Maxwell embarked upon a new kind of adventure. They had heard that sheep were selling in California for very high prices, so Kit suggested buying some from the Navahos, who always had too many and would gladly sell them for a few cents a head. At Río Abajo, Kit purchased 6,550 head and Maxwell bought about 2,000. Kit returned with his sheep to Rayado, where Tom Boggs, Henry Mercure, and John Bernavette and their men were waiting to go with him to California.

Kit led his party to Fort Laramie, then took the emigrant trail to California. They passed through the mountains during the summer; it was pleasant and easy traveling, with good grazing for sheep. On August 1, they arrived at their destination and sold their sheep to ranch-owner Samuel Norris for $5.50 a head. Maxwell arrived at Sacramento shortly thereafter with 1,700 of his original 2,000 sheep; Kit and his group had been more fortunate, losing only 50 head along the trail. From Carson River, Maxwell sent Kit a message, which he received at Sacramento, asking him to await his arrival so that they could travel back home together.

Kit went to San Francisco and stayed at the Niantic Hotel. He could hardly believe that it was the same town he had visited with Frémont only a few years before. It was a sleepy little village of perhaps two or three thousand inhabitants then; now it had a population of almost forty thousand.

While Kit and Boggs were in or near San Francisco, they visited Kit's younger brother, Lindsey, and his family at their ranch on the Russian River. Moses, Kit's older half-brother, was there, too. Robert, another brother, had come to California sometime in the fifties; with him was his nephew, Moses Briggs, son of Nancy Carson Briggs, Kit's sister.

Kit also saw Adaline for the last time. At Napa County he officiated at the laying of a cornerstone for Lilburn Boggs' house, which was the first building in the valley. His fame as a result of Frémont's writings made him recognized and sought after, so much so that he cut short his visit in San Francisco.

Maxwell took a steamer to Los Angeles, but no amount of talk would persuade Kit to accompany him. He said: "I would not travel on the sea, having made a voyage on that in 1846 and was so disgusted with it, that I swore that it would be the last time I would leave sight of land when I could get a mule to perform the journey." And by mule Kit went to Los Angeles, arriving there fifteen days after Maxwell.

Kit, Boggs, and Maxwell prepared for the long journey to New Mexico. Los Angeles had grown since Kit last saw it, but only slightly compared to the rapid strides of San Francisco. There were probably about two hundred people living there on Kit's last visit; now there were some two thousand, and the Spanish influence was dominant.

They were soon ready to leave and so set out. Kit says they passed a Pima village and from there, "on account of the scarcity of grass, we continued up the Gila to the mouth of the San Pedro." They traveled up this stream for three days, then cut across to the copper mines. From there they pressed on to the Río del Norte and through the Río Abajo country, where they had bought the sheep, to Taos, arriving there in December, 1853.

Before reaching home Kit learned from the Mormon delegate to Congress, Dr. John Milton Bernhisel, that he had been appointed Indian agent for the Moache Ute, Jicarilla Apache, and Pueblo Indians. The Apaches were considered the most savage of the 350,000 Indians governed by 100 agents and superintendents throughout the United States.

On January 9, 1854, after spending the holidays with his family, Kit reported for duty at the Ute agency. His bond (for $5,000) was signed by Carlos Beaubien and Peter Joseph and was dated January 6. Since his office was at Taos (on the west side of the plaza), he moved Josefa, their small son William, and his niece, Teresina Bent, there.

David Meriwether became governor of New Mexico Territory and ex officio superintendent of Indian affairs there on May 22, 1853. When Governor Meriwether investigated Indian affairs, he concluded that prior to leaving office, his predecessor had spent large sums on the Indians and had made lavish promises to them. Meriwether decided to be strict with his charges, not to coddle them, as he termed it, and to deal with them sternly. His strict ways were resented by the Indians, who got entirely out of hand during his administration. Long before anyone fully realized what was happening, the hungry, destitute Indians resorted to stealing, marauding, and finally war to get what they needed. There was little game left, thanks to the white man, and unless the government supported them, they were doomed to starvation.

It was under these conditions and in this tense situation that Kit Carson became Indian agent in New Mexico Territory. He was well qualified for the job, better by far, one might observe, than was Governor Meriwether for his position as superintendent.

Hardly had Kit established his office when trouble broke out. In February, the Apaches began plundering and stealing from the settlers. Lieutenant David Bell and his dragoons killed a number of Apaches, forcing the rest to retreat, in a fight at Red River. One or two soldiers were killed and several wounded. When Kit heard of the affair, he feared a general war would result. In March, just before he went to Santa Fe on business, he set out to visit a large band of Jicarilla Apaches who were camped about twenty miles from Taos. He went alone, and he talked of peace, trying hard to convince them that their hostility toward the whites would only result in punishment for themselves and their families. He insisted that they prove their sincerity by pledging to follow the line of peaceful conduct which he, as their agent, had laid down. The Apache chiefs, after expressing great pleasure at his being made their agent, assured Kit that they would keep the peace, but their assurance didn't fool Kit for a moment.

While Kit was in Santa Fe, the Indians got into trouble again, and Lieutenant J. W. Davidson of the First Dragoons and sixty dragoons of Company F were sent out against them. The Indians were well fortified in the Embudo Mountains about twenty miles southwest of Taos, and seeing that they outnumbered the troops, they decided to make a stand. The troops occupied the banks of a small stream next to the mountain upon which the Indians had established themselves. The dragoons fought their way up the mountain on foot, leaving their horses in charge of a few guards.

The Indians had the dragoons surrounded, firing upon them from every direction. Finally, Lieutenant Davidson was forced to retreat or face losing most of his men. As the whites withdrew, the Indians rushed them in great numbers, forcing them to turn and fight. Their arrival at camp was timely, for the Indians had rushed the guards and stolen some of the horses.

When the dragoons retreated, they left twenty-two men dead on the battlefield, and nearly every man in the company had a wound of some sort. This Indian victory, called the Battle of Cieneguilla, was fought on March 30, 1854. When Kit returned from Santa Fe the following day, he passed near the battlefield but did not see a single Indian.

On April 4, Lieutenant Colonel Cooke, "the very peppery man with a language," commanded a large force of regular troops against the Apaches. Kit Carson acted as guide and agent for the government. From a camp on the Río Puerco, Kit wrote to William S. Messervy, acting governor and superintendent, reporting that in his opinion the Apaches had been driven to war by the actions of the troops stationed in the vicinity of Taos and that the vigorous pursuit of the Apaches through the mountains had led them to believe that no quarter or mercy from the government would be given. He added: "It would be best for them to be sent for, and a fair and just treaty made with them."

Acting Governor Messervy did not agree with Kit, and neither did the Army, of course. This was the beginning of a long period during which Kit spent his time fighting for a square deal for the Indians; his earnest plea was to feed them and keep all promises made to them. Messervy's answer to Kit's appeal was:

> You will see that war actually exists between the United States and the Jicarilla Apache Indians and that it was commenced by the Indians themselves. I can not under any circumstances make peace with these Indians, much less make overtures to them. They are now beyond the control of this department, and until I have the assurance of General

Garland Commanding this Military Department, that they are chastised to the extent that faith can be placed in their promises of future good conduct, I shall listen to no terms of peace.

Now Governor Messervy had overstepped his authority when he declared war on the Apaches without the consent of Congress and the President, but the step was necessary. It was such acts as these, totally lacking in understanding of the Indians' problems, which kept them at war with the whites for so many, many years.

In the meantime, Kit and the dragoons chased the Apaches past the Arroyo Hondo down to its junction with the Río Grande, through deep canyons and across rock-filled river beds, to the village of Servilleta. Here they camped.

It took two days to pick up the trail of the Apaches, and in two days more they caught up with them. Charging the Indians, the dragoons killed several and captured all the camp equipment and a number of horses. One soldier was killed and one wounded. They continued the pursuit for many miles through a deep canyon, until they had killed seven more warriors and wounded many others, at which time they returned to the captured camp to spend the night.

The wounded man, with an escort of soldiers, was sent to Taos to receive medical aid. The others followed the Apaches for six days but could not overtake them. The Indians would break up into small bands and circle back. Thus when the soldiers followed a trail, they ended up at almost the same place from which they had started. This must have been amusing to Kit, who knew how difficult the Apaches were to trail.

When the escort was returning to the field from Taos, they met a Ute Indian. Thinking he was unfriendly, they captured him and took his weapons and horse, but he escaped and joined his tribe. Colonel Cooke and Kit were worried that the Utes might become angry and join the Apaches, so Kit was sent to Taos to talk to the Utes and explain that the soldiers had believed the man they captured to be an Apache. Kit returned the Indian's horse and weapons and told the Utes he hoped they would remain friendly. If they didn't, he said, they would be treated as enemies. They did remain comparatively peaceful during the long Indian wars, except on one occasion when they joined the Apaches in 1855.

A most serious incident with the Utes which required Kit's attention was the theft of thirty head of animals belonging to Juan Benito Valdez and Jesús María Sanchez. A military escort of sixteen men under Major Thompson and Lieutenant Davidson was sent to help Kit recover the animals. They pursued the Utes unsuccessfully for sixty or seventy miles northeast of Fort Massachusetts. They recovered only ten or twelve head, which the Utes had abandoned.

On March 21, 1854, Agent Carson reported to Messervy:

> The game in the Ute country is becoming scarce, and they are unable to support themselves by the chase and hunt, and the government has but one alternative, either to subsist and clothe them or exterminate them.

Kit was of the opinion that the Indians would have to be made to know and feel the power of the government before they would respect it enough to become peaceful. He felt, too, that the government had to accept its responsibility in regard to the Indians.

The war against the Apaches continued, with Major Brooks taking the field in pursuit of them. He met with little success. Kit said of him: "[He] had been in the field some 10 or 15 days and had not the fortune to meet any of the enemy." The Major saw many trails but didn't know which one to follow. In all probability, if he had chosen one to follow, he would have gone in a circle, finally arriving back where he started.

On May 23, Kit again left his agency to accompany the Army against the Apaches. Major James H. Carleton and his First Dragoons rode out of Taos on that day to Fort Massachusetts, from which point Captain Quinn and his scouts started west to find the Indians' trail. Kit and Major Carleton's group met Quinn three days later on the Huerfano River. It was apparent to Kit that from the place where Major Brooks had given up his pursuit, the Indians had headed for Mosca Pass. Sure enough, when they went through the pass, Kit found a place where the Indians had camped some days before. For six days they followed the trail through rugged ravines, canyons, and mountain passes. On the day they caught up with the Indians, Kit told Major Carleton that if the party met with no accident, they would overtake the Indians about two o'clock. The Major replied that if they did, he would buy Kit "one of the finest hats that could be procured in New York." Says Kit: "The Indians were found at the hour I had predicted. The Major fulfilled his promise presenting to me a hat he had directed to be made in New York,—and a fine one it was." Inside it was this inscription: "At two o'clock, Kit Carson from Major Carleton."

Now that they had discovered their quarry, Major Carleton ordered a charge. The Indians fled, with the dragoons hot on their heels. The brush around the encampment was thick, affording excellent cover, and in it Captain Quinn and three of his Indian scouts concealed themselves. Hoping to call back the Indians who were in hiding in the undergrowth, Quinn had one of his scouts give the rally call of the Apaches. Only two warriors and two squaws made their appearance, and they were immediately fired upon. One warrior was killed, and the others fled.

Major Carleton scoured the countryside, but the Indians had vanished. On the eleventh of June, the expedition returned to Taos.

When Kit was in Taos, the Indians visited him at his office and at his home east of the town plaza. He would sit on the long portal of his adobe house after work hours or on Sundays, smoking and talking with Indians who came to visit "Father Kit," as they affectionately called him. They considered him their true friend and benefactor.

The Utes came often to visit Kit; the Apaches, often drunk and sullen, stayed away. In the daytime they could be seen stumbling, intoxicated, around the village plaza. Taos livestock was driven out to graze during the day, then brought in to the community corral at night. The Indians were turned out before the gates were locked, and guards maintained their stations.

In September, 1854, Kit reported on the Utes:

They seem to manifest the most peaceful relations toward the United States and say they are desirous of remaining at peace with the United States. . . . They complain that they are poor and that the game is scarce . . . and that while all the Indians of the North are receiving presents, they are receiving none. . . . I would respectfully suggest that as the inclement season is now very near, that you, at an early day as possible call them together and make them presents of Blankets, Shirts & I deem this to be a matter of great importance.

Kit was again trying to see that the Indians were cared for properly. He knew what suffering they faced in the long winter months. He knew, too, that if they were hungry, they would resort to stealing.

In November, just before the Indians were called in for council and the distribution of presents, one of their number was killed by a Mexican who wanted to steal his coat. In the same month, a party of Pueblo Indians who were under Kit's agency was attacked by a party of Cheyennes or Arapahoes while they were in the Raton Mountains hunting deer and antelope. Twelve Pueblos were killed, among whom were some who had served with distinction against the Apaches under the command of Colonel Cooke. Kit reported the affair to Santa Fe and steps were taken to punish the guilty Indians, but nothing was accomplished.

The Utes did not fare very well as a result of being called in by Governor Meriwether to receive presents. They believed that some of the coats they received were contaminated because each chief who got a coat died of smallpox. To them, this meant that their white father had planned to destroy them with the coats, so they joined the Apaches in a raid on Costilla in northern New Mexico. The Jicarillas and Moaches were led by bold, handsome Chief Blanco of the Utes, whom Peters described as having a "lofty forehead and features as regular as if carved for sculptured perfection."

Again the dragoons were called out by Governor Meriwether. When Colonel Thomas Fauntleroy arrived at Cantonment Burgwin from Fort Union, there appeared in the regulars and volunteers such widely known men as Lieutenant Colonel Céran St. Vrain, Lieutenant Albert H. Pfeiffer, Alexander McDowell McCook,

Captain Manuel Antonio Chavez (a descendant of the conquistador DeVargas), and Kit Carson, who was acting as Indian agent and as guide to Fauntleroy.

Colonel Fauntleroy arrived in February of 1855 and in March received orders to take the field for battle. He had four companies of volunteers, about five hundred men, at his disposal.

No doubt Kit was glad to escape the tedious office routine, with its monthly reports, and be out in the open again. Governor Meriwether had returned his latest report, requesting more information. Kit was being too brief with his pen:

> I have to acknowledge the receipt of your report for the month of February last and to inform you that I apprehend it will not prove to be such a document as is desired by the Department at Washington.[2]

Colonel Fauntleroy's command rode from Taos to Fort Massachusetts, then traveled on to the Río del Norte, which they followed to the point where it leaves the mountains. From here they cut north to Saguache Pass, where they found the Indians in great numbers. A battle ensued and the Indians fled. An artillery detachment was left with the provisions while the rest of the troops pursued the Indians. Fauntleroy caught them on the headwaters of the Arkansas River a few days later and after a short battle defeated them. A few warriors were killed and some of the Indians' horses were captured. The weather became intensely cold and the passes covered with snow, forcing them to return to Taos. Kit said some of the days were as cold "as ever I experienced."

[2] Records reveal that Governor Meriwether detained Kit on the latter's trip to Santa Fe, actually placing him under temporary arrest until the inconsistencies in his accounts were cleared up.

14 ★ The Civil War

IN THE YEAR 1855 Sergeant Smith Simpson mustered out of the volunteers, stayed in Taos, married a Spanish woman, and reared a family. He later gave Edwin Legrand Sabin, author of *Kit Carson Days*, information about his friendship with Kit, saying that he did much of the clerical work and bookkeeping for Carson while he was Indian agent. Simpson's daughter, however, denies his statement. Perhaps he did help, but there is no record of his name as clerk or interpreter in any of the official correspondence while Kit was agent.

Kit did have some help with records, correspondence, and bookkeeping, and, according to Ute agency records, he apparently paid these men out of his own salary most of the time. The records show that he was allowed a certain yearly sum for an interpreter, but the first knowledge Governor Meriwether had of the situation was September 29, 1855, when he wrote Carson: "Charges for expenses of *self and clerk* at Santa Fé $15 when I am ignorant of any regulation which authorizes an Agent to have a clerk." Kit's correspondence had named John W. Dunn as interpreter and described him as of "steady habits, and attentive, industrious and skillful in the discharge of his duties." Other clerks and helpers on record in the agency office over the years of Kit's service were: C. Williams and J. P. Esmay and John Mostin, about whom Carson wrote on August 31, 1858: "I have in the employ of the Indian department John Mostin as interpreter, a native of Clinton County, New York, aged

29 years, at a salary of $500 per annum. He was appointed June 1, 1857 at the Agency."

Most of Kit's time was spent away from the office; he was either fighting Indians or trying to make peace with them. Colonel Fauntleroy rode against the Apaches again in April, 1855, this time with better results. Colonel St. Vrain routed the Indians at the Purgatoire River and captured their animals and equipment. Kit said of St. Vrain: "He immediately took the field again, and kept in pursuit of [the] Indians till a few days before the expiration of [his men's] service. If the Volunteers had continued in the service three months [longer] and had [been] under the command and sole direction of Colonel St. Vrain, there would never again have [been] need [of] any troops in this [part of the] country." Such was Kit's good opinion of St. Vrain's ability; however, the records show that long after St. Vrain was dead, and Kit, too, for that matter, there was at times a great need for troops in New Mexico.

About July, 1856, the negotiation of peace treaties with the Indians began. First, the Indians who were at peace were called in to the agency, and peace treaties and agreements made. Then, in July, the warring factions of both the Apaches and the Utes asked for peace; Governor Meriwether granted their request in August.

Orders from the Governor directed Kit to assemble the Jicarilla Apaches and the Capote Utes at Abiquiu on September 4 to receive their annuities. The next day, September 5, while some of the presents were being distributed, a Ute chief who was dissatisfied with his gifts raised his gun to shoot the Governor. The Indians standing near the irate chief quickly overpowered him before he could fire. A rumor was circulated that Agent Carson was the instigator of the disturbance. Upon hearing this report, Kit immediately wrote to the Governor, disclaiming any knowledge of the affair and stating that he was not present at the time of the disturbance. The Governor's answer reassured him that he had not heard the rumor and that the disturbance was a mild one.

The treaties, which were never fully lived up to by either the United States government or the Indians, provided for a yearly allotment of cash if the Indians would settle on some land of their choice and farm it. The treaties are long and involved, and both the government and the Indians agreed to responsibilities they couldn't possibly fulfill. Kit well knew that the Indians wouldn't keep their promises of peace, and of the United States he said:

> The Superintendent went on to Washington with his treaties, which were laid before the Senate. They have not been confirmed as yet, nor should they be, as they are not of a character to suit the people. The Apaches are now committing depredations daily which go unpunished, and in my opinion they may again commence hostilities ere long. The other tribes [Utes] will comply with their provisions, I think, and will not be hostile again if the government does not stop their supplies of provisions during such times as they cannot hunt.

The Utes and Apaches of Carson's agency roamed so wide an area that he could not comply with the Interior Department's requests to report on the exact number of Indians under his control. Their very freedom was a temptation for them to raid the settlers and steal horses. Kit knew all of this, and many times he must have looked the other way—unless the offenses were too serious to be disregarded. Then the troops were notified and the Indians were punished. Kit continued to talk peace to the Indians; he tried to persuade them to settle down to farming, but he must have known at the time that it was useless as well as almost impossible.

Military forts were being built from New Mexico to Oregon in order to protect settlers and travelers, but the Indians continued to raid the whites' corrals whenever they had the chance. Fort Union was established in 1851. Thirty miles north of Las Vegas and a hundred miles northeast of Santa Fe, in 1854 it became headquarters for the Northern Military District of New Mexico and general supply depot for all army detachments in New Mexico. Many other forts were erected and put into operation; a rough line of them stretched southward along the Río Grande to the Mexican border and on either side into Apache country and up through Ute and Navaho country.

Fort Union, however, was the post of importance to Maxwell and Kit. Although it retarded the growth of Mora, Taos, Costilla, Abiquiu, and Rayado, it helped the expansion of Cimarron and Las Vegas and virtually made Lucien Maxwell a success. It didn't impede the Indians much—they stole stock from the fort as well as from each other whenever they had the chance.

Kit seemed to have a way with the Indians. This relationship might have been due to the fact that he was completely unafraid of them. He was also able to understand their problems. Whenever there was trouble of any kind, Kit was summoned to the scene. He usually had the right approach and could calm the Indians as well as the whites and Mexicans. On one such occasion, Ute Chief Colorow gave quite a scare to Mora residents, who immediately sent for Kit.

Captain Robert Morris and his company of cavalry had picked up two Utes caught stealing stock and were on their way to deliver them to Agent Carson at Taos. Morris stopped at Mora to spend the night, requesting quarters for his men and forage for his horses as he halted in front of Colonel St. Vrain's store. This was provided, and the two Indian prisoners were put under guard. The mill corral where the soldiers and the two prisoners were housed was enclosed by a solid adobe wall with a heavy double gate. The troops were busy feeding their horses and grooming them for the night and the cooks were preparing dinner. Captain Morris was in St. Vrain's office, talking and having a glass of sparkling Catawba. Everyone, including Morris, knew that Colorow and his band had been in the valley for two weeks, quietly hunting and trading with the village residents.

It wasn't long after the animals had been fed that the guard heard a knock on the corral gate and, thinking it was Captain Morris, opened the gate. Facing him was Colorow, backed by some 150 war-painted warriors. Not a sound was made, no war whoops ejected, and Chief Colorow had on no war paint. Before the guard had a chance to cry out, two husky Indians rode in, grabbed the prisoners, who were sitting by the fire, threw them on their horses as silently as possible, and rode past the guards and into the mountains beyond at top speed. Colorow and his warriors made no attempt to follow the two Indians who rode away with the prisoners.

Captain Bob, with drawn saber, came on the run as soon as he heard and saw the Indians riding off. Colorow stood facing the Captain in silence. When Morris demanded an explanation of the guard, the latter told him that there had been a misunderstanding and that "my old *compadre* [Colorow] desires an explanation for the arrest of his people." The guard suggested that they talk to St. Vrain, who, he said, "knows and has the confidence of all Indians from Missouri to the Gila, and will soon show Colorow that you only intended to take the two bad Utes over to Kit for his action as agent."

The conference in St. Vrain's office (with all the painted, feathered warriors standing without) failed to gain Colorow's consent to return the two Utes. Messages were sent to Colonel Loring at Fort Union and Kit Carson at Taos, with the result that at dawn the next day, Kit arrived, and at ten o'clock that same morning, Colonel Loring, with two hundred riflemen, rode into Mora. Colonel Loring demanded that Kit bring the Indians in for a council. This Kit did, and in vain did the Army try to induce the Utes to return to their reservation. The Chief contended that his people were doing no harm and that they had to eat. Kit said nothing, but let the Army do all the talking.

From Tuesday until Friday, Colorow consistently refused to give up the two Utes. Finally, Colonel Loring delivered an ultimatum: if by tomorrow morning "at nine o'clock I do not see you and your people passing down the valley to Taos, it is war." Colorow, probably thinking discretion the better part of valor, had his band of Ute warriors and their families strung along the entire length of the San Gertrudes Valley on their way to Taos, with their agent, Kit Carson, accompanying them.

With all the Indians and extra soldiers gone from Mora, it seemed almost too peaceful when fifteen nearly naked Apache warriors appeared in the doorway demanding to know where Kit Carson was. When asked why they wanted the agent, they replied that Colorow's Utes had stolen all of their horses the night before! One of them motioned to his legs, saying that "Apache have good legs, can catch Utes," and away they ran in pursuit of the Utes. They caught up with Colorow after a run of thirteen miles, and Kit persuaded the Utes to return the stolen horses. All went their way in peace.

That summer of 1856, Kit accompanied Lieutenants William Magruder and William Craig of the First Dragoons on a hunting trip in the Raton Mountains. And this same year, Kit's old friend Frémont ran for president and was defeated. Thus the presidential election of 1856 did not affect Kit, as well it might have, but the next one would. Kit would again enter the army, this time to fight against the land of his birth.

Right now Kit had on his mind more pressing things than the distant rumblings of trouble between the states. Following the hunting trip, he began to write his final reports to his superintendent, for his term as agent for the Utes, Apaches, and Pueblos would end in 1857. Kit's estimate for funds necessary to operate his agency during the quarter ending in March, 1857, totaled $2,290.03; the next quarter's estimate was $1,387.50. These figures seem to tally with those of other agencies and are lower than some. Much of Kit's time was now taken up with trying to determine the extent of the boundary lines of the lands belonging to Indians under his agency.

With the expiration of his first term as Indian agent, Kit could look back at what could honestly be called a period of more serious trouble than most agents had encountered. The years had been marked by the Apache war, depredations, stealing, and murders, not to mention the tedious annoyance of clerical work. He had quieted the Utes more times than were recorded, and he had worked hard to protect his Indians, the poorest of all tribes, from exposure and starvation.

Kit was reappointed agent to the same Indians for a term to end with the adjournment of the next session of the United States Senate. He accepted the honor—if honor it may be called. His bond was signed on May 26, 1857, by himself, Peter Joseph, Thomas Boggs, James B. Woodson, and Ezra DePew. Meanwhile, on March 17, James L. Collins had succeeded David Meriwether as superintendent of Indian affairs in New Mexico.

As one might expect, Kit was better equipped to handle his second term than he had been for the first. He knew more about the red man's problems: poverty, disease, too much liquor—all of which were gifts from the white man. As their agent, Kit petitioned the government to feed and clothe his Indians in exchange for their land. More than that, he advised that they be kept away from the white settlements for reasons stated in his report of August 29, 1857. He said in part:

> It gives me great pleasure to state that the Mohuache band of Utah Indians for whom I am agent, are at this present date in a more prosperous condition than for years past. They are friendly disposed towards the United States, and are well satisfied with the treatment they receive from the government.

Kit explained that gifts were given out on the eighteenth and that the Indians seemed well satisfied, which, he pointed out, was an improvement over 1854, when they started hostilities after the gifts were distributed. Moreover, he stated, the Moache Utes were not yet contaminated by the white man's vices, particularly those of drunkenness and prostitution, and he recommended that they be removed, as far as was practicable, from the settlements and taught to farm for their subsistence. Troops should be stationed near them, he said, to protect them from hostile tribes, and he entertained no doubts that "by kind treatment they might be brought to a state of civilization in a short period." At that time there were 350 males and about 400 females.

In the same report, Kit mentioned the Tabeguache Utes, who had no agent. Since they were by far the largest tribe of Utes and since their main hunting grounds were in New Mexico, he suggested that an agent be appointed to reside among them. In a report one year later, it is interesting to note that the government had appointed an agent for the Tabeguaches. His name was Kit Carson:

Some 750 Tabeguaches were added to Kit's jurisdiction and received their gifts from the agency. In a report to Superintendent Collins, Kit states:

During the year [1857 to August 1858] the Indians committed few depredations: they stole some animals from the Mexicans, and the Mexicans also stole some from them. The Indians gave me the animals stolen by them, and I made the Mexicans return the animals they had stolen, thus satisfying both parties. I have visited the Indians as often as necessary during the year, and given them such articles as they require, principally provision.

It was in the report just quoted that Kit commented on his action to prevent the Tabeguache Utes from joining the "bloodless Mormon War." The Mormons had tried to induce the Utes into an alliance against General Albert S. Johnston. Kit successfully blocked the move:

> It being thought that the Utes would join the Mormons in their opposition to the entry of the United States troops into Great Salt Lake City, I caused the allowance of their provisions to be increased, to prevent such a course being pursued by them. No Utah, as far as I know, aided the Mormons.

Brigham Young had proclaimed: "If they [the government] dare to force the issue, I shall not hold the Indians by the wrist any longer for white men to shoot at. They shall go ahead and do as they please." But it turned out that Young didn't "hold the Indians by the wrist," as he had thought.

In November of 1857, a band of Moaches stole some horses in the Arkansas River area. Kit applied to Captain Morris, commanding at Cantonment Burgwin, for military assistance and was given five soldiers. They found the Indians "on the Conejos in a severe state of hunger." When the Moaches had given up the stolen horses, Kit presented them with some 102 bushels of wheat.

Kit's third appointment as Indian agent came on March 3, 1858 (his bond was signed by Peter Joseph, Lucien Maxwell and himself and dated July 27, 1858). He had signed up for what proved to be a restless period; the Mormons were at war with the United States, and the Navahos were trying to effect a peace with the Utes at Santa Fe. The Utes would not commit themselves, claiming that the Navahos were committing depredations against them at the very time they were trying to make peace. Carson, agreeing with his Utes, felt that this was no time to make peace with the Navahos, and nothing was accomplished along peace lines.

The peace conferences which were in progress between the Utes, Arapahoes, and Cheyennes suddenly terminated when the Utes killed some of the Cheyennes and Arapahoes. Chief Blanco of the Utes had a quarrel with the leader of a surveying party, and throughout the summer trouble brewed. Kit was busy trying to keep his Utes out of mischief, but it was small trouble as yet.

During the same period, the Navahos were giving their agent considerable trouble by warring with their Mexican neighbors, the Utes, and some of the Apaches. The Navahos were the wealthiest Indians in the Southwest and ranged over a wide area from the San Juan River—west of the Río Grande, east of the Colorado, and "between the thirty-fifth and thirty-seventh parallels of north latitude," about twenty-five thousand square miles. They were a powerful tribe and probably numbered more than eight thousand people. They had large herds of sheep and many horses, raised corn and wheat, and clusters of peach trees were scattered in the fertile valleys. There was no need for them to steal and plunder. Their weaving had been developed to such an extent that they were believed to surpass any other Indians on the continent in this art. They were never destitute of warm clothing, as were the Apaches and Utes.

Kit well knew that the Navahos looked upon any type of leniency as an admission of weakness. General Kearny's talks failed to impress them; indeed, they must have been highly amused at his tactics in 1846, for in sight of his command they drove off stock, some of it belonging to his troops. In 1848, Colonel Newby took the field against them, as had Walker and Kearny before him and Washington after; but, like his predecessors, he failed to force the Indians into peace. The failures only increased the Navahos' contempt for the federal government. They continued to raid and kill and steal. In 1851, Superintendent Calhoun had written:

The Navajos commit their wrongs from a pure love of rapine and plunder. They have extensive fields of corn and wheat, fine peach orchards, and grow quantities of melons, squash, beans and peas, and have immense flocks of sheep, and a great number of mules and horses of a superior breed. They have nothing of the cow kind. . . .

When Agent Greiner told Navaho Chief Armijo at the Jemez Springs Council that the people of the Río Abajo had complained about Navaho raids, Armijo replied:

My people are all crying in the same way. Three of our chiefs now sitting before you mourn for their children—who have been taken from their homes by the Mexicans. More than two hundred of our children have been carried off and we know not where they are.

The conference failed to produce any constructive results, as usual. Peace talks like this one would continue until Colonel Kit Carson took the field against the Navahos. Although he did not want it, Kit was to help conquer this mighty tribe.

At his agency in Taos, Kit Carson continued to supply his Indian charges with plenty of food and clothing. The Utes volunteered to fight the Navahos, who had now openly revolted against the United States. Two chiefs and eighteen warriors accompanied Kit to Santa Fe, where they enlisted as soldiers.

By April of 1859, the country between Pike's Peak and Valle Salado was overrun with miners and prospectors looking for gold, which had first been discovered in the vicinity of Pike's Peak. This was the only hunting grounds the Tabeguache Utes had, Kit wrote in his report, and he feared trouble with the whites. No serious trouble had yet developed, but bad feeling ran high.

In August, when the annuities were to be presented, a near riot developed when an Indian entered a field near the Río San Antonio to pluck an ear of corn. The Mexican who owned the cornfield nearly clubbed the Indian to death. Indians camped near by heard of it and were bent upon massacring all the Mexicans and Anglos in the vicinity. Kit had been summoned when the trouble started, and he was able to pacify the indignant Indians. He advised them to start for home at once, fearing that if they stayed, there would be more serious trouble.

The Tabeguaches, resentful about the miners' trespassing on their hunting grounds, had not appeared in August for their annuities, but in October, they informed Agent Carson that they were ready to make peace and receive their presents. In August they had fought with some miners, killing five of them and losing three braves, but now they wanted peace. They took their gifts and, according to Kit, seemed well satisfied.

The campaign of the fifties had drawn to a close. Kit had proved always to be fair to his charges and to his superintendent. Although he had always been "Father Kit" to the Indians, he did not spare the rod when the whites were threatened with annihilation as the Apaches raided settlement after settlement, and when the Indians had the upper hand and defeated Lieutenant Davidson and his dragoons, Kit had taken the field against them and had shown the Army how to deal with them. At the same time, his reports had contained a continuous plea for the government to feed and clothe the Indians and, above all, to keep the promises made to them.

At the beginning of the year 1860, the Indians under Kit's jurisdiction were comparatively quiet, but the unsettled state of the Union, with rumblings of war, was felt in Taos. Kit, a Southerner by birth, must have had moments of doubt about the Union. In his report to Superintendent Collins, he said he feared disruption of the Union and proposed that the Indians' extra expenditures wait until some decision came from Washington.

It was the quiet before the storm. Abraham Lincoln was elected President of the United States to serve one of the most turbulent terms of office in American history. He and Kit were both born in the same year, both in log cabins. Both had made their mark in developing the United States, and both would be gone before the sixties were out.

This year was the last Kit served as Indian agent, for in June, 1861, he resigned to fight for the preservation of the Union. Much of his last year in office was quiet, with few important happenings other than the usual need for more food and clothing for his charges. They would visit his office when their supplies were exhausted, and since they were always hungry, Kit always had Indian visitors.

William F. M. Arny succeeded Kit in July, 1861. The agency office, which had always been in Taos, was now moved to Cimarron, forty miles east, because Taos stills and Taos Lightning were always a temptation to the Indians. Arny reported the Moaches as friendly toward the United States, and from available records, it seems that they remained friendly all during the Civil War. Perhaps Kit's peace talk had meant something after all.

In 1860, Kit had suffered a fall which at the time seemed not too serious, but as things turned out, it was one of the factors contributing to his untimely death. The accident occurred during a hunting trip in the San Juan Mountains; his companions were all ahead of him, and none of them saw what happened. He told Josefa and Teresina that he was walking beside his horse on a steep slope when the animal fell and rolled for some distance. He became entangled in the reins, he said, and was dragged along. The fall sprained his shoulder and left him with a chest injury which later developed into an aneurysm. Although he rarely complained, he must have suffered a great deal during the last years of his life.

Although Kit had resigned as Indian agent, he continued to fight for the Indians' rights and to help them as long as he lived. Trouble with the Indians of his former agency was now only occasional, for he had done his job well. Fort Union had grown in size and strength, and this year, 1861, Congress appropriated $35,000 for the improvement of the Santa Fe Trail from Fort Union to Santa Fe via Las Vegas.

In August, Kit and St. Vrain protested to Colonel E. R. S. Canby about the withdrawal of regular troops from the Territory, saying that the volunteers were unable to protect public property and the lives of public officials. During the early phases of the Civil War, the Indians of New Mexico and Arizona had continued their plundering and were now meeting with little resistance. The troops, it seemed, were preparing to fight a different kind of war.

The Navahos were still committing depredations, although they were supposedly in a state of armistice. According to Governor Connelly's report to Washington:

> Extermination by the sword or by starvation is our only remedy for the evils which they have caused and will continue to cause our people so long as there is one in existence. Something might perhaps be done by the Government in the way of colonizing, placing each tribe upon a reservation. . . .

Year after year, the same verdict had been rendered by governors, generals, and agents and troops sent against the Navahos, only to return defeated. This year was no exception.

The Civil War stirred up the Utes, Kiowas, Apaches, and Navahos, and the Confederates tried hard to use these Indians against Union troops. Kit must have been very concerned about the situation, for just after he resigned he joined the Army and on July 26, 1861, was ranked as Lieutenant Colonel. On August 31, he was rated as "Commander of Battalion New Mexico Volunteers for duty on the Plains," and on September 20, his rating was listed as *"Colonel Present."* There is no evidence of muster into service here, since the rank of colonel was made possible for him by the resignation of Colonel Céran St. Vrain on that date.

While Kit was in Taos, the American flag was torn down in the plaza, an action which aroused the entire village. Kit, St. Vrain, Captain Simpson, and five others went to the mountains and cut a long cottonwood pole. To it they nailed the flag of the Union, then set it up in the center of the plaza. Colonel Carson, with his hand on his gun, gave orders that the flag would fly day and night. He posted two men at the old Bent–St. Vrain store to guard it, for he knew there were many Southern sympathizers in Taos.

When the fighting broke out, Kit's old friend Frémont was in Europe. He promptly offered his services to his country and returned home—after first making arrangements for war purchases. He was made brigadier general and given command of the Department of the West, with headquarters at St. Louis.

The First New Mexico Volunteer Infantry was soon mobilized,

with Christopher Carson as its colonel. In October, the men were sent to Albuquerque for training, staying there until the end of January, 1862. Kit's wife and children soon joined him at Albuquerque, which seemed to make him very happy for he loved them dearly.

On January 31, Josefa and the children returned to Taos. Kit, with eight companies of his First New Mexico Volunteers, moved out of Albuquerque to join other forces at Fort Craig under Colonel Canby. On February 21, within sight of Fort Craig, they fought in the Battle of Valverde. General Henry Hopkins Sibley's Confederates routed the Union Army, by-passed Fort Craig, and marched on to Albuquerque.

The battle started in the morning when Colonel Roberts' Union troops advanced toward Sibley's Confederates. The Río Grande divided the two armies. Company K, with two field pieces, crossed the river to set up a steady fire at the Confederates. Union men and horses were badly wounded, scores killed, and many drowned as they tried to cross the river. Colonel Carson's regiment fought bravely beside the conspicuous Colorado Pike's Peakers, whose gray blouses with red stripes in front made a ready target for Sibley's men. The Union forces had the upper hand until a few hours before sundown; then it became apparent that they were taking a bad beating. Canby's army, or what was left of it, retreated some six miles to Fort Craig after burying its dead under a flag of truce. Of the Confederate soldiers, 36 men were reported killed, and 150 wounded were taken to Socorro and Albuquerque. Canby reported three officers and 65 men killed, three officers and 157 enlisted men wounded, and one officer and 34 enlisted men missing. Kit, with his usual luck, came out unscathed.

Colonel Carson's report to Colonel Canby related his own part in the battle:

> About 1 o'clock in the afternoon I received from Colonel Canby the order to cross the river, which I immediately did, after which I was ordered to form my command on the right of our line and to advance as

skirmishers toward the hills. After advancing some 400 yards we discovered a large body of the enemy charging diagonally across our front, evidently with the intention of capturing the 24-pounder gun, which, stationed on our right, was advancing and doing much harm to the enemy. As the head of the enemy's column came within some 80 yards of my right a volley from the whole column was poured into them, and the firing being kept up caused them to break in every direction. Almost at the same time a shell from the 24-pounder was thrown among them with fatal effect. They did not attempt to reform, and the column supported by the gun on the right, was moving forward to sweep the wood near the hills, when I received the order to retreat and recross the river. This movement was executed in good order. The column, after crossing the river, returned to its station near Fort Craig, where it arrived about 7 o'clock in the evening.

From all accounts of the Battle of Valverde, Colonel Carson and his regiment performed creditably before they were ordered off the field.

Kit and his men waited at Fort Craig for orders, which came on March 31:

> Headquarters Department of New Mexico.
> Fort Craig, N. Mex., March 31, 1862.
>
> Col. C. Carson:
>
> Colonel: You are charged with the duty of holding this post. Your command will consist of seven companies of your own regiment, two of the Second, and one of the Fourth Regiment New Mexican Volunteers. The convalescents, as they become effective, will add to your strength, and I am instructed by the colonel commanding to say that the objects in view of the plan of operations require that it should be held to the last extremity. The manner of doing this is left to your judgment and discretion, in both of which he has the utmost confidence. The force of the enemy in the Mesilla will not allow him to make a regular attack upon the post, but it may be attempted by surprise. To guard against this he desires that you will exercise yourself and exact from all of your command the most unremitting vigilance.
>
> The sick and wounded left in your care will of course receive every attention, and the colonel commanding desires me to say that any ex-

penditures that will add to their comfort or conduce to their recovery
will be fully authorized.

Very respectfully, sir, yr obed serv't,
Wm. J. L. Nicodemus,
Captain Twelfth Infantry,
Actg. Asst. Adj't. Gen.

The Colorado Volunteers and Canby's regulars relieved Kit of
his Fort Craig assignment, and by the middle of May, 1862, he
was in Albuquerque organizing the First New Mexico Cavalry.
On October 12, he and his five companies were at Fort Stanton to
take the field against the Apaches.

I5 ★ Apaches and Navahos

FORT STANTON, located on the Río Bonito in present-day Lincoln County, New Mexico, had been abandoned by Federal troops on August 2, 1861, and in 1862, Colonel Carson and his regiment found it in a deplorable condition. Doors, windows, and everything removable had been carted away, leaving only the walls standing. The surrounding farms and settlements had been abandoned when the fort closed down because the settlers could no longer live safely without the fort's protection from the Indians.

Colonel Carson's orders were to garrison the fort with one company of soldiers and hunt Indians with the other four companies. Long, written instructions and orders arrived almost daily from Kit's commanding officer, General James Henry Carleton. It was his plan, the General explained to Kit and outlined to Washington, first to wage war against the Mescalero and Gila Apaches and then subdue the Navahos.

Long before Kit was aware of it, General Carleton and Governor Connelly decided that he was the most competent man available to command troops against the Apaches and Navahos. Although when approached on the subject Kit was not at all enthusiastic about it—he argued that the Indians could be brought to terms without war—he nevertheless obeyed orders.

Colonel J. Francisco Chavez, Governor Connelly's stepson, was chosen as second in command. With four companies, he moved into the Navaho country to establish Fort Wingate, a site selected by General Canby.

General Carleton's orders to Kit were that "all Indian men of the Mescalero tribe are to be killed whenever and wherever you can find them. The women and children will not be harmed, but you will take them prisoners, and feed them at Fort Stanton until you receive other instructions about them." But Carson did not always kill the men as he was ordered to do. Within a few weeks after his campaign started, he captured five hundred men, women, and children and sent them to Santa Fe.

The last week in October or the first in November, 1863, Captain James Grayton, while on scout duty with his troops, came upon a band of Apaches. According to orders, he fired upon them, killing, among others, two important chiefs, Manuelito and José Largo (Long Joe). Seventeen horses and mules belonging to the Apaches were captured. Apparently, from orders received by Colonel Carson on November 25, there was subterfuge in this attack:

> If you are satisfied that Graydon's attack on Manuelita and his people was not fair and open, see that all the horses and mules, including two said to be in the hands of one Mr. Beach, of Manzana, are returned to the survivors of Manuelito's band.

It became apparent, too, that Charles Beach was responsible for the unfair acquisition of the horses and mules and the killings because the next day he was ordered arrested as "an improper person to reside in the Mescalero country."

Not only war but army trouble inside Fort Stanton occupied Kit's time and energy. The second week in November, during his absence, the loosely disciplined garrison at Fort Stanton went on a rampage: two murders occurred at headquarters shortly after. Dr. J. M. Whitlock, a close personal friend to Kit, arrived at Fort Stanton to ask Kit to sign a recommendation for his appointment as surgeon with the reorganized militia. He entered the fort's store to look for Kit and there met Captain James "Paddy" Grayton, who had been with Kit in the Battle of Valverde. Grayton, who was very popular with the men, had been a liquor dealer between his two periods of soldiering, and it was this activity which had caused trouble between him and Dr. Whitlock. While Grayton was stationed at Patos, in Mescalero country, Dr. Whitlock had written to the Santa Fe newspapers accusing Grayton of luring Apaches into camp, getting them drunk, and then ordering his soldiers to shoot them down in cold blood.

Now Captain Grayton demanded that Dr. Whitlock retract the statements he had given the newspaper, adding that they reflected upon his honor. Dr. Whitlock steadfastly denied any untrue statements, saying he could prove everything he had written, and refused to retract anything. Grayton then challenged him to a duel and went to his tent for a pistol. When he returned, Dr. Whitlock was ready for him, and both men fired. Whitlock's first bullet missed completely, but his second inflicted a mortal wound, lodging near Grayton's heart. One of Grayton's bullets had wounded Dr. Whitlock in the wrist, at the same time shattering the grip of his pistol. Captain Grayton's comrades carried him to his tent, where he died. Dr. Whitlock threw his useless pistol away, entered the store, took a shotgun from the rack, loaded it, and stood waiting. When he heard the soldiers returning to the store, he left by a back entrance, but they saw him and shot him down. His body was thrown into a near-by ditch, and soldier after soldier from Grayton's Company H passed by to shoot at it. It was hit some 130 times.

At this point, Colonel Carson arrived on the scene and "long roll" was sounded. The soldiers fell in. Kit ordered Grayton's Company H disarmed, from the lieutenant down to the lowest private. "I'll have you scoundrels to swing before sunset!" he thundered. No one had ever seen him in such a rage before.

Later, some of Kit's fellow officers persuaded him to do nothing rash, but to arrest the ringleaders in the affair and turn them over to the civil authorities. After Grayton's funeral, which was preached by an army chaplain, Father Damasio Taladrid, Fort Stanton again settled down to fight Mescalero Apaches.

As Colonel Carson pursued the Mescalero Apaches from Fort Stanton, the campaign against the Gila Apaches was in full progress at Mesilla under the leadership of General John R. West's California Column. General Carleton's orders to West were to give the Indians no quarter, to make no peace or hold no conferences with them. West sent scouting parties to look for the Gilas, with specific instructions to seek out Chief Mangas Coloradas.

It wasn't long before Red Sleeves and his band were sighted near Piños Altos. Captain E. D. Shirland and twenty men persuaded him to go to Fort McLane, where he was confined as a prisoner of war, and told that he would be shot if he tried to escape. Under the agreement of his custody, he was assured that his family could join him and that all of them would be housed, fed, and well treated. At midnight on January 18, 1863, a sergeant and three privates went on guard duty, and about one o'clock, Red Sleeves was shot and killed. General West was awakened soon after the shooting and told that Mangas Coloradas had made three unsuccessful attempts to escape between midnight and one o'clock and that "even with a murderous Indian whose life was clearly forfeited by all laws, either human or divine, the good faith of the U.S. Military authorities was in no way compromised."

General West explained why Red Sleeves was not reunited with his people as had been promised: "His detention prevented this, and being apprehensive that his people would scatter, alarmed at his absence, I decided to pursue and punish them." In the chase West mentions, Captain William McCleave, First cavalry, California Column, killed eleven of the Gila Apaches and wounded the widow of Mangas Coloradas on January 29.

General Carleton's purpose in getting Red Sleeves out of the way might have been to gain access to the rich ore in Apache country. Carleton says in his Report No. 319:

> Unless I am compelled by Confederate Forces to abandon the rich country about Piños Altos and on the Río Prieta, it will be held permanently. Our troops have already killed Mangus Colorado, his son, his brother, and some sixty of his braves, and I am still prosecuting hostilities against the Gila Apaches, and propose to do so until people can live in that country, and explore and work the veins of precious metals which we know abound there with safety. The country along

the Río Prieta, and further down the Gila, gives promise of richness in gold and silver. I have two companies out now surveying a road from Fort Craig to Fort West.

Colonel Carson reported to Carleton on January 4, 1863: "The Pecos and Bonito Valleys might now be cultivated without danger of Indian depredations." The next month, Kit was in Santa Fe, then in Taos for a leave with his family. The campaign at Fort Stanton was labeled a success. About four hundred Mescaleros were held at Bosque Redondo, and the others had supposedly fled to join their neighbors, the Gilas.

While Kit Carson was still in Taos, Colonel J. Francisco Chavez arrived (February 1) at Fort Wingate to prepare for his campaign against the Navahos as ordered by General Carleton:

Send for Delgadito and Barboncito again and repeat what I before told them, and tell them that I shall feel very sorry if they refuse to come in; that we have no desire to make war upon them and other good Navajoes; but the troops cannot tell the good from the bad, and we neither can nor will tolerate their staying as a peace party among those against whom we intend to make war. Tell them they can have until the twentieth day of July of this year to come in—they and all those who belong to what they call the peace party; that after that day every Navajo that is seen will be considered as hostile and treated accordingly; that after that day the door now open will be closed. Tell them to say this to all their people, and that as sure as the sun shines all this will come true.

Carleton's General Orders No. 15, issued in Santa Fe on June 15, 1863, stated the many reasons for going to war against the Navahos:

I. For a long time past the Navajo Indians have murdered and robbed the people of New Mexico. Last winter, when eighteen of their chiefs came to Santa Fé to have a talk, they were warned, and were told to inform their people that, for these murders and robberies, the tribe must be punished, unless some binding guarantees should be given that in [the] future these outrages should cease. No such guarantees have yet been given; but, on the contrary, additional murders and additional robberies have been perpetrated upon the persons and property of our unoffending citizens. It is therefore ordered that Colonel Christopher Carson, with a proper military force, proceed without delay to a point in the Navajo country known as Pueblo Colorado, and there establish a defensible depot for his supplies and hospital, and thence to prosecute a vigorous war upon the men of this tribe until it is considered, at these headquarters, that they have been effectually punished for their long-continued atrocities.

The new post was called Fort Canby, in honor of General E. R. S. Canby, Kit's commander at the Battle of Valverde.

In Kit's command there were a few officers and men from the California Column and some regulars from Fort Union, which, with his field staff and regiment, amounted to some 27 officers, 260 infantrymen, and 476 cavalrymen. Kit had asked for permission to use Utes as guides and spies. While he was still in Taos on leave, this was granted, and he picked them then and there. Kit had also asked permission for the Utes to keep captured Navaho women and children, and although General Carleton seemed in favor of this arrangement in letters to Washington—for he had kept slaves at one time himself—he refused permission. Kit was instructed to send all Navaho captives, without exception, to Santa Fe. General Carleton authorized Kit to pay twenty dollars for every usable horse and a dollar for every sheep captured and delivered to him.

On July 10, General Carleton made a trip to Los Piños, twenty miles south of Albuquerque, where Colonel Carson's troops were mobilizing, in order to have a last conference with Kit. Carson's nine companies, six to be mounted, were headed by nine captains. In all, Kit commanded 736 men and officers.

Arriving first at Fort Wingate, Kit's unit marched into the heart of the Navaho country, to Fort Defiance, where a band of Utes reported to Kit, telling him that they were ready to fight their bitter enemies the Navahos. Kit gave them food and weapons and sent them on a scout. A week later they reported back: they had killed eight Navaho men and had captured four women and seven children.

Although the Navahos were not fighters like the Apaches, they held their own against U. S. troops at the outset. They even stole Kit's favorite horse—within pistol shot of his tent—and ran off army sheep and goats while he was camped at Black Rock near Fort Canby; just beyond rifle range, they butchered and cooked some of the animals! Their little victories were short lived, however, and the Navaho Nation later paid a terrific price for them.

The Navahos were not prepared for a long siege of any kind, for they barely subsisted from season to season. If their crops failed and there was no surplus of grains, they resorted to plunder in order to feed their people. With this in mind, General Carleton planned to starve them into submission. To expedite matters, the General ordered Kit to destroy the Indians' grain fields, vegetable gardens, and peach trees.

A pastoral people, the Navahos lived in family communities, each ruled by a head chief. Each community had its own living to make, its own governing to do. One chief could make a treaty for his own people, but he could not make an agreement for other chiefs, since there was no central government. Thus Colonel Carson had to search out each family group and send them to Fort Canby for transfer to Bosque Redondo, as he had been ordered to do. He was not to make any treaties or hold any conferences with them. This had been tried before, and treaties made by one set of families would be disregarded by the others. General Carleton therefore planned to take them out of their country and educate their children, contending that "on a reservation, until they can raise enough to be self-sustaining, you can feed them cheaper than you can fight them."

On July 25, Colonel Carson ordered Major Cummings to bring in all the wheat and corn on the Río de Pueblo Colorado; the corn was to be dried and used to feed army animals. Cummings and his men brought grain to Fort Canby, but the Navahos retaliated for their loss by killing the Major. At the time of his death, he was alone with a civilian, contrary to Colonel Carson's "positive instructions"; he had left his command before, and he and the unarmed civilian evidently expected no attack. A concealed Indian shot the Major in the stomach and he fell dead on the spot. Colonel Carson sent his body to Fort Defiance with the report: "His death is the result of his rash bravery."

On July 24, Kit had sent Captain Culter to Santa Fe with the resignations of Chaplain Taladrid and Captain McCabe. He requested that "you accept them, as well as all others which I may forward to you, as I do not wish to have any officer in my command who is not contented or willing to put up with as much inconvenience and privations for the success of the expedition as I undergo myself."

When Companies G and H arrived at Fort Defiance on August 2, their horses were in such poor condition that Colonel Carson was forced to dismount Captain Pfeiffer's company and leave the horses at the fort. On August 5, Kit moved out with twelve companies on a thirty-day scouting trip, moving south toward Zuñi Pueblo. Two hours out, they discovered and destroyed some seventy acres of corn. No Indians were sighted until they camped in a field of corn and wheat, when two were seen in the vicinity. Sergeant Romero, with fifteen men, was sent out after the Indians; he failed to find them but captured one of their horses.

The next day, they met some of Captain Pfeiffer's detail, who had been dispatched on the fourth to scout the country to the right and left of Kit's route. With them were eleven Navaho women and children, and a hundred head of sheep and goats. A woman and child had been killed by the soldiers when they tried to escape; the child was reported killed accidentally. Captain Pfeiffer returned about midnight with two children and a horse, reporting that he had destroyed five acres of corn.

After sending the prisoners to Fort Defiance, Colonel Carson and his command continued toward Zuñi. Within fifteen miles of that place, they captured five Moqui Indians, who, when questioned, stated that many Navahos with large herds of animals were camped near their villages. It rained the next day and they made camp, but on the following day the sky cleared and about five o'clock in the evening, Carson left camp with Companies D, G, and K, 75 men from Companies H and M, and 30 mounted men of Company M, as well as the Ute spies, marching all night to arrive at the canyon west of the Moqui villages. The Navahos took flight, but Captain Pfeiffer, with 30 cavalrymen, captured 1,000 head of sheep and goats. Captain Berney's company captured 25 horses and 100 sheep and goats, while the Utes captured two women and three children, killing one man and taking 18 horses and two mules. One wounded Indian man escaped and was later reported dead by one of the Moquis, who told Kit that he was not only one of the most powerful Navaho chiefs, but also the worst.

The Utes in Kit's command now returned home, and Kit took Major Thompson and a one-hundred-man detail to chase some Navahos who were reported near Oraibi village. The Indians were too far ahead, and Kit did not overtake them. While he was absent from camp, the Navahos stole seven mules which had strayed too far. Lieutenant Hubbell and a soldier, who had been lost, returned to camp while Kit was away. Upon his return, Kit ordered the entire camp, except his immediate command, to proceed to some springs twelve miles west of the Moqui villages. Later, he and his men joined them.

About two in the morning of the fifteenth, the camp was aroused by a party of raiding Navahos trying to run off the animals. A few volleys scattered the Indians before they could steal any animals. There was an abundance of good grass and plenty of water at this spot, so Kit stayed a few days to give both men and animals a rest.

On the morning of August 20, Colonel Carson's command left the Pueblo Colorado to make an examination of the Cañon de Chelly area. In this vast Navaho country, the corn and wheat were ripe, and they found large quantities of ripe pumpkins and beans. Now the Cañoncito de los Trigos, with a small, clear stream running through its three miles, has perpendicular cliffs some 150 feet high. Kit tried to lay an ambush for the returning Indians with 25 men under Captain Pfeiffer, but the Indians escaped. On the twenty-second, however, they discovered the bodies of two Indians, presumably killed shortly before the Utes returned home. Just as they reached a large cornfield where they were to camp, they discovered a Navaho man. He was pursued and killed and his horse wounded in the neck. Next morning, Kit wrote:

Arrived at the west opening of Cañon de Chelly, but could find no water; about twelve miles farther found abundance of running water and good grass, and encamped. I made a careful examination of the country on this day's march, particularly in the immediate neighborhood of Cañon de Chelly, and am satisfied that there are very few Indians in the cañon, and these of the very poorest. They have no stock, and were depending entirely for subsistence on the corn destroyed by my command on the previous day, the loss of which will cause actual starvation, and oblige them either to come in and accept migration to the Bosque Redondo, or to fly south to Red River to join the wealthy bands now there. I am inclined to think they will adopt the first of these courses.

Apparently, the Navahos were hiding from Kit. His guide informed him that when General Canby had encamped there for several days in 1860, the Navahos were numerous and boldly came in sight of the troops in large groups on the high mesas above the road. Needless to say, the Navahos realized that if they showed their heads above the cliffs now they would be shot at by the soldiers. Only occasionally did the troop come upon an Indian unaware, and then he was shot if he was unable to make his escape.

On the twenty-fifth, they marched fifteen miles northeast; the next day, they traveled about twelve miles southeast through excellent stock-raising country, but still saw no Indians. On the twenty-seventh, they crossed the stream that runs through the eastern opening of the Cañon de Chelly and camped on a branch of it some four miles farther on. Kit was of the opinion that both these streams could be blocked off, compelling the Indians who took refuge in this stronghold to abandon it for lack of water.

When they were about seven miles out, after leaving camp on the twenty-eighth, Kit sent out Companies D and H; that night he sent out two detachments—one under Lieutenant Dowlin and the other under Captain Everett. Dowlin discovered one Indian, who escaped but left his horse and saddle; the latter had a bullet hole in it. Everett didn't see a single Indian.

Upon his arrival at Fort Canby, Kit was confronted with the embarrassing fact that during his absence, some of his men had killed an Indian who came to the camp with three of his fellows under a flag of truce. "I cannot but regret that they were not better received, and kept until my arrival," said Kit in his report. Two of the Indians escaped; the seventy-year-old one who stayed was called Little Foot. He told Kit that he came from the marshes southeast of Zuñi and that he had come to make arrangements to comply with the wishes of the commanding general for his people, who were destitute, to go to Bosque Redondo or anywhere the general wanted to send them. Kit believed him and set him free, with instructions to have his people at the fort in twelve days.

August hadn't been much of a success as far as military campaigns were concerned, but at least Kit had a fair idea that the Navahos had fled to Salt River with their stock. Since Salt River was near the San Francisco Mountains in Apache country, within easy striking distance from Pima villages, Kit suggested that operations be continued from there.

For twenty-seven days during September, Kit was away from the fort scouting for Navahos. First he searched the Little Colorado, with three Zuñi Indian guides furnished by the Zuñi governor and twenty others who tagged along to show their friendship for the whites and their enmity to the Navahos. On the first part of the trip, water was scarce and good grass for the horses was hard to find. The Navahos had disappeared, or stayed well hidden from Carson's command, as he reported on his return:

> This scout, I am sorry to say, was a failure as regards any positive injury inflicted upon the Navajos; but the fatigue and hardships undergone by my command are fully compensated for by increased knowledge of the country, and of the haunts of the Navajos with their stock.

From any other colonel in the United States Army, this would seem like an overly optimistic view of the situation, but as will be seen later on, Colonel Carson did acquire the knowledge he needed for his later victory over the Navahos. With such information he was better able to carry out General Carleton's orders to subjugate the Navahos and force them to go to Bosque Redondo reservation.

Kit was not only having trouble finding the Navahos, he also had trouble throughout the fall of 1863 with his animals, which had been continually in the field without proper rest and food. Operating as he was in a barren country where grass was mighty scarce and the supply of water uncertain, the horses became so exhausted that Kit had to send his scouting parties out on foot. He respectfully suggested that the horses be wintered on the Río Grande and said that he would continue his winter campaign on foot. As a consequence, on October 6, some seventy-five men left the post—unmounted.

Chief Little Foot, who had promised to return to Fort Canby with his people for transfer to Bosque Redondo, failed to make his appearance, and Kit sent soldiers to hunt for him at Chusco. Finally, after a long search, Little Foot and his people were found and sent to the reservation.

On November 15, after the horses had been sent to winter on the Río Grande, Colonel Carson and Companies C, D, G, H, and L of the First Cavalry, New Mexico Volunteers, left Fort Canby to explore the country west of the Oraibi villages. Sergeant Andrés Herrera, with thirty men of Company C, was sent on a trial scouting trip of twenty miles to overtake a small party of Navahos. They killed two, wounded two, and captured fifty head of sheep and one horse. They destroyed a recently deserted Navaho village and returned to the main camp in time to join Carson's main company, now on its way to Oraibi, where it arrived on the twenty-first.

The Navahos had been committing depredations against most of these villages, so the Hopis were ready to wage war against the Navahos when Kit arrived. Numbering about four thousand, they were in a deplorable state. Having no water for irrigation, they had to depend on the rains to make their crops. For miles around the country was barren and desolate. Kit felt that the government should do something about their condition, so he recommended that the few years of accrued Navaho annuities be given to them. Whether the Navaho annuities were received by the Oraibis is unknown, for there is no record of such in the official files.

The Moquis who joined Carson's command were of some service as scouts, but nothing spectacular was accomplished in routing the

Navahos, who seemed adept at keeping well away from the troops. As he was returning to their village (by a different route), he saw in the distance the smoke of an Indian camp. He took a few officers and fifty infantrymen to raid the camp, but the Indians spotted them as they charged down the hill. The Navahos escaped, leaving their clothing, shields, one horse, and four oxen, which they had probably stolen, behind them.

At his main post of operations—Fort Canby—Colonel Carson prepared to examine the Cañon de Chelly again. He had not done so sooner because his last trip to that vicinity had convinced him that there were few Navahos there. However, he was not to leave on this expedition until January 6, 1864, for there were reports to be made and preparations to be executed for the long trip.

The main obstacle confronting Kit was the procurement of a messenger between Fort Canby and Fort Wingate—a very dangerous duty which, he told his superiors, he did not feel like ordering any of his soldiers to undertake. The Army had tried to hire a civilian for this job, at good wages, but to no avail. So Kit suggested:

> I therefore respectfully ask that [Captain Asa B. Carey] be authorized to pay a compensation to the soldier who may be found to carry the express. This I understand was done under like circumstances in the Florida War, and by General Canby during the late invasion of this Territory by the Texans. . . . Until the action of the General commanding is made known, the officers of the command have agreed to subscribe from their pay a sufficient compensation, and I trust that speedy measures will be taken to relieve them from an expense not expected of them by the Government.

At the west end of Cañon de Chelly, Kit established a supply depot and base of operations. He set up another base at the east end, sending supplies there by pack train. The two sections were to be in close communication.

When he arrived at the west post on January 12, Kit dispatched Sergeant Herrera and fifty men to scout for Navahos. At daylight, Herrera discovered a trail and, following it rapidly, overtook a band of Navahos as they were entering the canyon. They killed eleven

Indians, captured two women and two children, and took 130 head of sheep and goats.

In the meantime, Colonel Carson, with his staff and escorts, reconnoitered from the main base of operations and took a detour to the right of the previous day's march, striking the canyon about six miles from its mouth. They proceeded up it some five or six miles on the south rim until they saw several Indians on the opposite side. Since they could not find a way to descend the almost perpendicular cliffs and since the Indians were well out of rifle range, they could do them no harm. When Kit returned to his base, he made a report, commenting on Sergeant Herrera's success:

> This is the second occasion which I have had to record my sense of the energy and ability displayed by the Sergeant in the successful carrying out of my orders, and I respectfully recommend him to the favorable notice of the General commanding.

With a three-day ration in haversacks, Kit sent out two forces to operate on each side of the canyon. On the north side were companies D and E, commanded by Captain Joseph Berney; on the south side, commanded by Captain Asa B. Carey, were companies B and G, accompanied by Colonel Carson, who was now worried about Captain Pfeiffer's command, sent out from the east base.

They found the place where Herrera had had his fight and found five wounded Indians, to whom Dr. Short administered medical aid. Kit expressed a belief that they would recover. The section then proceeded to a point where the view of the canyon to its eastern terminus was unobstructed. They were unable to discover any signs of Captain Pfeiffer and his command, nor did they find any Indian signs. Kit satisfied himself of the feasibility of flanking the south side of the Cañon de Chelly from west to east without much difficulty, for there were no extensive intersecting canyons to delay progress.

On his return to camp, Kit was met by three Indians, under a flag of truce, requesting permission to come into camp with their people for transfer to Bosque Redondo. They said their people were in a starving condition because their crops had been destroyed. Permission was granted, and they were to report no later than ten o'clock the next morning. By that time, sixty Indians had arrived. They told Kit they would have surrendered long before but they thought this was a war of extermination and had only learned the true state of affairs from the old captive Kit had sent back to them. Kit issued them some meat, and they returned to the canyon to collect the rest of their people. Kit directed them to meet him at the main post in ten days. They all arrived as promised and were put in charge of Captain Carey's command.

That same day, the Captain got his wish to go through Cañon de Chelly. Kit says in his report of January 23:

> This command of seventy-five men I conferred upon Capt. Carey at his own request, he being desirous of passing through this stupendous cañon. I sent the party to return through the cañon from west to east, that all the peach orchards, of which there were many, should be destroyed as well as the dwellings of Indians. I sent a competent person with the command to make sketches of the cañon, which, with written descriptions of the cañon by Captain Carey, in the shape of a report I respectfully enclose.

Much to Kit's relief, when he returned to headquarters he found Captain Pfeiffer and his command, intact, with the interesting news that they had completed the march through the Cañon de Chelly from east to west without a single casualty. They brought in ninety women and children, had killed one man, and had found two Indians frozen to death. Kit forwarded Captain Pfeiffer's long, interesting report to General Carleton.

Pfeiffer's prisoners, put under guard, were soon joined by four of their fellows captured by Captain Berney, whose men had killed two other Indians. Then came four warriors from the mountains to tell Kit that many well-to-do Indians wanted to come into his camp but were afraid. Kit furnished the most intelligent of these warriors with provisions and sent him to tell the Navahos that they would be fully protected if they surrendered with the intention of settling at Bosque Redondo.

Kit left three companies with Major Sena and returned to Fort Canby. He now felt that he had accomplished all he could in the Cañon de Chelly; he also wanted to be at Fort Canby when the Indians came in. Then, too, he had to keep his scouts on the move to bring in any remaining Navahos.

On January 23, Colonel Carson reported from Fort Canby that he had more than five hundred Navahos ready to transport to Santa Fe in two days, and Cabaro Blanco, a Navaho chief, assured Kit that over a thousand more were on their way to the fort. The last sentence in Kit's report was: "I do not think I am premature in congratulating the general commanding on the speedy and successful result of his measures to restore permanent peace and security to the people of New Mexico."

The Navaho campaign was deemed such a success that General Carleton, who had consistently refused Kit a leave to visit his family in Taos for a few days, now granted him one for the last week of January. In Santa Fe, Kit conferred with officials regarding the problem of feeding Navahos en route to and after their arrival at Bosque Redondo. Hundreds of Navahos were waiting at Fort Canby to be taken to the Bosque Redondo—waiting to march across three rivers, the Río Puerco, the Río Grande, and the Pecos, against the warning of their medicine men.

While Kit visited his family, friends and thrill-seekers alike came to hear about the Cañon de Chelly campaign, something, it is presumed, which Kit did not care to discuss. From all appearances, this campaign was a success. Before the end of 1864, almost nine thousand Navahos would be sharing the Bosque with their natural enemies, the Apaches. General Carleton had mistakenly painted the Bosque as the perfect place for the Apaches and Navahos, whom he described as coming from the same stock and speaking the same language. Kit, if asked, could have told him differently, or perhaps he did, but the mistake was already made when Carleton informed Washington that the Bosque Redondo was the answer to the Navaho and Apache problem.

Assistant Adjutant General Cutler lavishly praised the men who fought in the Navaho campaign. He told of their hardships in the frozen, snow-covered Cañon de Chelly, fighting their way over mountains and through "hitherto inaccessible regions" to pursue the wily enemy. General Carleton's report to General Thomas in Washington, dated February 7, said in part:

> This is the first time any troops, whether the country belonging to Mexico or since we acquired it, have been able to pass through the Cañon de Chelly. . . . Colonel Washington, Colonel Sumner, and many other commanders have attempted to go through it, but have had to retrace their steps. It was reserved for Colonel Carson to be the first to succeed. . . .

But Kit Carson was not the conqueror of the Navahos; he was only one of many such officers, all obeying orders. Nor did he traverse the canyon from one end to the other; his officers did that for him. Credit or blame was due no one individual, but reports continued to single out various officers for praise, as one submitted by Captain Asa B. Carey shows:

> True, Carson's campaign was a great success; indeed it was the last war against the Navajos, but to General Carleton belongs the credit of its success, inasmuch as he pursued them to a reservation and confined them to it.

By April 10, 1864, Colonel Carson was again making his reports from Fort Canby. He had, at that time, some 216 Navahos at the post and recommended that "as they are poor the sooner they go to work to raise grain, the better." It is evident in later events how little attention the government paid to Kit's plea in behalf of the Indians, but he still tried:

> It is here and en route that we must convince them by our treatment of them of the kind intentions of the Government towards them, otherwise I fear that they will lose confidence in our promises, and desert also. [He is here referring to the escape of some one hundred Indians headed by Chief Juanico's son while they were en route to the Bosque Redondo under Captain McCabe.] As suspicion enters so largely into

the composition of the Indian character the greatest possible care must be taken not to awaken it by acts contrary to the promises. I think one pound of beef or of flour, wheat or corn, is entirely too small an allowance for an able bodied Indian for one day.

General Carleton could see the value of the pastoral and mineral lands that the Navahos had surrendered to the United States: "a country whose value can hardly be estimated—the mere pittance, in comparison, which must be given at once to support them, sinks into insignificance, as a price for their natural heritage."

Colonel Carson sent to headquarters a list of the Navaho chiefs who had sued for peace with the suggestion that Sergeant Herrera might be able to ascertain how many followers each chief had, thereby arriving at the approximation of their strength. This census was not for the purpose of paying the Navahos for their land, but for General Carleton to make sure that all the Navahos were at the Bosque Redondo. His effort for subjugation was much better planned and more vigorous than his plan to feed and clothe the Indians when they arrived at the reservation.

About the middle of summer, Kit was appointed acting superintendent over the Indians at Bosque Redondo, reporting from Fort Sumner to the Bosque on July 11, 1864. Among other duties, he had to compile a record of births and deaths, teach the Indians to farm, and see that food was properly distributed. Difficulties arose, or, rather, continued, between the Navahos and Apaches. The crops failed, "attacked by cutworms," and by fall it was obvious that Carleton's odious plan had failed miserably: thousands of Indians were starving.

Carleton deferred making his report to Washington until October 30, with no more explanation than that he wanted to be sure:

I have delayed making a formal report on the important matter of subsisting the Navajo and Apache Indians now on the Bosque Redondo Reservation, until I could learn definitely the probable result of the harvest in this Territory. Everything at Bosque Redondo was a success this year except the corn crop. We had a field of nearly three thousand acres, which promised to mature finely, when, after it had tasselled, and the ears formed, it was attacked by what they call here the cut worm, or army worm, and the whole crop destroyed.

It was impossible to rush in enough food for thousands of starving Indians. Carleton, who knew what was happening, wrote to the commanding officer, Brigadier General Marcillus M. Crocker, at Fort Sumner:

> Tell the Navajos to be too proud to murmur at what cannot be helped. We could not foresee the total destruction of their corn crops. . . . tell them to work hard, every man and woman, to put in large fields next year, when if God smiles on our efforts, they will, at one bound be forever placed beyond want and be independent. . . .

Many hundreds of them were placed beyond want of any kind through starvation that winter of 1864–65. Kit did not witness this horrible situation, for in the fall of 1864, he was ordered to Fort Bascom to fight the Kiowas and Comanches.

The free Navahos were still at war with the troops in November, when Kit left, and they continued to harass the settlers. About 7,000 Navahos were at the reservation, but there were many who had not surrendered. The Apaches, who numbered about 3,500, had already deserted the Bosque Redondo by the hundreds, but it was not until January 15, 1867, that the Navahos were released from bondage. On that day, the War Department formally relinquished authority over the Navahos, transferring them back to the Bureau of Indian Affairs in the Department of the Interior.

16 ★ Adobe Walls

COLONEL CARSON arrived at Fort Bascom on November 10, 1864, with 321 enlisted men and 14 officers. By September, 1864, General Carleton was forced to relax his campaign against the Navahos in order to fight the Kiowas and Comanches.

For some time the two tribes had been troublesome. Believing the troops would be away indefinitely, fighting Navahos, the Plains Indians had attacked wagon trains and had murdered civilians at Walnut Creek that summer. They robbed a wagon train belonging to merchant Ambrosio Armijo at Pawnee Fork, and at Pawnee Rock they attacked the Allison train, killed and scalped five men, and carried off as captives five small boys. On October 22, 1864, General Carleton said he had ordered his men

> not only to take the field promptly but to accomplish all that can be accomplished in punishing these treacherous savages before the winter fairly sets in. They have wantonly and brutally murdered our people without cause, and robbed them of their property; and it is not proposed that they shall talk, and smoke, and patch up a peace, until they have, if possible, been punished for the atrocities they have committed. To permit them to do this would be to invite further hostile acts from them as soon as the spring opens and our citizens once more embark on their long journey across the plains.

General Carleton's avid desire to punish the Plains Indians could have cost the Army a large number of troops and Kit Carson his life. The Sioux, who later wiped out Custer's men at the Little Big

Horn, were fewer in number and had fewer guns than the Plains Indians at Adobe Walls, which was the most significant Indian battle, in point of Indian strength, ever to have occurred west of the Mississippi River. The Indians had their side of the problem. They owned the country from the Platte to Texas, according to Kiowa Chief Dohasan, and did not wish the white man in it to kill their buffalo and other game and to make roads. They had agreed to let the white man travel the Santa Fe Trail, but they specified that he must keep to the trail. When the white man hadn't kept his word, the Indians had retaliated. Thus the Arapahoes and Cheyennes joined the Kiowas and Comanches in one last battle to protect their homeland from invasion by white destroyers.

Colonel Carson had recruited 75 Ute and Jicarilla Apache scouts and fighters from Lucien Maxwell's ranch on the Rayado. The Army had expected to enlist Navahos from Bosque Redondo, since a number of them had expressed willingness to enlist, according to Carson's letter of October 18, 1864, to General Carleton, but the Utes, who were willing to fight with the Apaches, were not willing to fight side by side with the Navahos. It was also a probability that the Apaches would have objected if asked.

Two howitzers, under the command of Lieutenant George H. Pettis of the California Column, were brought up by pack mule. Colonel Carson's command was to co-operate with General Blunt's troops from Fort Larned, although Kit was in full command by order of General Carleton. For the Indian scouts and fighters, Kit had successfully requisitioned 100 rifles, 6,000 rounds of ammunition, 120 blankets and shirts, and, for old Chief Ka-ni-at-ze, one extra horse. His command was organized as follows: Colonel Christopher Carson, First Infantry, New Mexico Volunteers, commanding; Colonel Francisco P. Abreu, First Infantry, New Mexico Volunteers; Major William McCleave, First Cavalry, California Volunteers; Lieutenant Benjamin Taylor, Jr., U.S. Fifth Infantry; Surgeon George S. Courtright, U.S. Volunteers; Captain Joseph Berney, Company D, First New Mexico Cavalry and his command, mounted; Lieutenant Sullivan Heath, Company K, with all of Johnson's men then at Fort Union and Fort Bascom; Captain Merriam, Company

M, First California Cavalry; Captain Witham's cavalry; Captain Emil Fritz, with cavalry from Fort Sumner; Captain Charles Deus's Company M, First New Mexico Cavalry, from Fort Bascom; Lieutenant Edmiston, Company A, First Veteran Infantry, California Volunteers; and Lieutenant Pettis, Company K, First Infantry, California Volunteers, "with two howitzers, two pounds each, mounted on prairie carriage."

On November 12, 1864, the column left Fort Bascom: 14 commissioned officers, 321 enlisted men, 75 Indian scouts, 27 wagons, an ambulance, and 45 days' supplies. Their destination was Adobe Walls, in present-day Hutchinson County, Texas Panhandle, a Bent–St. Vrain trading post built in 1845–46 for trade with the Comanches. On the fourth day out, the column passed the place where, in the fall of 1849, Carson, acting as guide for Major Grier's troops, had surprised the Apaches who were holding Mrs. White.

They proceeded cautiously through the Indian country. After being delayed two days by snowstorms, on Thursday afternoon, November 24, they camped at Mule Springs, about thirty miles west of Adobe Walls. This day was the second nationally established Thanksgiving Day as designated by President Lincoln's proclamation, but there was no celebration for the Army.

While some of the man were eating supper—it was nearly sundown—the Indian scouts suddenly sprang to their feet and started talking excitedly in their own language. When some of the officers questioned Colonel Carson about their excitement, he replied that the quick, sharp eyes of the Indians had made out the approach of the two scouts he had dispatched that morning. Lieutenant Pettis had failed to see the scouts, who were some two miles off, and he thought it remarkable that the Indians knew they were approaching. And what was more remarkable to the young Lieutenant was that while the scouts were still far off on the hillside they had conveyed to the Indians in camp that they had found the enemy. When the scouts arrived in camp, they immediately sought out Colonel Carson to inform him that they had found indications that a large body of Indians with many horses and cattle had moved that very morning.

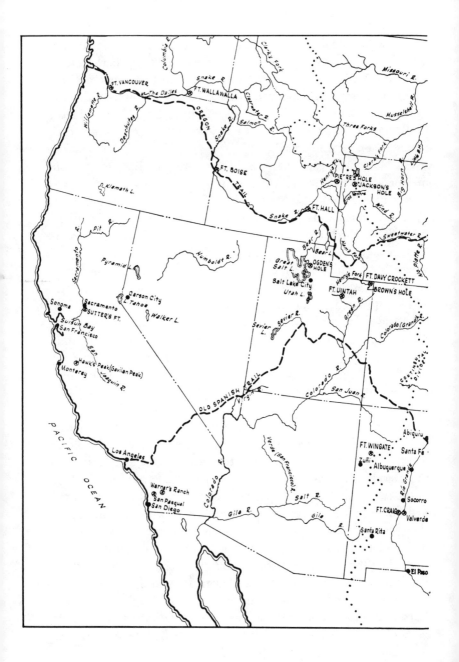

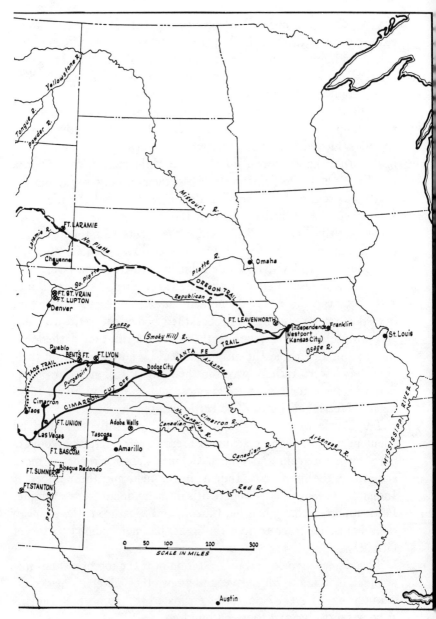

KIT CARSON COUNTRY, 1826–1868

Colonel Carson ordered all cavalry and the two howitzers to be ready to move without delay. That night, they covered fifteen miles, and at midnight a halt was made to await daylight. No talking was allowed, no smoking or fires permitted. A heavy frost added to the discomfort of silent waiting.

At dawn, Colonel Carson mounted his horse and gave orders for the column to move down the Canadian River. The Indians were wrapped in their buffalo robes, which stood up high above their heads; their knees drawn up nearly at right angles, they were a peculiar sight to Pettis, who described their "funny appearance."

Kit was telling Pettis about a dream he had had the night before when they heard a voice on the opposite side of the river shouting to "come here." Kit knew the scouts had found enemy pickets and therefore ordered Major McCleave, with Company B and one of the New Mexico detachments, to cross the river. The scouts, who amused Pettis with their strange garb, disappeared into a thicket near the river. A moment later they came riding out, devoid of their heavy buffalo robes, their bodies covered with paint and profusely decorated with feathers. With a yell they dashed into the stream. The three Indian pickets had by now jumped on their ponies and were racing away for their camp. Colonel Carson ordered his main force to attack at once; and he followed with Lieutenants Heath and Pettis. The battle was on.

The Battle of Adobe Walls has been colorfully described by Lieutenant Pettis, whose account differs in some respects from reports by Kit Carson and others. Colonel Carson's report is more accurate in the number of Indians in the field and the number of Indian lodges, but Pettis' report fills in many details. For example, Pettis reported that when he, Carson, and Heath put the spurs to their horses in order to join the fight, his men seemed to forget fatigue.

The battery arrived and took position near the top of a small hill occupied by Carson, McCleave, and a few other officers. They could see fighting on every side. Pettis estimated the number of Indians at between twelve and fourteen hundred.

With a mass of Indians such as this, it didn't look promising for the Army. Kit Carson ordered battery fire, and the astonished Indians rose high in their stirrups, gazed in wonder, then turned and fled to their village. By the time the fourth round was fired, there wasn't an Indian within range.

Surgeon Courtright had converted a corner of the old fort into a hospital. The walls were high enough, Pettis said, to give ample protection to the wounded and the horses.

Colonel Carson ordered the command to unsaddle, water and stake the horses, and eat breakfast—haversack rations, raw bacon and hardtack—declaring the enemy would not attack again. Hardly had they finished eating when Kit observed, through his binoculars, a large force of Indians advancing from a village about three miles east of Adobe Walls. Almost before his men had resaddled and mounted they found themselves surrounded by a thousand Indians ready for battle. The Kiowas were under the command of chief Dohasan, or Little Mountain, among whose aides were Stumbling Bear and White Bear. One of the Apache chiefs was Iron Shirt.

The battle lasted until sundown. During the afternoon, fresh Indian fighters arrived in parties of from five to fifty until an estimated three thousand were on the field. Carson's report, short, as usual, stated that the Indians were mostly Kiowas, with a small number of Comanches, Apaches, and Arapahoes, all armed with rifles and all displaying more daring and bravery than he had ever before witnessed. His report gave army casualties as "two soldiers killed, ten wounded, 1 Indian killed, and five wounded, and a large number of horses wounded. It is impossible for me to form a correct estimate of the enemies loss, but from the number I saw fall from their horses during the engagement, I cannot call its loss less than sixty in killed and wounded." Pettis estimated, from what an Indian eyewitness told him, "nearly one hundred killed and between one hundred and one hundred and fifty wounded."

All during the fighting, when the army bugler sounded an order, someone on the Indian side sounded the opposite call, to which the army men responded with shouts and laughter. Kit said it was not an Indian but a white man who had the bugle, but who it was, was never known. He kept it up all day, much to the merriment of the soldiers.

The officers and the men wished to fight through and capture a large Indian village down the river, but Carson hesitated. His horses were badly used up, his supplies were running low, and he knew the necessity of protecting his rear. So, a little after three o'clock in the afternoon, he gave orders to retreat the way they had come and to destroy the Indian village they had sighted on their arrival.

Guessing the Army's intent, the Indians renewed their attack, and for a while Colonel Carson had serious doubts about the outcome. "The Indians charged so repeatedly," he said, "and with such desperation that for some time I had serious doubts for the safety of my rear, but the coolness with which they were received by Captain Berney's command, and the steady and constant fire poured into them, caused them to retire on every occasion with great slaughter."

Finding it impossible to delay the troops' march to their village, the Indians set fire to the tall grass in Carson's rear. The wind whipped the fire forward with great fury, causing the command to come up on the double. Kit fired the valley on his front and retired to a piece of high ground on his right flank and ordered battery action, which may very well have saved his command.

Just before sundown they reached the Apache village, which was now crowded with Indians trying to save their belongings. A couple of shells from a howitzer, followed by a charge, drove the Indians to the far end of the village. One detail destroyed the village while another kept the remaining Indians in check. Iron Shirt, who refused to leave the doorway of his lodge, was killed where he stood.

At dark the company commanders reported that their ammunition was nearly exhausted. Kit had the wounded loaded on ammunition carts and gun carriages and, not knowing where his supply train was, marched his men away from the scene. Three hours later, they saw fires in the distance. Approaching with caution, they were relieved to find the supply train—intact and unharmed.

Colonel Carson was prepared to fight throughout the next day, but the Indians only hovered near, out of howitzer range. They were shrewd enough to know that if they avoided getting too close, the shells could do them little, if any, harm.

On Sunday, after breakfast, much to the consternation of all the officers and most of the men, Carson gave the order to saddle up and begin the retreat. The majority still wanted to attack the Comanche village, but the order to retreat stood, for Carson had twenty-five wounded men and many wounded animals and he was not willing to tempt fate again. He later admitted that the Indians had thrashed him but at the same time he thought he had taught them a severe lesson. Pettis wrote:

> They also said that the Indians claimed that if the whites had not had with them the two "guns that shot twice" referring to the shells of the mountain howitzers, they would never have allowed a single white man to escape out of the valley of the Canadian, and I may say, with becoming modesty, that this was also the often expressed opinion of Colonel Carson.

General Carleton was proud of Carson's success. He said in a letter to Kit that the "brilliant victory" was "another green leaf to the laurel wreath which you have so nobly won in the service of your country. That you may long be spared to be of still further service, is the sincere wish of your obedient servant and friend, James H. Carleton." And well Carleton might be proud, for Kit had helped to subjugate the Navahos and had now come out of an almost impossible situation with the Plains Indians at Adobe Walls.

On December 20, Colonel Carson was back at Fort Bascom, where he spent his birthday and Christmas. The day after Christmas, he received orders that if the hostile Indians (and the Plains Indians seemed to have quieted somewhat since the Sand Creek affair and the Battle of Adobe Walls) were no longer dangerous, his command was to be disbanded or distributed, its colonel to proceed to Taos to await further orders.

At last a leave was in store for Kit. In January, 1865, he was in

Taos with Josefa, where he remained most of the time until May of 1866. The Carsons now had five children: William (Julian, as his mother called him), born October 1, 1852; Teresina, June 23, 1855; Christopher, June 13, 1858; Charles (named for Governor Bent and also for the Carsons' first child, who died in infancy), born August 2, 1861; and Rebecca, named for Kit's mother, born April 13, 1864. On December 23, 1866, another daughter, Stella (Estifanita), was born.

Sitting with eight of his companions-at-arms, all of whom served with him in New Mexico, Kit had his picture made in Santa Fe at the Montezuma Lodge. With him were Colonel Edward H. Bergman, U.S. Volunteers; Colonel C. P. Cleaver; General N. H. Davis; Colonel H. M. Enos; Dr. Basil K. Norris; General J. C. McFerran; General D. H. Rucker; and Kit's commanding officer in the Navaho campaign, General James H. Carleton.

It must have been very gratifying for Kit to receive the thanks of his general in a letter dated January 30, 1865, in which General Carleton also expressed pleasure at Kit's staying in the service:

> It gratifies me to learn that you will not leave the service while I remain here. A great deal of my good fortune in Indian matters here— in fact nearly all with reference to the Navajos, Mescalero Apaches, and Kiowas,—is due to you, and it affords me pleasure always to acknowledge the value of your service.

Although when Kit left Fort Bascom the Plains Indians were quiet, it was just the lull before the storm, for they soon struck wagon trains on the Santa Fe Trail with renewed vengeance. Troop escorts were necessary for all travelers along the trail, with orders that every soldier was to have his "musket in hand at all times."

Temporary cantonments were springing up along the wagon route to protect the traveler. In May, Colonel Carson was ordered to establish a camp of three companies at or close to Cedar Springs (near Cold Springs on the Cimarron route, in what is now the Oklahoma Panhandle) to protect and assist the wagon trains traveling to and from the States. General Carleton believed that in his new camp, to be called Camp Nichols, Kit could have "a talk with some of the chiefs of Cheyennes, Kiowas, and Comanches, and impress them with the folly of continuing this bad course." It took more than talks by Kit Carson to quiet the fury which the Sand Creek Massacre had created in the hearts and minds of the Indians.

Carleton's confidence in Colonel Carson's ability is noted in a letter of instructions dated May 8:

> In my opinion, your consultations and influence with the Indians of the plains will stop the war. . . . I have full faith and confidence in your judgment and in your energy.

Colonel Carson, who was a brigadier general by brevet as of March 13, 1865, for "gallantry in the battle of Valverde and distinguished services in New Mexico," took up his station at Camp Nichols with orders to maintain a well-disciplined camp and to report everything in full.

Knowing Kit's easy-going nature, Carleton had impressed upon him the fact that he should have adequate defenses thrown up against sudden Indian attacks, maintain pickets at strategic posts, and keep his guards well armed. He warned Kit to have reveille under arms so that the men would have their weapons in hand at all times. He said:

> If the Indians behave themselves, that is all the peace we want, and we shall not molest them; if they do not, we will fight them on sight and to the bitter end. The war is over now, and, if necessary, 10,000 men can at once be put into the field against them. Tell them this. It is a short speech, but it covers the ground. You know I don't believe much in smoking with Indians. When they fear us, they behave.

But Kit believed that smoking with the Indians did help him to solve some of the problems he had to face with them. He believed they should be allowed to air their grievances; they had many complaints against the white man. Treaties had been made and broken. The Navahos and Apaches had been conquered and sent to Bosque Redondo, only to break out and be hunted down by the Army and brought back in irons. While Kit smoked the peace pipe with the Indians, he learned things he would not otherwise have known.

Not long after Camp Nichols was established, Kit was called away to serve on a special treaty commission appointed by order of the President and to testify, with William Bent and others, on the Indian problem. On March 3, Congress had set up a "traveling Joint Special Committee of three members of the Senate and four of the House" for the purpose of "directing an inquiry into the condition of the Indian tribes and their treatment by the civil and military authorities of the United States." Reasons for the investigation by the President centered around the recent charge that Colorado citizens had fired into an Indian camp flying the American flag, killing women and children of all ages. This happened after the naked bodies of the Hungate family, with stakes driven through them by the Indians, had been displayed in the Denver market place. Still another reason for the inquiry was that the military persecuted Indians whom the agents and superintendents insisted were innocent of lawlessness. Another phase of the investigation was to be "the Indian Reservation Plan."

Kit Carson firmly believed that the reservation was the only hope for peace. Speaking of the Utes, he said: "They are a brave, warlike people; they are rather small size, but hardy, and very fine shots. I would advise however, that they be put on a reservation, as they cannot live much longer as now; they are generally hungry, and killing cattle and sheep, which will bring on war. . . . I think that every effort should be made to secure peace with the Cheyennes and Arahapoes before any war is prosecuted against them, in view of the treatment they have received." He also presented the particular problems of the Cheyennes and Arapahoes by saying that it had been publicly stated that Colorado authorities, expecting their troops to be sent east, "aggressed an Indian war so that the troops would have to remain at home." Kit said that he knew of no hostilities perpetrated by the Indians previous to the attack; this confirmed William Bent's testimony. He felt that the Kiowas were hostile against the government without just cause, and the other tribes were compelled to be hostile.

The Comanches were quite unfriendly just now. "I think," said Carson, "if proper men were appointed and proper steps taken, peace could be had with all the Indians on and below the Arkansas, without war. I believe that, if Colonel Bent and myself were authorized, we could make a solid, lasting peace with those Indians. I have much more confidence in the influence of Colonel Bent with the Indians than in my own."

In his oral sworn testimony, Colonel Carson expounded upon the reasons why the Navahos had to be taken from their own country to a reservation. He told of the impossibility of changing their way of life, referring to their continued forays with the Mexicans, in which they would go into Mexican country to steal stock, women, and children. He stated there were wealthy Navahos who wanted to live in peace, but the poorer ones were in the majority, and they had no head chief to control them.

When I campaigned against them eight months, I found them scattered over a country several hundred miles in extent. There is no suitable place in their country—and I have been all over it—where more than two hundred could be placed. If located in different places, it would not be long before they and the Mexicans would be at war. If they were scattered on different locations, I hardly think any number of troops could keep them on their reservation. The mountains they love cannot be penetrated by troops. There are cañons in their country thirty miles in length, with walls a thousand feet high, and when at war it is impossible for troops to pass through these cañons, in which they hide and cultivate the ground. In the main Cañon de Chelly they had some two or three thousand peach trees, which were mostly destroyed by my troops. Colonel Sumner, in the fall of 1851, went into the Cañon de Chelly with several hundred men and two pieces of artillery; he got into the cañon some eight or ten miles, but had to retreat out of it at night. In the walls of the cañon they have regular houses built in the crevices, from which they fire and roll huge stones on an enemy. They have regular fortifications, averaging from one to two hundred feet from the bottom, with portholes for firing. No small arms can injure them, and artillery cannot be used. In one of these crevices I found a two-story house. I regard these cañons as impregnable. . . .

He further stated that some of the Mexicans objected to the Navahos' being put on a reservation because then they, the Mexicans, could no longer steal from them.

In his written testimony, Kit touched on the fact that the Indians' hunting grounds were being encroached upon by white civilization:

> Instead of forcing them backwards before its steady advance, civilization now encircles them with its chain of progress, and each year, as it passes away, sees the chain drawing rapidly closer around the hunting grounds of the red men of the prairies.

Focusing directly on the heart of the Indian trouble, he said:

> Indian agents, appointed solely by political influence, are often swayed by feelings of personal gain in the transaction of their business, making the government appear to act in bad faith towards the savages; then making promises, impossible to fulfil, to shield themselves from attack, they excite feelings of hostility that can only be quenched in blood. To this cause, and that of repeated acts of aggression on the part of the numerous reckless frontiersmen that swarm upon the borders of the Indian territory, may be attributed many, if not most, of our recent Indian war, massacres, and murders, extending from Minnesota to California.

Colonel Carson felt that the white settler needed protection, but at the same time he stressed the government's obligation to the Indian

> whilst high motives of right impel us, out of respect to ourselves and duty to the Indians, to protect our citizens, assist in the settlement of the almost unknown interior of our country, and relieve and assist while controlling the red man of the west, as their hunting grounds vanish before the sturdy energy of the pioneer and backwoodsman.

Kit described the Indians' way of life:

> There is nothing inimical in the bold, courageous, marauding Co-

manche—the wild, treacherous, nomadic Apache—the hardy, industrious agricultural Navajo, or the lazy, degraded, almost brutalized Digger. These tribes are types of the different North American Indians, and from these, or a more extensive list carefully prepared, classifications should be made to govern officers intrusted with their removal, for it is not probable that reservations can be set apart for each tribe; and where several are located together, the nearer their characters assimilate the greater will be the success, whilst the danger will decrease in the same proportion, for one wild tribe looks down on another with contemptuous pride—strange to us, but perfectly natural to their untutored minds, as they possess a less degree of skill in the barbaric virtues of murder, violence, and theft.

He listed three causes of the rapid decrease of the Indians: "continued cruel wars among themselves, prevalence of venereal diseases, and the use of intoxicating liquors." The last-named cause, he said, was the direct result of their contact with the white man, and "humanity and justice demand that prompt measures be taken to arrest their fatal progress."

In closing his testimony, Kit had this to say:

I am indulging in no chimerical or utopian idea in believing that in the next generation civilization can advance undisturbed into the vast interior of our country, whilst from the reservations the hum of busy, productive industry will resound, and the prayers of Christianity be heard from every tribe, and America stand proudly foremost among nations as the exemplar of mercy, humanity, and philanthropy, as she now does of civilization and progress.

Major Pfeiffer was in charge of Camp Nichols during Kit's absences and continued in that role until the last of the year, when the camp was ordered evacuated. In August, Kit forwarded to General Carleton a letter from Senator Doolittle, along with two "telegraphic dispatches" which Doolittle had received from Secretary of War Stanton. Senator Doolittle, chairman of the committe of inquiry, had a special mission for Colonel Carson, namely, trying to effect with the Plains Indians "a cessation of hostilities so that their chiefs and important warriors would be friendly disposed to meet with the commission in council to make peace treaties." Carson was the mediator who knew the dangers involved if the Indians thought these overtures of peace evolved from fear rather than a sincere desire for peace.

For Carson's escort, the General had selected Adjutant Tanfield, suggesting that Kit pick up a guide at Fort Bascom and reminding him to keep daily records of his talks with the Indians and to make daily reports. By October 14, Kit had paved the way for the commissioners to hold council with the Arapahoes and Cheyennes of the Upper Arkansas at Bluff Creek, some forty miles south of present-day Wichita, Kansas. Although the meeting was not significant historically, it did award the Indians their claims of property damages from Chivington's Sand Creek Massacre. The Indians were given land and their annuities were restored; they could hunt at large, providing they kept at least ten miles from the public roads.

On October 7, 1865, a treaty with the Apaches was signed, and the next day saw one with the Comanches and the Kiowas of Little Mountain. It is interesting to note here that all of the 650 treaties signed over a century have been violated or completely disregarded by one or both parties, usually the United States government.

That same fall, Kit made a trip east. He stopped at Fort Leavenworth, where General Rusling noted the visit in his diary, then went on to Missouri, where he must have had some misgivings about having fought against the South, for his family were all Southerners. However, according to family tradition, he was quite warmly received. He also visited St. Louis, Washington, and even New York on this trip, and at least one photograph was made of him at the time by Mathew Brady. He also visited General Sherman, who later educated his oldest son, William.

Kit returned to and spent his time in Taos, Santa Fe, at Maxwell's large house on the Rayado, and at Bosque Redondo. Honor came to him on April 6, 1866, when President Andrew Johnson signed the document confirming his appointment as brevet brigadier general in the U.S. Army. His commander, General Carleton, was mustered out of volunteer service on April 30, 1866, and reassigned on July 31 as lieutenant colonel of the Fourth U.S. Cavalry. Kit accepted his own reduction to lieutenant colonel when he was assigned as commander of the important post of Fort Garland, Colorado, on August 11. With him he took Josefa and their five children, in addition to his niece, Teresina Bent, who came to visit.

Kit's job at Fort Garland was to keep peace with the Indians and to see that they didn't get liquor. There were few men living more qualified to handle the job than Carson because he respected the rights and privileges of the Indians and the Indians knew it. Peace with the Indians was all important now, and no man was so certain to insure it as Kit Carson.

In September, 1866, Kit again saw General Sherman, who came to Fort Garland for a short visit. During Sherman's stay at the fort, Governor Cummings and Brigadier General James F. Rusling came for conferences with the Ute Indians, "of which chief Ouray [The Arrow] was the principal feature, and over whom Carson exercised a powerful influence," as Sherman later expressed it. A preliminary talk, with the Governor present, was held on September 21 in Kit's office. The Indians were urged to accept the reservation plan, outlined by the Army, which was to be presented to them later. On September 23, about thirty miles from the fort, on the Río Grande, the council was convened. Kit translated the proposals into Spanish, gesticulating profusely to Chief Ouray, who in turn translated them into Ute for the Indians. Sherman was so impressed with Kit's ability to handle the Indian problem that he wrote: "These Red Skins think Kit twice as big a man as me. Why, his integrity is simply perfect. They know it and they would believe him any day before me." Rusling said that Kit "returned their confidence by being their most steadfast and unswerving friend."

General Rusling developed a great liking for Kit during his stay at Fort Garland. He described Kit in the following words:

> He certainly bore the marks of exposure, but none of the extreme "roughing it" that we had anticipated. . . . His head was a remarkably good one, with the bumps of benevolence and reflection well developed. His eye was mild and blue, the very type of good nature, while his

voice was as soft and sympathetic as a woman's. He impressed you at once as a man of rare kindliness and charity, such as a truly brave man ought always to be. As simple as a child, but brave as a lion, he soon took our hearts by storm, and grew upon our regards all the while we were with him. We talked and smoked far into the night each evening we spent together.

When speaking in English, Rusling said, Kit often hesitated for the right word, but in Spanish and Indian "he was as fluent as a native." He later recalled that when he was at Fort Garland, Kit's "hair was already well-silvered and he had a well-knit frame and full deep chest, a noticeably broad and open brow and a full square jaw and chin, that evidently shut as tight as Sherman's or Grant's when necessary." Impressed with Kit's conscientiousness, he quoted him as often saying, "Now, stop, gentlemen! Is this *right*? *Ought* we to do this? *Can* we do it? Is this like human nature?" It was characteristic of Kit to test problems by the moral law. "I think," said Rusling, "that was the predominating feature of his character— his perfect honesty and truthfulness—quite as much as his match-less coolness and courage." But Kit's old injury had flared up, and he complained of pain in his chest. He no longer rode horseback, but traveled in an ambulance.

In the summer of 1867, trouble with the Indians again broke out when a Ute chief named Kaneache (or Kaniatse) had an argument with an army officer in which threatening language was used on both sides. Even though Maxwell interfered and averted a battle, Kaneache remained hostile to the *anglos* and Mexicans and made a raid on the cornfields of the Purgatoire Valley, claiming the soil and the crops. The Mexicans retaliated by killing Kaneache's son. Troops from Fort Stephens, a camp near Spanish Peaks, came to the Mexicans' rescue but were resisted by the Indians, who killed several soldiers. Chief Kaneache, who had been one of Carson's scouts in the Navaho and Kiowa campaigns, tried to persuade Chief Ouray and the Tabeguaches to join him, but instead, says Ban-croft, "Chief Ouray placed all his people under the surveillance of Fort Garland, commanded by Col. Carson, and repaired to the

Purgatoire to warn the settlers." Kit sent Chief Shawno and some Tabeguache braves to bring in Kaneache, dead or alive. Kaneache and another hostile chief were captured and brought to Kit, who sent them on to Fort Union.[1]

[1] Kit was commander at Fort Union from December 23, 1865, until April 21, 1866, when he was transferred to Fort Garland as commanding officer. He went to Fort Union from Camp Nichols.

17 ★ Death of Kit Carson

ON NOVEMBER 22, 1867, Kit Carson, brevet brigadier general, was the last man in his regiment to be mustered out of service. He had already moved his family from Fort Garland to Boggsville, about two miles from Las Animas, where Thomas O. Boggs and his wife, Rumalda, had settled on the Purgatoire River. Teresina Bent Scheurich and her mother, who visited the Carsons at the fort, had returned to Taos.

The Indian fights, the Civil War, and the campaigns of the sixties had taken their toll of Kit's failing health, but in January, 1868, the Indians and the government were again demanding Kit's services. The Utes had been invited to Washington to discuss their grievances and to talk over another treaty settlement, and the commissioner of Indian affairs urged Kit to accompany the Utes to the capital. Josefa also wanted him to take the trip in order to consult specialists regarding the pains in his chest.

Although it was a great tax upon his failing health he, characteristically, was always ready to promote the welfare of the Utes, who regarded him in the light of a father, according to Dr. Tilton.

So it was that in February, 1868, Kit started for Washington. He traveled by stagecoach to Fort Hayes; from there he took a train to St. Louis, where he was met by Colonel Albert G. Boone (grandson of Daniel Boone), who accompanied him to Washington to add his experience to the Ute council.

In Washington, General Frémont, along with other celebrities, called on Carson at the house where the conference members were staying. In his ill condition, the company, attention, and publicity he received proved to be almost too much for Kit at times, while at other times he seemed to enjoy the attention accorded him.

The treaty, which was concluded on March 2, settled the Utes on a reservation of some 15,120,000 acres in western Colorado. It extended from the White River on the north to the Río de los Piños on the south. The government promised that no one except agents, officers, and government men could "enter, reside, pass over or settle upon the confines of this reservation." The ink was scarcely dry before white settlers began to violate the agreement.

In New York, Philadelphia, and Boston, Kit consulted specialists, who gave him little, if any, hope of recovery. In Boston, on March 25, wearing his colonel's uniform, he had his last picture taken. In New York, he just missed seeing his friend Captain Pettis, who had heard that Kit was in the East.

From Boston, Kit returned, by way of Chicago, to Council Bluffs, where he took the Union Pacific to Cheyenne, Wyoming. From there he went by stage to Denver. At the Planter's House he rested in bed a few days in order to recuperate and to gather strength for the stage trip to La Junta. There his wife and Tom Boggs met him on April 11 and drove him home. Soon after arriving in Boggsville, he made a trip to Fort Lyon to consult Dr. H. R. Tilton, assistant surgeon of that post. He was tired and very ill; he complained of the need to cough and said he couldn't breathe when he was lying flat. The pain in his chest grew progressively worse, for an aneurysm was pressing on the pneumogastric nerve, causing spasms in the bronchial tubes.

On April 13, 1868, another daughter, Josefita, was born to the Carsons. Ten days later, Mrs. Carson died. She was buried at Boggsville, close to the Carson-Hough place. The shock and grief at losing his beloved wife seemed to be more than Kit could bear. However, for the sake of his seven motherless children, Kit made a brave effort to resume the task of living, as is indicated in a letter to Aloys Scheurich, his last:

Mouth of Purgatoire River
May 5, 1868

Dear Compadre:

I have received your letter and it has been a satisfaction to me to hear that you are well. I arrived here on the 11th of last month, sick and worn out, but began to improve from that time and would be comparatively healthy if the misfortune, loosing my wife hadn't happened. Those were trying days for me. My health is improving now and I am very apt to be on the other side of the mountains by the end of this month; it is almost necessary for me to go, as much on account of business as for the sake of my health, to avoid the heat during the summer months.

You have had before this the particulars of my wife's death and I need not repeat them here. My children are well.

We are farming as much as can be done without going to any great expense. I had a ditch taken out and everything works well in that respect. I intended to build me a house, but as I apprehend some trouble about our land, I decided to wait until matters are settled.

Now I have told you of my intentions and prospects, I expect you will appreciate the interest I am taking in you and yours and let me know what your calculations are for the future.

It is my intention to send my wife's corpse to Taos, as soon as the weather is cool enough to do so and have taken the necessary steps to have this done, even if I myself should be called away, she will rest as close to her family as possible. I have given the necessary orders to have my own body, if I should die, and that of my wife's sent together to Taos, to be buried in our graveyard near Elfigo. I want neither her nor myself to be buried in the church.

My best regards to the old lady, Teresina and your boy, who I am told is a fine child.

Please tell the old lady that there is nobody in the world who can take care of my children but her and she must know that it would be the greatest of favors to me, if she would come and stay until I am healthier and may make such arrangements as would suit her. She has two children here and is among those nearest to her.

The country has changed much since she was here last, no danger of Indians now. A greater number of people are living here, than then.

If she should determine to come, let me know immediately, and I will send a carriage for her. Chipita Gorda is nursing the baby, which is doing very well, but still I am anxious to get another nurse.

Remember me to all my friends, more particularly Miller, and don't delay to give an answer.

Yours truly,
C. Carson.

As Kit's condition became steadily worse, Dr. Tilton was called more frequently to see him. Each time he was called, he had to cross the river, which was swollen by spring floods, and he finally suggested that Kit be moved to his own quarters at Fort Lyon, which was done on May 14. Aloys and Teresina Scheurich and Mrs. Bent arrived the day after Kit was moved. Tom Boggs took Aloys to Fort Lyon, where Aloys remained with Kit while Mrs. Bent and her daughter took charge of the Carson children.

The move, Dr. Tilton said, enabled him to make Kit much more comfortable. "In the interval of his paroxysms, he beguiled the time by relating past experiences. I read Dr. Peters' book, with the hero my auditor; from time to time, he would comment on the incidents of his eventful life. It was wonderful to read of the stirring scenes, thrilling deeds, and narrow escapes, and then look at the quiet modest, little man who had done so much."

The day after Kit arrived at the post hospital, he made his will, which he dictated to Aloys Scheurich, naming Tom Boggs as his executor:

Fort Lyon.
Pueblo County.
Colorado Territory.
May 15th, 1868.

I, Christopher Carson, a resident of Pueblo County, Colorado Territory, knowing the uncertainty of life, and being now of sound mind, do make this, my last Will and Testament.

TO WIT:

First. It is my will, that of my cattle, numbering from one hundred

275

to two hundred head, such only, shall be sold, from time to time, as may be necessary for the support of my children; the balance to be retained, with the increase, for the benefit of my children.

Secondly. It is my will, that my seven yoke of steers, and two ox wagons, shall be kept by my administrator, for the use and support of my children.

Thirdly. It is my will, that my four horses and one carriage, shall be kept by my adminstrator, for the use and support of my children.

Fourthly. It is my will, that my house and lot, with all the improvements, in Taos N. M., be sold by my administrator for a sum, not less than one thousand dollars, the proceeds to be used for the benefit of my children. If the property, above named, will not bring the sum of one thousand dollars, it is my will that it be rented annually, and the amounts so received, used for the benefit of my children.

Fifthly. It is my will, that my furniture in my house in Taos, N. M., be sold by my administrator, and the proceeds used by him, for the benefit of my children.

Sixthly. It is my will, that some two or three pieces of land, lying in the Valley of Taos, N. M., the titles to which are in my wife's name, be rented, from year to year, to the highest bidder, and the sums so received, be used by my administrator, for the benefit of my children.

Seventhly. It is my will, that the accruing interest, at the rate of ten per cent per annum, on a Promissory Note for the sum of three thousand dollars, drawn in my favor, and signed by L. B. Maxwell, of Cimmaron, N. M., be paid to my administrator, the amount so received, to be used by him, for the burial expenses of myself and wife.

Eighthly. It is my will, that my administrator gets security for the Promissory Note of three thousand dollars, drawn in my favor, and signed by L. B. Maxwell, of Cimmaron, N. M., and failing in that, to collect the note, and loan the money on good security, and at the highest rate of interest obtainable. The annual interest to be used by him, for the support of my children.

Ninthly. It is my will, that any moneys which may be due me from Mr. Myer of Costilla C. T. and Mr. Rudolph the sutler of Fort Garland, C. T. be paid over to my administrator, to be used by him for the support of my children.

Tenthly. It is my will, that any moneys which may be due from Mr. L. B. Maxwell, for cattle sold to Mr. Frank Pape, be paid to my ad-

ministrator, the amount so received, to be used by him, for the support
of my children.

Lastly. I hereby appoint *Mr. Thomas O. Boggs,* of Pueblo Co., Col.
Ter., my administrator, to carry out the provisions of this, my last will,
and testament.

Signed this 15th day of May,
One thousand eight hundred and
sixty-eight, in the presence
of   C. Carson
J. A. Fitzgerald
H. R. Tilton
Recorded, October 6, 1868
    M. G. Bradford
      Probate Judge
Filed in Probate Court, June 1, 1868, M. C. Bradford, Judge

Aloys stayed with Kit day and night. The officers of the post paid
him marked attention and respect, and he never lacked visitors and
admirers when he felt like receiving them. True to mountain fashion,
his bed consisted of a blanket and a buffalo robe on the floor of Dr.
Tilton's quarters, but he was comfortable only in a semireclining
position. He was not permitted to smoke, and since swallowing
solid food would make his condition worse, his only nourishment
consisted of liquids.

Dr. Tilton spent most of his time doing what he could to relieve
Kit's pain. "I explained to him the probable mode of termination
of the disease," he said, "that he might die from suffocation or more
probably the aneurysm would burst and cause death by hemorrhage.
He expressed a decided preference for the latter mode."

Kit's disease progressed rapidly, and he calmly contemplated his
approaching death. Several times he remarked to Dr. Tilton: "If
it was not for this [pointing to his chest], I might live to be a hundred years old."

As the attacks of dyspnea grew worse, Dr. Tilton used chloroform
to lessen Kit's suffering. "I was compelled," related Dr. Tilton, "to
give chloroform to relieve him, at considerable risk of hastening

a fatal result; but he begged me not to let him suffer such torture, and if I killed him by chloroform while attempting relief, it would be much better than death by suffocation."

The night of May 22 was the most comfortable Kit had spent for some time. However, he coughed up some blood, which indicated that the end was near. About the middle of the afternoon on May 23, Kit asked Aloys Scheurich to cook him a good meal, saying he was tired of the soft food they had been giving him. With Dr. Tilton's approval, Aloys prepared a buffalo steak and some coffee. Kit ate heartily and asked for his old clay pipe. The doctor consented. Kit smoked and talked with Aloys. Dr. Tilton was lying on the bed, listening.

Suddenly Kit called out: "Doctor! Compadre! Adios!" Said Tilton: "I sprang to him, and seeing a gush of blood pouring from his mouth, remarked, 'This is the last of the General.' I supported his forehead on my hand, while death speedily closed the scene. . . . Death took place at 4:25 p.m., May 23, 1868."

The flag was at once lowered to half-mast, and the funeral was announced for ten o'clock the next morning. Word was sent to Boggsville, to inform Kit's family and friends of his death.

The Reverend Gamaliel Collins, post chaplain, officiated at the funeral. Kit's body was laid in a hand-made casket lined with the wedding dress of Captain Casey's wife. Paper flowers from the bonnets of the women at the post were the only floral arrangements available.

One mile from Fort Lyon, the casket was consigned to relatives and friends from Boggsville, and from there it was conveyed, under military escort, to Kit's last home, where he was laid to rest beside his beloved Josefa.

News of Kit Carson's death flashed from one end of the continent to the other. From Fort Lyon, Colorado Territory, went this message:

Kit Carson died at this post between the hours of four and five o'clock, afternoon, this day, from disease of the heart under which he had been laboring since his return from the east. He had been removed to the fort some ten days since, so that Dr. Tilton, the post surgeon, could give better attention than if he had remained at his brother-in-law's, Mr. Boggs, some five miles distant.

The *Rocky Mountain News,* the *New York World,* the *Missouri Republic,* the *Washington Intelligencer,* the *Santa Fé New Mexican,* the *Pueblo Chieftain,* and some of the California papers carried resolutions of respect from Kit's brothers-at-arms, as well as news stories of his death. Appleton's *Annual American Cyclopaedia* for 1868 devoted a column of its obituary section to Kit, as much space as most of the ranking military men commanded.

Although it was Kit's wish to be buried in Taos, it was more than a year before his body and that of Josefa were taken there—in a wagon driven by "Dutch Joe" through Raton Pass. They were buried in a small cemetery on the eastern outskirts of the village, and their graves remained neglected until the Taos Masons erected marble headstones in 1908. Kit had become a Mason when he joined the Montezuma Lodge in Santa Fe on April 22, 1854. On December 27, 1859, he transferred his membership to the newly formed Bent Lodge 294 in Taos, and when it discontinued, he rejoined the Montezuma Lodge—January 7, 1865. He became a Master Mason on December 28, 1854.

The cemetery has been incorporated into present-day Kit Carson Memorial Park, which surrounds the small graveyard. Here, above Kit's grave, the American flag flies day and night to commemorate the year 1861, when Kit nailed the flag to the Taos-plaza pole. The Stars and Stripes also fly day and night on Taos plaza in commemoration of this event.

The West has honored Kit Carson's memory. Many of his mementos are preserved in Sacramento, Denver, and the Kit Carson Museum in Taos, New Mexico. There is a large painting of Kit at Fort Garland, and in Denver, on the dome of the Capitol, there is also a picture of him. The Civic Center at Denver also honors his memory with a pioneers' monument done in bronze by Frederick MacMonnies. Kit Carson Highway goes through Taos and many parts of New Mexico and Colorado.

Spokane, Washington, has a Mount Kit Carson and a Kit Carson Park. In Carson Park at Trinidad, Colorado, there is a splendid equestrian statue of Kit by Augustus Lukeman. There is a Kit Carson Pass in the Sierra Nevada Mountains, a town named Carson in Colorado, a Fort Carson in Colorado, and Carson City, the capital of Nevada.

Of all the monuments erected to Kit's memory, the one at Santa Fe, in front of the Federal Building, is perhaps the most significant because of its inscription, a short sentence which sums up Kit's life in four simple words: "He led the way."

Notes on Sources

Chapter 1
FAMILY BACKGROUND

ALEXANDER CARSON SOUGHT RELIGIOUS FREEDOM: F. Tom Carson, *Carson Family History* (hereafter referred to as *Carson History*), 9, 11; Blanche C. Grant, "Notes and Documents on the Life of Christopher Carson" (hereafter referred to as "Grant's notes"); the late John Young-Hunter to Blanche Grant, Taos, 1936; John Young-Hunter's address at the Carson Commemorative Birthday Dinner, Sagebrush Inn, Taos, December 24, 1950; Calvin D. Cowles, "The Genealogy of Five Allied Families"; Edwin L. Sabin, *Kit Carson Days:1809–1868* (hereafter referred to as "Sabin, 1 vol."), 1.

EARLY RELIGION IN PENNSYLVANIA: Marvin C. Wilbur (ed.), *Presbyterian Plan Book*, 10; George P. Fisher, *History of the Christian Church*, 573; Albert H. Newman, *A History of the Baptist Church in the United States* (Philadelphia, 1915), 197, 209.

THE CARSONS' AND BOONES' PIONEERING VENTURES: Edwin L. Sabin, *Kit Carson Days, 1809–1868: Adventures in the Path of Empire* (hereafter referred to as "Sabin, 2 vols."), I, 1–6; Grant's notes; Theodore Roosevelt, *The Winning of the West* (hereafter referred to as "Roosevelt"), I, 176; John Bakeless, *Daniel Boone, Master of the Wilderness* (hereafter referred to as "Bakeless"), *passim*; John H. Wheeler, *Historical Sketches of North Carolina* (Philadelphia, 1851); Cecil B. Hartley, *The Life of Daniel Boone*,

16; John Walton, "Ghost Writer to Daniel Boone," *American Heritage*, Vol. VI, No. 6 (October, 1955), 10–13, 95.

CARSONS IN EARLY NORTH CAROLINA; KIT'S FATHER AND GRANDFATHER: Sabin, 2 vols., chaps. I and II, *passim;* William H. Foote, *Sketches of North Carolina* (New York, 1846), 78–188; *Carson History*, 10; Roosevelt, I, V, *passim;* Grant's notes.

FOUNDING OF KENTUCKY: William Fleming, "Journal in Kentucky" (hereafter referred to as "Fleming"); Sabin, 2 vols., I, 2; *Carson History*, 33; Bakeless, chaps. I and II, *passim*, 87, 88; Roosevelt, II, *passim*, 11, 39.

PURCHASE OF KIT'S BIRTHPLACE; DESCRIPTION: Madison County (Kentucky) Court House Records, Deed Book E, 257; Grant's notes; Charles Carson to Blanche Grant, June 20, 1930, Colorado.

Chapter 2
KIT'S EARLY LIFE

KIT'S BIRTHPLACE; MIDDLE NAME: Grant's Notes; Milo M. Qaife (ed.), *Kit Carson's Autobiography* (hereafter referred to as *Autobiography*), 3; Mary Ann Carson Rubey (hereafter called "Mary Ann") to Mrs. J. F. Hawley (hereafter called "Mrs. Hawley"); Sabin, 2 vols., I, 3; Blanche C. Grant (ed.), *Kit Carson's Own Story of His Life* (hereafter referred to as *Own Story*), 9; Edward S. Ellis, *Life of Kit Carson* (hereafter referred to as "Ellis"), 5.

CARSONS AND BOONES IN EARLY KENTUCKY: Grant's notes; Lewis Collins, *History of Kentucky, passim;* Bakeless, chap. II, *passim*, 364; Madison County (Kentucky) Court House Records, Deed Book, 1811.

BOONE'S JUSTICE TREE: Fleming; Bakeless, 372.

CARSONS MOVE TO UPPER LOUISIANA: Grant's notes; Teresina Bent Scheurich (hereafter called "Teresina") to Charles Carson, 1901, Colorado; George H. Carson to Blanche Grant, *circa* 1930; *Autobiography*, note 3; Mary Ann to Mrs. Hawley in an interview with Blanche Grant, 1929; Charles Carson to Blanche Grant, "Kit Carson as a Missourian: The Life of the Great Plainsman Who Considered This His Home State," *Kansas City Star Magazine,* September 13, 1925 (hereafter referred to as "Carson, *Kansas City Star*"); Sabin, 1 vol., 6.

DESCRIPTION OF KIT; EARLY SCHOOLING FOR LAW: Grant's notes; J. H. Widber's unpublished MS in Bancroft Library; Captain Charles A. Montgomery's description of Kit, copy owned by author; DeWitt Clinton Peters, *Pioneer Life and Frontier Adventures* (hereafter referred to as "Peters"), vii–x, *passim; Carson History,* 36; Carson, *Kansas City Star;* George H. Carson to Blanche Grant; Sabin, 2 vols., I, 2.

ALEXANDER, FIRST CARSON TO GO WEST: H. M. Chittenden, *The American Fur Trade of the Far West* (hereafter referred to as "Chittenden"), I, 149, 186; Washington Irving, *Astoria* (hereafter referred to as *Astoria*), I, 182, 210–16, 247, 250–51, and II, 10–11, 196.

FAMILY ACTIVITIES; THE WAR; LINDSEY'S DEATH: *Carson History,* 34–37; Howard County (Missouri) Tax and Marriage Records; George H. Carson to Blanche Grant; *Own Story,* note 1; Grant's notes; Missouri Fur Company records; Teresina to Charles Carson; *Autobiography,* note 2; Mrs. Hawley to Blanche Grant.

Chapter 3
CARAVAN AT INDEPENDENCE

KIT RAN AWAY: Sabin, 2 vols., I, 8, 16; *Own Story,* 9; Mary Ann to Mrs. Hawley as told to author in 1951; *Carson History,* 36; Grant's notes; Teresina to Charles Carson; Teresina to Rumalda Luna Boggs (hereafter called "Rumalda"), 1905; *Missouri Intelligencer,* October 6, 1826; F. T. Cheetham, *Kit Carson: Pathbreaker, Patriot, Humanitarian* (hereafter referred to as "Cheetham"), 3; Charles Burdett, *The Life of Kit Carson, the Great Western Hunter and Guide* (hereafter referred to as "Burdett"), 4.

CARSON WITH BENT, NOT ST. VRAIN, IN 1826: Thomas M. Marshall, "St. Vrain's Expedition to the Gila in 1826," *Southwestern Historical Quarterly,* Vol. XIX, No. 3, 251–60; Grant's notes; Teresina to Charles Carson that by Kit's own statement he met

Charles Bent on the 1826 caravan, not Céran St. Vrain; Charles F. Coan, *A History of New Mexico* (hereafter referred to as "Coan"), I, 302; Louis Houck, *A History of Missouri*, III, 146.

PREPARATION AND JOURNEY TO SANTA FE: Josiah Gregg, *Commerce of the Prairies* (hereafter referred to as *Commerce*), chaps. II and III, *passim;* "The Osage Treaty," 3883; John S. C. Abbott, *Kit Carson, the Pioneer of the West* (hereafter referred to as "Abbott"), chaps. I and II, *passim,* 32; Peters, 30; *Own Story*, 10; *Commerce*, 41–42; D. M. Kelsey, *A History of Our Wild West* (New York, 1928), 227; Grant's notes; Colonel Henry Inman, *The Old Santa Fé Trail,* 408, 409; Teresina to Charles Carson concerning Bent's leaving caravan; Kit Carson to Teresina; Sabin, 2 vols., I, 20; Rumalda to Teresina, 1903; Governor Bent's proclamations; William G. Ritch Collection, Huntington Library, 1697–1715.

CARAVAN ARRIVAL AND DESCRIPTION OF SANTA FE: *Commerce,* 62, 63; Grant's notes; Esteban de Terreros y Pando, *Diccionario Castellano,* definition for *gringo;* Ralph E. Twitchell, *Leading Facts of New Mexican History* (hereafter referred to as "Twitchell"), II, 174; James F. Meline, *Two Thousand Miles on Horseback* (hereafter referred to as "Meline"), 152–53; Chittenden, II, 504 n. 9, 519; George Frederick Ruxton, *On the Old West*, 290–92.

KIT IN TAOS WITH KINCAID; MEETS PADRE MARTINEZ: Ellis, 7; George H. Carson to Blanche Grant; Peters, 30; Abbott, 33–34; Charles Carson to Blanche Grant; Kit to Teresina; L. Pascual Martinez to author, 1939.

TAOS INDIANS: Coan, I, 26; John C. Bourke, *The Moaquis of Arizona* (New York, 1884), 3–4; Edgar L. Hewett, *Ancient Life in the American Southwest,* 210–11; Lewis H. Garrard, *Wah-To-Yah* (hereafter referred to as Garrard), 194–95; Blanche C. Grant, *When Old Trails Were New* (hereafter referred to as *Old Trails*), *passim.*

Chapter 4
TRIP TO CALIFORNIA
EL PASO AND CHIHUAHUA TRIPS: *Own Story*, 11; Grant's notes;

Rumalda to Teresina concerning Kincaid's death and Christmas in Chihuahua; Abbott, 41; Ellis, 8; George B. Grinnell, "Bent's Old Fort and Its Builders," Kansas Historical Society *Publications* (1919–1922); General Thomas James, *Three Years Among the Indians and Mexicans*, 155.

On the Way to California: Ellis, 9–11; *Own Story*, 12–14; Coan, I, 303–304; E. C. Worchester, "The Weapons of the American Indians," *New Mexico Historical Review*, Vol. XX, No. 3, 233; Joseph J. Hill, "Ewing Young in the Fur Trade in the Far Southwest, 1822–1834," *Oregon Historical Quarterly*, Vol. XXIV, No. 1 (March, 1923); Burdett, 12–19; Peters, 37–43; Grant's notes; Rumalda to Teresina concerning Kit's visit to the Navaho chief.

Visit California Missions: Ellis, 12–15; *Own Story*, 15–16; Abbott, 62–63; William H. Davis, *Seventy-five Years in California*, 6, 7.

Trouble at Los Angeles; Return Trip: *Own Story*, 17–21; Hubert H. Bancroft, *History of California* (hereafter referred to as "Bancroft, *California*"), III, 174; Abbott, 74–78; Burdett, 54–61; Ellis, 22–26, quote from Young; Jonathan T. Warner, "Reminiscences of Early California—1831 to 1846," Historical Society of Southern California *Annual Publications*, Vol. VII (1907–1908); Bancroft, *California*, III, Young's letter to Captain Cooper.

Back in Taos; Indian Ceremonials: Grant's notes; *Own Story*, 20; Frank Waters, *Masked Gods*, 198; Coan, I, 47; Earle R. Forrest, *Missions and Pueblos of the Old Southwest*, 88; Twitchell, I, 29; M. Morgan Estergreen, "When Taos Dances," *New Mexico Magazine*, Vol. XXVIII, No. 8 (August, 1950), 16, 40; Rumalda to Teresina concerning Kit's invitation to Indian dances and his meeting Charles Bent in Taos.

Chapter 5
THE CARSON LUCK

Big Moses and Kit in Taos: Grant's notes; Rumalda to Teresina, 1904; Sabin, 2 vols., I, 62.

Trip to Rockies with Fitzpatrick: Ellis, 27; *Own Story*, 20–21; Hubert H. Bancroft, *The Works of Hubert Howe Bancroft*

(San Francisco, 1889), III, 175; Miss A. J. Allen (comp.), *Ten Years in Oregon*, 160; Bernard De Voto, *Across the Wide Missouri* (hereafter referred to as "De Voto"), 438; Chittenden, I, 471–76; Grant's notes; Rumalda to Blanche Grant; Bert G. Phillips to author.

KIT MEETS SINCLAIR; JOINS GANTT: *Own Story*, 21; Peters, 59–65; Ellis, 28.

CROW FIGHT: *Own Story*, 22–24; Peters, 62–65; Milo L. Whittaker, *Pathmakers and Pioneers of the Pueblo Region*, 84–86; Grinnell, "Bent's Old Fort and Its Builders," *loc. cit.*, 36.

COUREURS DE BOIS; COMMENT ON TRAPPERS: Burdett, 66–67; *Astoria;* Washington Irving, *The Adventures of Captain Bonneville*, 86; Timothy Flint, *The Personal Narrative of James Ohio Pattie of Kentucky.*

CACHE STOLEN; AMBUSH: *Own Story*, 26–29; Grant's notes; "The Mountainmen and Their Part in the Opening of the West," Missouri Historical Society *Bulletin*, Vol. III, No. 4, 158; Peters, 68–69.

TO BAYOU SALADE; HAPPY HUNTING GROUNDS; TAOS AGAIN: Grant's notes; Rumalda to Teresina, description of Bayou Salade; Abbott, 105–106; *Astoria*, 265–66; *Own Story*, 27–29; Rumalda to Teresina concerning conversation of trappers on way to Taos.

THE FUR EMPIRE: Elizabeth L. Gibhart, *The Life and Adventures of the Original John Jacob Astor, passim;* Chittenden, *passim;* Frank Waters, *The Colorado*, 170.

LEE AND KIT RETURN TO ROCKIES; KIT CHASES CALIFORNIA INDIAN: *Own Story*, 30–31; Ellis, 51–58; Grant's notes.

GRIZZLY EXPERIENCES: *Own Story*, 31–32; Ross Kimball to author about grizzlies' claws; Henry Howe, *Historical Collections of the Great West*, 306; Grant's notes.

Chapter 6
EVENTFUL YEARS

CAMP WITH FRIENDLY TRIBE; TROUBLE WITH BLACKFEET: Burdett, 126–28; *The Forty-fifth Report of the Bureau of American*

Ethnology to the Secretary of the Smithsonian Institution (1930);
Peters, 118; *Autobiography*, 41–43.

BLACKFOOT BATTLE; SUMMER RENDEZVOUS: Grant's notes; Rumalda to Teresina, 1903; *Own Story*, 33–35; Ellis, 72–76; Abbott, 121–23; Meline, 250–51; Ellis, 66–72; Sabin, 1 vol., 155–77, *passim.*

FIGHT WITH SHUNAR; ARAPAHO MARRIAGE: *Autobiography*, 42–44; Samuel Parker, *Journal of an Exploring Tour Beyond the Rocky Mountains*, 76; Cheetham, 6; Sabin, 1 vol., 200–201; Grant's notes; Rumalda to Teresina about Arapaho marriage; Captain James Hobbs, *Wildlife in the Far West* (hereafter referred to as "Hobbs"), 448.

WINTER CAMP; CREASING; INDIAN FIGHTS: Grant's notes; W. E. Webb, *Buffalo Land*, 306; *Commerce*, 367–70; Charles Larpenteur, *Forty Years a Fur Trader*; *Autobiography*, 48–55; Washington Irving, *A Tour on the Prairies* (hereafter referred to as *Tour*), 117–20; J. Frank Dobie, *The Mustangs*, 144–45; Sabin, 2 vols., I, 273; George W. Kendall, *Narrative of the Texas Santa Fé Expedition* (hereafter referred to as "Kendall"), *passim*; Sabin, 1 vol., 177; DeVoto, 371, 391, 442 n.12; Grant's notes; Kit to Teresina on Old Bill Williams.

DEATH OF WAA-NIBE; ADALINE TO MISSOURI: Grant's notes; unpublished letters from Mrs. Amick, Kit's niece; Sabin, 1 vol., 201; Stanley Vestal (Walter Campbell), *Kit Carson, the Happy Warrior of the Old West* (Boston and New York, 1925), 178.

OLIVER WIGGINS; KIT AT BENT'S FORT: Grant's notes; unpublished letters from Oliver Wiggins; *Autobiography*, 64; John D. Hunter, *Manners and Customs of the Western Indians*, 295; Grinnell, "Bent's Old Fort and Its Builders," *loc. cit., passim.*

INVOLVED IN CHARLES BENT'S AFFAIRS; JOSEFA: Sabin, 2 vols., I, 283–84; Bent Family Bible; Grant's notes.

Chapter 7
EXPLORING WITH FRÉMONT
FROM CHOUTEAU'S LANDING TO FORT LARAMIE: *Autobiography*,

65–67; John C. Frémont, *The Exploring Expedition to the Rocky Mountains, Oregon and California* (hereafter referred to as "Frémont, *Exploring*"), 5–122, *passim;* Charles Preuss, *Exploring with Frémont* (hereafter referred to as "Preuss"), xxii, xxiii, 3, 13, 17, 28, 29; Grant's notes; unpublished letters from Oliver Wiggins; *Tour,* 189–91.

To SOUTH PASS AND RETURN: John C. Frémont, *Memoirs of My Life* (hereafter referred to as *Memoirs*), 118, 119–60; Kit Carson's baptismal certificate (1842) and marriage certificate (1843).

Chapter 8
FRÉMONT'S SECOND EXPEDITION

ARMIJO AND THE TEXANS: *Commerce,* 79 n.19; *Autobiography,* 68–69; *Missouri Historical Review,* Vol. XXII, 93–94; Kendall, *passim;* Coan, II, 311–16; Bancroft, *California,* XII, 323–30; Grant's notes.

KIT JOINS SECOND EXPEDITION: Frémont, *Exploring,* 141–42; Grant's notes; *Memoirs,* 169–410.

Chapter 9
THIRD EXPEDITION WITH FRÉMONT

KIT IN TAOS; PADRE MARTINEZ: Grant's notes; Teresina Bent Scheurich letters; L. Pascual Martinez, "Padre Martínez"; Ralph E. Twitchell, *The Military Occupation of New Mexico: 1846–1851* (hereafter referred to as "Twitchell, *Occupation*"), 134; William A. Keleher, *Maxwell Land Grant: A New Mexico Item* (hereafter referred to as *Maxwell Grant*), 29.

KIT AND OWENS AT RAYADO: *Autobiography,* 88; *Memoirs,* 427.

KIT WITH FRÉMONT: *Memoirs,* 411–610, *passim; Autobiography,* 88–104; Garrard, 158; Chittenden, II, 797; Bancroft, *California,* XII, 16–21; Grant's notes; Carson file, Huntington Library; Abbott, 249; *Washington Union,* June, 1847; *Own Story,* 65–77; *California Star,* April 1, 1848.

GAVILAN FORT: Bancroft, *California,* XII, 12–22; Thomas O. Larkin's official correspondence; *Autobiography,* 94; Martin's narrative; John A. Sutter, *Personal Reminiscences*, 145–48; Bancroft, *California*, XX, 747.

BEAR FLAG: Walter Colton, *Deck and Port*, 390–91; Bancroft, *California*, XXII, 146, 334 n.9, 408, 411, 415–19, 425, 430; Irving B. Richman, *California under Spain and Mexico*, *1535–1847*, *passim*; Joseph W. Revere, *A Tour of Duty in California*, *passim*; Preuss, 119 n.67; Benjamin M. Read, *Illustrated History of New Mexico* (hereafter referred to as "Read"), 417, 439; L. Bradford Prince, *Historical Sketches of New Mexico from the Earliest Records to the American Occupation* (hereafter referred to as "Prince"), 307; Larkin, *Documented History of California*, ix, 121; James M. Cutts, *The Conquest of California and New Mexico*, 246–47.

Chapter 10
GUIDE TO KEARNY

CARSON ON DISPATCH DUTY; GUIDE TO KEARNY: *Autobiography*, 109–12; Bancroft, *California*, XVII, 336, 340; *Memoirs*, 568; Alexander W. Doniphan, *Doniphan's Expedition* (hereafter referred to as "Doniphan"), 208–24; W. H. Emory, *Notes of a Military Reconnaisance from Fort Leavenworth in Missouri to San Diego* (hereafter referred to as "Emory"), 55–126; Twitchell, *Occupation*, 56; Read, 441; Coan, II, 335–36; Ellis, 190.

BATTLE OF SAN PASQUAL: Bancroft, *California*, XXII, 341–47; *Autobiography*, 111–16; Doniphan, 226–30; Grant's notes; Emory; Abraham Johnson's journal.

CARSON AND BEALE CRAWL TO SAN DIEGO; Abbott, 262; Grant's notes; *Autobiography*, 116; Sabin, 2 vols., II, 537–39; Ellis, 192–96; *Memoirs*, 588–89; Bancroft, *California*, 356.

BATTLE OF SAN GABRIEL; PEACE TREATY: *Autobiography*, 117; Sabin, 1 vol., 229; *Memoirs*, 600; Bancroft, *California*, XXII, 392 n.11, 396, 397, 425–33; Emory.

Chapter 11
REVOLT IN TAOS

GOVERNOR BENT'S MURDER: Bancroft, *California*, XVII, 430–33;

Coan, II, 341–44; Prince, 315–17; Twitchell, *Occupation*, 124–33; Rumalda to Bert Greer Phillips, 1904; Garrard, 182, 187; Colonel Price's official report.

CARSON TO ST. LOUIS AND WASHINGTON ON DISPATCH DUTY: *Autobiography*, 119–20; Sabin, 2 vols., I, 564, 570; Peters, 308; Grant's notes; "An Interview with Jessie Benton Frémont," *The Land of Sunshine Magazine* (February, 1897); *Washington Union*, June 15, 1847; Grant's notes; House Ex. Doc. No. 17, 31st Cong., 1st sess., 247; Elizabeth Benton Frémont, *Recollections, passim;* William T. Sherman, *Memoirs of General William T. Sherman* (hereafter referred to as "Sherman"), I, 46–47.

Chapter 12
ON DISPATCH DUTY

OVER THE SPANISH TRAIL: Sherman; George D. Brewerton, *Overland with Kit Carson* (hereafter referred to as "Brewerton"), 37–200, *passim;* Treaty of Guadalupe Hidalgo; Coan, I, 315; Grant's notes; *Memoirs*, 200.

CARSON BACK IN NEW MEXICO: *Weekly Reveille*, July 31, 1848; *Autobiography*, 125–26; Sabin, 2 vols., II, 602–603.

TO ST. LOUIS AND WASHINGTON: Thomas H. Benton, *Thirty Years' View*, II, *passim*, LeRoy Hafen, "Mountain Men," *Colorado Magazine*, Vol. XI, No. 5, 174.

BACK IN TAOS; GUARD DUTY: Ellis, 205; *Autobiography*, 129; Preuss, 152; Grant's notes; F. Stanley, *Fort Union (New Mexico)* (hereafter referred to as *Fort Union*), 3, 11; *Maxwell Grant*, 29, 67.

CARSON TO THE RESCUE OF MRS. WHITE: *Autobiography*, 131–36; Ellis, 207–10; Peters, 339–51; Burdett, 345–46.

Chapter 13
INDIAN AGENT

BENT'S FORT: David S. Lavender, *Bent's Fort* (hereafter referred to as "Lavender"), 301–302, 314–15, 318–19.

ADVENTURES; TWO PISTOLS AS A GIFT: *Autobiography*, 136–41; Burdett, 349–50; Peters, 369–77; Ellis, 213.

To St. Louis and Return: Grant's notes; Hobbs, 448; Lavender, 320; *Autobiography*, 142–43; *Fort Union*, 311.

Last Trapping Spree; Home Again: *Autobiography*, 146; Burdett, 355–61; Peters, 395–404; Twitchell, II, 340; Sabin, 2 vols., II, 627, 631, 632; Venita Reche McPherson to author.

Carson and Maxwell Take Sheep to California: *Autobiography*, 146–47; Grant's notes; Boggs file, Bancroft Library.

Appointment as Indian Agent and Service: *Autobiography*, 149–56; Ellis, 227; Peters, 423; Grant's notes; agency letters and superintendent's records, Santa Fe; Messervy to Carson, April 13, 1854; Carson to Messervy; Carson to Commissioner of Indian Affairs, June 30, 1854.

Chapter 14
THE CIVIL WAR

Agent's Reports and Duties: Mrs. Albert Gusdorf (Simpson's daughter) to author, 1946; Letters from Meriwether to Carson, March 10, 1855, September 29, 1855, and August 31, 1858; Carson to Commissioner of Indian Affairs, June 30, 1855; Carson, *Kansas City Star*.

Peace Treaties; Fort Union: *Autobiography*, 168; *Fort Union*, 86–90, 202; Carson to Meriwether, September 17 and 20, 1856.

Carson Reappointed; More Indian Trouble: Carson's agency reports, August 29 and September 1, 1857; Sabin, 1 vol., 647; William A. Keleher, *Turmoil in New Mexico, 1846–1868* (hereafter referred to as *Turmoil*), 52–59.

Carson Reappointed Again; Suffers Fall: Grant's notes; Sabin, 2 vols., II, 680; Army records, National Archives.

Flag Torn Down at Taos: *Old Trails*, 163.

Battle of Valverde: *Turmoil*, 170, 201; Records of the Rebellion, Series 1, Vol. IX; Coan, I, 371–74.

Chapter 15
APACHES AND NAVAHOS

Trouble at Fort Stanton: *Turmoil*, 285, 290; Indian Agency

Official Records hereafter referred to as "Official Records"), Series L, Vol. XV, 576; Sabin, 2 vols., II, 704.

CHIEF RED SLEEVES: *Turmoil*, 486–92; Official Records, Series L, Vols. XV, 229, and L, part 2, 296; Carleton to Samuel J. Jones, April 27, 1863; Carson to Carleton, January 4, 1863.

CAMPAIGN AGAINST THE NAVAHOS: Carleton to Chavez, June 23, 1863; *Santa Fé New Mexican*, June 15, 1863; Coan, I, 378; Carson to Carleton, August 19, 1863; Carson to Captain Benjamin J. Culter, August 31, October 5, December 6, and December 20, 1863, and two letters dated January 22, 1864; Official Records, Series L, Vol. XXIV, 77; *Turmoil*, 369; *Santa Fé New Mexican*, February 18, 1864; Carleton to Thomas, February 7, 1864; General Asa B. Casey to Edwin L. Sabin, 1909; Carson to Carleton, April 10, 1864; Carleton to Thomas, October 30, 1864; Carleton to General Marcellus M. Crocker, October 31, 1864; Superintendent Michael Steck to Commissioner of Indian Affairs, October 16, 1864.

Chapter 16
ADOBE WALLS

CARLETON'S ORDERS; PREPARATION: *Santa Fé Gazette*, October 29, 1864; Edgar I. Stewart, *Custer's Luck* (Norman, 1955), *passim;* Sabin, 2 vols., II, 728; Carson to Carleton, December 4, 1864; Records of the Rebellion, Series 1, Vol. XLI, part 1; Carleton to Carson, December 15, 1864.

BATTLE OF ADOBE WALLS: Captain George H. Pettis, *Kit Carson's Fight with the Comanche and Kiowa Indians*, 8–12, 19–34.

CARSON CHILDREN: Boggs' report as executor and administrator of Carson's will, 453.

CAMP NICHOLS; CARSON A PEACE DELEGATE: Sabin, 2 vols., II, 754; Carleton to Carson, May 8 and August 2, 1865; Kit Carson's oral and written testimony, Fort Lyon, Colorado Territory, August 19, 1865.

CARSON TO WASHINGTON; FORT GARLAND APPOINTMENT: Grant's notes; Kit Carson Museum Records, Taos; Ellis, 248–49, 253–54; Sabin, 2 vols., II, 767; Hubert H. Bancroft, *History of Nevada, Colorado and Wyoming, 1540–1888*, Vol. XXV, 471n.

Chapter 17
DEATH OF KIT CARSON

MUSTERED OUT OF THE ARMY: Grant's notes; Army records, National Archives.

ACCOMPANIES UTES TO WASHINGTON: Abbott, 344; Sabin, 1 vol., 489; Grant's notes; Treaties of the United States of America, National Archives; Charles Scheurich to author.

CARSON MOVES TO FORT LYON; LAST WILL AND TESTAMENT: Abbott, 345–46; Grant's notes; Charles Scheurich to Blanche Grant; Dr. Tilton to John S. C. Abbott.

THE GENERAL IS GONE: Abbott, 347; Sabin, 1 vol., 498; Grant's notes; Charles Carson to Blanche Grant.

LAST TRIBUTES: Ellis, 260.

Bibliography

BOOKS

Abbott, John S. C. *Kit Carson, the Pioneer of the West*. New York, Dodd & Mead, 1874.

Adams, Samuel H. *The Santa Fé Trail*. New York, Random House, 1951.

Allen, Miss A. J. (comp.). *Ten Years in Oregon: Travels and Adventures of Doctor E. White and Lady West of the Rocky Mountains*. Ithaca, 1848.

Alsop, F. W. *The Life Story of Albert Pike*. Little Rock, n.d.

Alter, J. Cecil. *James Bridger, Trapper, Frontiersman, Scout and Guide: A Historical Narrative*. Salt Lake City, Shepard Book Company, 1925.

Arnold, Elliott. *The Time of the Gringo*. New York, Alfred A. Knopf. 1953.

Bakeless, John. *Daniel Boone, Master of the Wilderness*. New York, William Morrow & Company, 1939.

Bancroft, Hubert H. *History of California*. 3 vols. San Francisco, The History Company, 1886.

———. *History of Arizona and New Mexico*. San Francisco, The History Company, 1889.

———, *History of Nevada, Colorado and Wyoming, 1540–1888*. San Francisco, The History Company, 1890.

Bate, W. N. *Frontier Legend*. N.p., Owen G. Dunn Company, 1954.

Bell, Margaret E. *Kit Carson, Mountain Man*. New York, William Morrow & Company, 1952.

Benton, Thomas H. *Thirty Years' View*. 2 vols. New York, 1879.

Bloom, Lansing B., and Thomas C. Donnelly. *New Mexico History and Civics*. Albuquerque, University of New Mexico Press, 1933.

Brandon, William. *The Men and the Mountain: Frémont's Fourth Expedition.* New York, William Morrow & Company, 1955.

Brewerton, George D. *Overland with Kit Carson: A Narrative of the Old Spanish Trail in '48.* New York, Coward-McCann, 1930.

Burdett, Charles. *The Life of Kit Carson, the Great Western Hunter and Guide.* New York, Grosset & Dunlap, 1902.

Camp, Charles L. *Kit Carson in California.* Cleveland, Arthur H. Clark Company, 1922.

Carson, Christopher (Kit). *Kit Carson's Own Story of His Life.* Ed. by Blanche C. Grant. Taos, 1926.

———. *Kit Carson's Autobiography.* Ed. by Milo M. Quaife. Chicago, The Lakeside Press, 1935.

Carson, F. Tom. *Carson Family History.* Washington, Ward & Paul, 1956.

Cather, Willa. *Death Comes for the Archbishop.* New York, Alfred A. Knopf, 1955.

Cheetham, F. T. *Kit Carson: Pathbreaker, Patriot, Humanitarian.* N.p., El Palacio Press, 1930.

Chittenden, H. M. *The American Fur Trade of the Far West.* 2 vols. Stanford, 1954.

Claussen, W. E. *Cimarron—Last of the Frontier.* Privately printed, 1948.

Cleland, Robert G. *This Reckless Breed of Men: The Trappers and Fur Traders of the Southwest.* New York, Alfred A. Knopf, 1950.

Coan, Charles F. *A History of New Mexico.* 3 vols. Chicago and New York, American Historical Society, 1925.

Collier, Edmund. *The Story of Kit Carson.* New York, Grosset & Dunlap, 1953.

Collier, John. *Indians of the Americas.* New York, New American Library, 1947.

Collins, Lewis. *History of Kentucky.* Louisville, 1877.

Colton, Walter. *Deck and Port, or, Incidents of a Cruise in the U. S. Frigate Congress to California.* New York, 1850.

Conner, Sabra. *On Sweetwater Trail.* Chicago and New York, The Reilly & Lee Company, 1928.

Cooke, Philip St. George. *Scenes and Adventures in the Army.* Philadelphia, 1857.

Cutts, James M. *The Conquest of California and New Mexico.* Philadelphia, 1847.

Davis, William H. *Seventy-five Years in California*. San Francisco, John Howell, and Chicago, R. R. Donnelley & Sons, 1929.

De Voto, Bernard. *Across the Wide Missouri*. Boston, Houghton Mifflin Company, 1947.

Dobie, J. Frank. *Coronado's Children: Tales of Lost Mines and Buried Treasures of the Southwest*. Boston, Little, Brown & Company, 1930.

————. *The Mustangs*. Boston, Little, Brown & Company, 1952.

Doniphan, Alexander W. *Doniphan's Expedition*. Cincinnati, J. A. and U. P. James, 1848.

Duffus, Robert L. *The Santa Fé Trail*. New York, Toronto, and London, Longmans, Green and Company, 1930.

Easton, Jeanette. *Narcissa Whitman*. New York, 1941.

Ellis, Edward S. *Life of Kit Carson*. New York, Chalterton-Peck Company, 1899.

Emory, W. H., *Notes of a Military Reconnaissance from Fort Leavenworth in Missouri to San Diego*. Washington, Wendell and Van Benthuysen, 1848.

Favour, Alpheus, H. *Old Bill Williams, Mountain Man*. Chapel Hill, University of North Carolina Press, 1936.

Fergusson, Erna. *Our Southwest*. New York, Alfred A. Knopf, 1952.

Fergusson, Harvey. *The Rio Grande*. New York, Tudor Publishing Company, 1945.

Field, Matthew C. *Prairie and Mountain Sketches*. Ed. by Kate L. Gregg and John Francis McDermott, Norman, University of Oklahoma Press, 1957.

Fisher, George P. *History of the Christian Church*. New York, 1931.

Flint, Timothy. *The Personal Narrative of James Ohio Pattie of Kentucky*. Cincinnati, John H. Wood, 1831.

Forrest, Earle R. *Missions and Pueblos of the Old Southwest; Their Myths, Legends, Fiestas, Ceremonies, With Some Accounts of the Indian Tribes and Their Dances and of the Penitentes*. Cleveland, Arthur H. Clark Company, 1929.

Frémont, Elizabeth Benton. *Recollections*. New York, 1912.

Frémont, Jessie Benton. *Far West Sketches*. Boston, 1890.

————. *The Will and the Way Stories*. Boston, 1891.

Frémont, John C. *The Exploring Expedition to the Rocky Mountains, Oregon and California*. Buffalo, George H. Derby and Company, and Cleveland, Smith, Knight & Company, 1850.

296

————. *Memoirs of My Life*. Chicago and New York, Bedford Clarke & Company, 1887.

French, Joseph L. *The Pioneer West*. Boston, Little, Brown & Company, 1923.

Garrard, Lewis H. *Wah-To-Yah*. Ed. by Ralph H. Bieber. Glendale, Arthur H. Clark Company, 1938.

Garst, Shannon. *Jim Bridger*. Boston, Houghton Mifflin Company, 1952.

Gibhart, Elizabeth L. *The Life and Adventures of the Original John Jacob Astor*. New York, Bryan Printing Company, 1915.

Grant, Blanche C. *Taos Today*, Taos, 1925.

————. *When Old Trails Were New: The Story of Taos*. New York, The Press of the Pioneers, 1934.

————. *Dona Lona: A Story of Taos and Santa Fé*. New York, Wilfred Funk, 1941.

Gray, William H. *A History of Oregon*. Portland, 1871.

Gregg, Josiah. *The Story of the Indian*. New York and London, D. Appleton and Company, 1924.

————. *Diary & Letters of Josiah Gregg*. Ed. by Maurice Garland Fulton. 2 vols. Norman, University of Oklahoma Press, 1941, 1944.

————. *Commerce of the Prairies*. Ed. by Max L. Moorhead. Norman, University of Oklahoma Press, 1954.

Grinnell, George B. *Beyond the Old Frontier*. New York, 1913.

Haines, Helen. *History of New Mexico from the Spanish Conquest to the Present Time, 1530–1890*. New York, New Mexico Historical Publishing Company, 1891.

Harris, Burton. *John Colter: His Years in the Rockies*. New York and London, Charles Scribner's Sons, 1952.

Hartley, Cecil B. *The Life of Daniel Boone, the Founder of the State of Kentucky*. New York and Chicago, A. L. Burt Company, n.d.

Hayden, F. U. *The Great West*. Bloomington, Charles R. Brodix, 1880.

Hayes, A. A. *New Colorado and the Santa Fé Trail*. New York, Harper & Brothers, 1880.

Hewett, Edgar. L. *Ancient Life in the American Southwest, with an Introduction on General History of the American Race*. New York, Tudor Publishing Company and Bobbs-Merrill Company, 1930.

————, Reginald G. Fisher. *Mission Monuments of New Mexico*. Albuquerque, University of New Mexico and School of American Research, 1943.

Hobbs, Captain James. *Wildlife in the Far West*. Hartford, Wiley, Waterman and Eaton, 1872.

Horgan, Paul. *Great River: The Rio Grande in North American History*. 2 vols. New York, Rinehart & Company, 1954.

Houck, Louis. *A History of Missouri*. 3 vols. Chicago, 1908.

Hough, Emerson. *The Way to the West*. New York, Bobbs-Merrill Company, 1903.

Howe, Henry. *Historical Collections of the Great West*. Nashville, J. S. Johnson, 1852.

Hunter, John D. *Manners and Customs of the Western Indians*. Philadelphia, 1823.

Hurd, C. W. *Boggsville, Cradle of the Colorado Cattle Industry*. Published by Boggsville Committee and printed by Bent County (Colorado) *Democrat*, n.d.

Inman, Colonel Henry. *The Old Santa Fé Trail*. New York, The Macmillan Company, 1897.

———. *The Great Salt Lake Trail*. New York, The Macmillan Company, 1898.

Irving, Washington. *Astoria, or, Anecdotes of an Enterprise Beyond the Rocky Mountains*. Philadelphia, Carey, Lea and Blanchard, 1836.

———. *The Adventures of Captain Bonneville*. New York, John B. Alden, 1887.

———. *A Tour on the Prairies*. Ed. by John Francis McDermott. Norman, University of Oklahoma Press, 1956.

James, General Thomas. *Three Years Among the Indians and Mexicans*. St. Louis, Missouri Historical Society, 1916.

Keleher, William A. *Maxwell Land Grant: A New Mexico Item*. Santa Fe, Rydal Press, 1942.

———. *The Fabulous Frontier*. Santa Fe, Rydal Press, 1945.

———. *Turmoil in New Mexico: 1846–1868*. Santa Fe, Rydal Press, 1952.

Kelsey, D. H., *History of Our Wild West*. New York, Willey Book Co., 1928.

Kendall, George W. *Narrative of the Texas Santa Fé Expedition*. London, Landos, Wiley & Putnam, 1844.

Kincaid, Robert L. *The Wilderness Road*. Indianapolis and New York, Bobbs-Merrill Company, 1947.

Larkin, *Documented History of California*, N.p., n.d.

Larpenteur, Charles. *Forty Years a Fur Trader.* New York, Francis P. Harper, 1898.

Lavender, David S. *The Big Divide: The Lively Story of the People of the Southern Rocky Mountains from Yellowstone to Santa Fé.* Garden City, Doubleday & Company, 1949.

———. *Bent's Fort.* Garden City, Doubleday & Company, 1954.

Lea, Aurora Lucero-White. *Literary Folklore of the Hispanic Southwest.* San Antonio, The Naylor Company, 1953.

Loomis, Noel M. *The Texan–Santa Fé Pioneers.* Norman, University of Oklahoma Press, 1958.

Lummis, Charles F. *The Land of Poco Tiempo.* New York, Charles Scribner's Sons, 1933.

McCracken, Harold. *Portrait of the Old West.* New York, Toronto, and London, McGraw-Hill Book Company, 1952.

McIntyre, John T. *In the Rockies with Kit Carson.* Philadelphia, Pen Publishing Company, 1913.

Magoffin, Susan Shelby. *Down the Santa Fé Trail into Mexico: The Diary of Susan Shelby, 1846–1847.* Ed. by Stella M. Drumm. New Haven, Yale University Press, 1926.

Meadowcroft, Enid L. *The Story of Davy Crockett.* New York, Grossett & Dunlap, 1952.

Meline, James F. *Two Thousand Miles on Horseback.* New York, 1873.

Moody, Ralph. *Kit Carson and the Wild Frontier.* New York, Random House, 1955.

Muzzey, David S. *Notes on the Ecclesiastical History of New Mexico.* Banning, California, 1898.

———. *An American History.* Boston, Ginn & Company, 1925.

Newman, Albert H. *The History of the Baptist Church in the United States.* Philadelphia, 1915.

Otero, Miguel A. *My Life on the Frontier, 1864–1882: Incidents and Characters of the Period when Kansas, Colorado and New Mexico Were Passing through the Last of their Wild and Romantic Years.* Vol. I. New York, The Press of the Pioneers, 1935.

———. *My Life on the Frontier, 1882–1897: Death Knell of a Territory and Birth of a State.* Vol. II. Albuquerque, University of New Mexico Press, 1939.

Parker, Samuel. *Journal of an Exploring Tour Beyond the Rocky Mountains.* Ithaca, 1840.

299

Parkman, Francis. *The Oregon Trail*. Boston, Little, Brown & Company, 1936.

Parsons, Elsie Worthington Clewes. *Taos Tales*. New York, American Folklore Society and J. J. Augustin, 1940.

Peters, DeWitt Clinton. *Pioneer Life and Frontier Adventures: An Authentic Record of the Romantic Life and Daring Exploits of Kit Carson and His Companions from His Own Narrative*. Boston, Estes and Lauriat, 1881.

Pettis, Captain George H. *Kit Carson's Fight with the Comanche and Kiowa Indians; Personal Narrative of the Rebellion*. Santa Fe, New Mexico Printing Company, 1908.

Phillips, Catherine C. *Jessie Benton Frémont, a Woman Who Made History*. San Francisco, John Henry Nash, 1935.

Pike, Albert. *Prose Sketches and Poems*. Boston, 1834.

Polk, James K. *Polk: The Diary of a President, 1845–1849*. Ed. by Allan Nevins. New York, 1929.

Preuss, Charles. *Exploring with Frémont*. Ed. by Erwin G. and Elisabeth K. Gudde. Norman, University of Oklahoma Press, 1958.

Prince, L. Bradford. *Historical Sketches of New Mexico from the Earliest Records to the American Occupation*. New York, Leggat Brothers, and Kansas City, Ramsey, Millett and Hudson, 1883.

Quaife, Milo M. (ed.). *The Southwestern Expedition of Zebulon M. Pike*. Chicago, The Lakeside Press, 1925.

Quimby, George T. *Indians of the Western Frontier*. Chicago, Chicago Natural History Museum, 1954.

Read, Benjamin M. *Illustrated History of New Mexico*. Santa Fe, New Mexico Printing Company, 1912.

Revere, Joseph W. *A Tour of Duty in California*. New York, C. S. Francis & Company, 1849.

Rich, William G. *Illustrated New Mexico*. Santa Fe, New Mexico Printing and Publishing Company, 1883.

Richman, Irving B. *California under Spain and Mexico, 1535–1847*. Boston and New York, Houghton Mifflin Company, 1911.

Ridge, John Rollin (Yellow Bird). *The Life and Adventures of Joaquín Murieta, the Celebrated California Bandit*. Norman, University of Oklahoma Press, 1944.

Roosevelt, Theodore. *The Winning of the West*. 6 vols. New York, The Current Literature Publishing Company, 1905.

Ross, Alexander. *The Fur Hunters of the Far West.* Ed. by Kenneth A. Spaulding. Norman, University of Oklahoma Press, 1956.

Ross, Marvin C. (ed.). *The West of Alfred Jacob Miller (1837).* Norman, University of Oklahoma Press, 1951.

Rusling, James F. *Across the Continent.* New York, 1874.

Russell, Osborne. *Journal of a Trapper.* Boise, Idaho, 1921.

Ruxton, George Frederick. *In the Old West, As It Was in the Days of Kit Carson and the Mountain Men.* Ed. by Horace Kephart. New York, The Macmillan Company, 1924.

———. *Ruxton of the Rockies.* Ed. by LeRoy R. Hafen. Norman, University of Oklahoma Press, 1950.

Ryus, W. H. *The Second William Penn.* Kansas City, Frank T. Riley Publishing Company, 1913.

Sabin, Edwin L. *Adventuring with Kit Carson and Frémont.* Philadelphia and London, J. B. Lippincott Company, 1912.

———. *Kit Carson Days: 1809–1868.* Chicago, A. C. McClurg & Company, 1914.

———. *Kit Carson Days, 1809–1868: Adventures in the Path of Empire.* 2 vols. New York, The Press of the Pioneers, 1935.

Schmitt, Martin F., and Dee Brown. *Fighting Indians of the Southwest.* New York, Charles Scribner's Sons, 1948.

Seymour, Flora Warren. *The Boys' Life of Frémont.* New York and London, The Century Company, 1928.

———. *The Story of the Sioux Indians.* Girard, Kansas, Haldeman-Julius Company, n.d.

Sherman, William T. *Memoirs of General William T. Sherman.* 2 vols. New York, 1875.

Simpson, J. H. *Report of Exploration Across the Great Basin, in 1859.* Washington, 1876. Appendix Q contains "Journal of an Exploration of the Mary or Humbolt River, Carson Lake, and Owens River in 1845," by Edward M. Kern.

Stanley, F. *The Grant that Maxwell Bought.* Denver, 1952.

———. *Fort Union (New Mexico).* Washington, The World Press, 1953.

State Historical Society of Colorado. *Bent's Fort on the Arkansas.* Denver, 1954.

Stevenson, Augusta. *Kit Carson, Boy Trapper.* Indianapolis and New York, Bobbs-Merrill Company, 1945.

Stewart, Edgar I. *Custer's Luck*. Norman, University of Oklahoma Press, 1955.

Stewart, George R. *Names on the Land*. New York, Random House, 1945.

Stone, Irving. *Men to Match My Mountains: The Opening of the Far West, 1840–1900*. Garden City, Doubleday & Company, 1956.

Tallant, Robert. *The Louisiana Purchase*. New York, Random House, 1952.

Terreros y Pando, Esteban de. *Diccionario Castellano*. Madrid, 1787.

Thomas, Alfred B. *The Plains Indians and New Mexico, 1751–1778*. Albuquerque, University of New Mexico Press, 1940.

Thwaites, Reuben G. *Early Western Travels*. Cleveland, Arthur H. Clark Company, 1905.

Tilton, Henry R. *The Last Days of Kit Carson*. Grand Forks, 1939.

Tinkle, Lon. *13 Days to Glory: The Siege of the Alamo*. New York, McGraw-Hill Book Company, 1958.

Tomlinson, Everett T. *Scouting with Kit Carson*. Garden City, Doubleday & Company, 1916.

Twitchell, Ralph E. *The Military Occupation of New Mexico: 1846–1851*. Denver, The Smith-Brooks Company, 1909.

———. *Leading Facts of New Mexican History*. 5 vols. Cedar Rapids, The Torch Press, 1911.

Upham, Charles W. *Life, Explorations and Public Service of John Charles Frémont*. Boston, Tichnoe and Field, 1856.

Victor, Frances F. *The River of the West*. Hartford, R. W. Bliss & Company, 1870.

Waters, Frank. *The Man Who Killed the Deer*. Denver, University of Denver Press, 1942.

———. *The Colorado*. New York, Rinehart & Company, 1946.

———. *Masked Gods: Navaho and Pueblo Ceremonialism*. Albuquerque, University of New Mexico Press, 1950.

Webb, James J. *Adventures in the Santa Fé Trade, 1844–1847*. Glendale, Arthur H. Clark Company, 1931.

Webb, W. E. *Buffalo Land*. Cincinnati and Chicago, E. Hannafard & Company, 1873.

West, Nathaniel. *The Ancestry, Life, and Times of Hon. Henry Hastings Sibley, LL.D.* St. Paul, Pioneer Press Publishing Company, 1889.

Whittaker, Milo L. *Pathbreakers and Pioneers of the Pueblo Region,*

Comprising A History of Pueblo from the Earliest Times. N.p., Franklin Press Company, 1917.

Wilbur, Marvin C. (ed.). *Presbyterian Plan Book.* New York, 1956.

Wissler, Clark. *Indians of the United States: Four Centuries of Their History and Culture.* New York, Doubleday, Doran & Company, 1940.

Wood, Dean Earl. *The Old Santa Fé Trail from the Missouri River.* Kansas City, E. L. Moudenhall, 1951.

ARTICLES

Baca, Jesús María. "Apologia of Presbyter Antonio J. Martínez," *New Mexico Historical Review,* Vol. III, No. 4 (October, 1928).

Boggs, Thomas O. "Early Scouts and Plainsmen," *Colorado Magazine,* Vol. VII (July, 1930).

Estergreen, M. Morgan. "When Taos Dances," *New Mexico Magazine,* Vol. XXVIII, No. 8 (August, 1950).

Francis, E. K. "Padre Martínez: A New Mexico Myth," *New Mexico Historical Review,* Vol. XXXI, No. 4 (October, 1956).

Grinnell, George B. *"Bent's Old Fort and Its Builders,"* Kansas Historical Society *Publications,* Vol. XV (1919–1922).

Hafen, LeRoy. "Mountain Men," *Colorado Magazine,* Vol. XI, No. 5.

"An Interview with Jessie Benton Frémont," *The Land of Sunshine Magazine* (February, 1897).

"Kit Carson as a Missourian: The Life of the Great Plainsman Who Considered This His Home State," *Kansas City Star Magazine* (September 13, 1925).

Marshall, Thomas M. "St. Vrain's Expedition to the Gila in 1826," *Southwestern Historical Quarterly,* Vol. XIX, No. 3.

Moody, Marshall D. "Kit Carson, Agent to the Indians in New Mexico, 1853–1861," *New Mexico Historical Review,* Vol. XXVIII (January, 1953).

"The Mountainmen and Their Part in the Opening of the West," Missouri Historical Society *Bulletin,* Vol. III, No. 4.

Ross, Nancy W. "Murder at the Place of Rye Grass," *American Heritage,* Vol. X, No. 4 (August, 1959).

Viles, Jonas. "Old Franklin: A Frontier Town of the Twenties," *Mississippi Valley Historical Review,* Vol. IX, No. 9 (March, 1923).

Walton, John. "Ghost Writer to Daniel Boone," *American Heritage,* Vol. VI, No. 6 (October, 1955).

Warner, Jonathan T. "Reminiscences of Early California—1831 to 1846," *Historical Society of Southern California Annual Publications*, Vol. VII (1907–1908).

Worchester, E. C. "The Weapons of American Indians," *New Mexico Historical Review*, Vol. XX, No. 3.

MANUSCRIPTS AND DOCUMENTS

Bancroft, Hubert H. "History of California." Vallejo MS, Vol. III. Berkeley, Bancroft Library.

Bent, Charles. Collected letters. Santa Fe, Museum of New Mexico. Mexico Archives.

Bent Family Bible. Taos, Kit Carson Museum.

Berry, John. Bill of sale for land sold to Lindsey Carson (photostat).

Boggs, Thomas O. Report as executor and administrator of Kit Carson's last will and testament (photostat).

Boggs file. Berkeley, Bancroft Library.

Carson, Christopher (Kit). Baptismal certificate (photostat).

———. Burial certificate (photostat).

———. Last will and testament, handwritten by Aloys Scheurich (photostat).

———. Marriage certificate (photostat).

———. Oath of allegiance to the government of the United States. (photostat).

Carson file. Includes Ralph E. Twitchell's documents on the Navaho expedition. Santa Fe, Museum of New Mexico Archives.

———. Berkeley, Bancroft Library.

Cowles, Calvin D. "The Genealogy of Five Allied Families." Unpublished MS. Washington, Rare Book Division, Library of Congress.

Fleming, William. "Journal in Kentucky." Unpublished MS relating to Daniel Boone and others (included in Draper MS). Madison, Wisconsin Historical Society Library.

Grant, Blanche C. "Notes and Documents on the Life of Christopher Carson." Unpublished MS, 1935. Owned by author.

House Ex. Doc. No. 17, 31st Cong., 1st sess. Washington, National Archives.

Indian Agency letters and official correspondence. Washington, National Archives.

Indian Agency Official Records, Series L, Vols. XV and XXIV. Washington, National Archives.

Indian treaties and other international acts of the United States of America, Washington, National Archives.

Kit Carson Museum records. Taos, Kit Carson Museum.

Map of the Old Santa Fe Trail (photostat). Owned by *New Mexico Magazine*.

Martinez, L. Pascual. "Padre Martínez." Folio 1082, New Mexico Archives. Albuquerque, Coronado Library, University of New Mexico.

"The Osage Treaty." Item No. 3983, William G. Ritch Collection. San Marino, Huntington Library.

Records of the Rebellion, Series 1, Vol. IX. Includes reports by Price, Johnson, Emory, Pettis, and others. Washington, National Archives.

LETTERS

Bent, Charles. Collected letters. Santa Fe, Museum of New Mexico.

Carson, Christopher (Kit), to Aloys Scheurich (last letter Carson wrote). Owned by Charles Scheurich.

Grant, Blanche C., to author.

Hewett, Edgar L., to Blanche C. Grant.

McPherson, Venita Reche, to author.

Phillips, Bert G., to author.

Rubey, Mary Ann Carson, to Mrs. J. F. Hawley. Published in the *Kansas City Star*, September 13, 1925.

Scheurich, Teresina Bent. Collected letters. Owned by Blanche C. Grant.

NEWSPAPERS

Boonelick Advertiser.

California Star (Los Angeles), April 1, 1848.

Daily Union (Washington, D. C.)

Kansas City Star, 1925.

Missouri Intelligencer.

Santa Fé Gazette, October 29, 1864.

Santa Fé New Mexican.

Washington Union (Washington, D. C.), 1847.

Weekly Reveille.

Index